C000128919

Ralph Brookfield

Ralph Brookfield trained as a molecular physicist, worked as a copy editor, software engineer, and freelance writer, ran his own software business, then became an award-winning director of technology in the digital television industry.

Since 2012, he has pursued his passions as a tutor, writer, and amateur musician. He is married, has two grown-up children, and is a founder member of the infamous Hanwell Ukulele Group in West London.

First published in the UK in 2021 by SUPERNOVA BOOKS
67 Grove Avenue, Twickenham, TW1 4HX

Supernova Books is an imprint of Aurora Metro
www.aurorametro.com

@aurorametro FB/AuroraMetroBooks

On the Trail of Americana Music text copyright © 2021 Ralph Brookfield

Interviews reproduced courtesy of Brumby Media Group © 2021

Cover design copyright © 2021 Aurora Metro Books

Editor: Cheryl Robson

With thanks to: Marina Tuffier, Bella Taylor, Jo Colton

Images: Brumby Media, Al Stuart, Cheryl & Steve Robson, John Morgan, Library of Congress, stockshots, public domain.

All rights are strictly reserved. For rights enquiries contact the publisher: info@aurorametro.com

We have made every effort to trace all copyright holders of photographs included in this publication. If you have any information relating to this, please contact editor@aurorametro.com

No part of this publication may be reproduced, stored in or introduced into a retrieval system, or transmitted in any form, or by any means (electronic, mechanical, photocopying, recording or otherwise without the prior permission of the publisher. Any person who does any unauthorised act in relation to this publication may be liable to criminal prosecution and civil claims for damages.

This book is sold subject to the condition that it shall not, by way of trade or otherwise, be lent, resold, hired out, or otherwise circulated without the publisher's prior consent in any form other than that in which it is published and without a similar condition being imposed on the subsequent purchaser.

Printed in the UK by Short Run Press, Exeter, UK.

ISBNs:
978-1-913641-09-2 (print version)
978-1-913641-10-8 (ebook version)

"A deep, inquisitive dive into the Americana story so far. In the best possible way, Ralph Brookfield's roots are showing."
– Paul Sexton

ON THE TRAIL OF
AMERICANA
MUSIC

BY

RALPH BROOKFIELD

SUPERNOVA BOOKS

Acknowledgements

Love and thanks to my wife Moira and to my family for their support and for putting up with my lack of attention inevitable at certain stages of the process.

Special thanks to publisher Cheryl Robson of Aurora Metro/Supernova for making this book possible, and for access to the interviews she made available from the forthcoming Brumby Media documentary on this subject. Much of the material within was gathered as a team effort, and this is acknowledged in the text with a non-regal "we".

Thank you to all the contributors named in this book and its index. I beg forgiveness for any inadvertent omissions.

There are many other friends and helpers whom I also thank for the personal support I needed to complete this book, and all these kind people have freely given particular help behind the scenes:

Sue Bremmer, Geraint Evans, Susan Furber, Ed Hopwood, Matt McManoman, Ronan MacManus, Noel Martin, Elizabeth Mulloy, Enda Mulloy, Pat Mulloy, John Murry, Phil Odgers, Elly O'Keeffe, Finn Panton, Geoff Price, Paul Riley, Robert Salmons, Ian Sephton, Paul Sexton, David Sinclair, Diana Stone, Al Stuart, Chris Tulloch, Jade Williams

CONTENTS

PREFACE   7

THE HISTORY OF AMERICANA MUSIC   11

DIFFERENT STRANDS IN US AMERICANA MUSIC   43

AMERICANA MUSIC IN THE US TODAY   75

AMERICANA MUSIC IN AUSTRALIA   93

AMERICANA MUSIC IN BRITAIN   117

IRISH AMERICANA MUSIC   143

CANADIAN AMERICANA MUSIC COMES OF AGE   163

EUROPEAN AND OTHER OFFSHOOTS   175

WOMEN CALL THE SHOTS   187

WHERE TO NEXT?   199

ENDNOTES   206

INDEX   227

The Bluebird Cafe, Nashville. Photo Brumby Media

PREFACE

"It's better to burn than it is to rust"

– Neil Young

After over 40 years of writing and playing music, I'm finally launching my first full-length album with a band of brothers and sisters I've befriended along the way. I've hired a small café-bar with an upstairs music room for the launch party. Off the back of the *Bandcamp* release I've been booked to open a major summer festival – the first time I've ever been invited to play such a high-profile event. The band is in great form after a gig the previous weekend to try out of some of the songs in a local cellar club. The mood lighting is set, the stage is ready, and we're raring to go. It's March 6, 2020.

A month later, we're all in total lockdown, the summer festival is cancelled along with our local carnival and all the other gigs I was planning to use to work up a bigger band for the big festival show. I pull the album off distribution hoping for a relaunch in more normal times (will they ever come?) and release instead an EP of new material made at home, with drums added remotely and separately by my son's friend, Oliver Lyu, in his studio. The EP is tinged with all the research I've started doing for this book: a bit of slide guitar, harmonica and, for the first time in a long time, some discrete wang-bar work on the electric guitar. I've even been inspired by a recent Lilly Hiatt tune.

My interest in Americana stems from many years of sessions with other grassroots musicians in local bars and other venues in London. For this journey along the multi-forked trail that is Americana music, I have taken advantage of the Covid-19 constraints during the pandemic to interview (online) musicians from the grassroots up, who have generously given of their unusually free time to share experiences of how American Roots music has informed their own musical journeys.

I was commissioned by publisher and filmmaker Cheryl Robson to write this book drawing heavily on film interviews she had conducted on three continents with her husband Steve for a documentary film about Americana Music which they are developing for media production company Brumby Media Group. The project stalled due to the Covid-19 pandemic and will resume in 2021. The film has captured the thoughts of dozens of industry insiders and aspirants during the years 2017–2018, when Americana music was really exploding into the public consciousness in the USA, UK, and Australia and provides a fascinating record of a musical movement. Where quotes are not referenced in the text, the source is this material, repurposed for this book.

Apart from the documentary material, I have used the power of online media for my research: my own socially distanced interviews, and online sources referenced in the endnotes. But most of all, I have listened to countless hours of recorded performances and studio-made material posted by the artists, by their representative labels or management, and by ordinary enthusiasts for the music. Finally, there is the more conventional bibliography of movies and literature on the music. To all the contributors who have informed my work I offer heartfelt thanks, and those who have contributed actively and directly I acknowledge elsewhere in this book separately by name.

My purpose has been to range over the good music that is being made today that owes an audible debt to the music of America that existed before the advent of recording technology.

This is the definition I think works best for the term 'American Roots music', and the term used by The Americana Music Association to define its mission. There exists such a vast catalogue of such music around the world that it is of course impossible to include more than a tiny fraction of everything worthy of public mention. I have naturally coloured my selection with my personal tastes but have tried to avoid over concentrating on artists who have climbed to a high level of exposure by virtue of commercial success.

I have also tried to represent the circular ocean currents of influence from other continents that have contributed significantly, both to American Roots and to contemporary Americana. African and European musical traditions fused with those of 'Latin' America and indigenous Americans to form American Roots music, which, once it became recorded and published, was then re-exported to almost every region in the world – notably Australia, Europe, Japan, and other countries where American culture was widely consumed. The circles joined and remained unbroken in the age of mass media through phenomena such as the 'British invasions' of popular music into the US in the 1960s through to the 1990s (the heyday of the international record industry), and the post-WWII international boom in 'Celtic' music that spread internationally from the late 1950s onwards.

Then there is Australia. Country music evoking the mountains and prairies of America exerts a strong cultural pull on that nation of wide-open wilderness and rural landscapes, ringed with cities full of people never more than a few generations away from their own pioneering immigrants. It's also no surprise that some of the Australian Country musicians began to explore their own country's indigenous musical heritage by working with traditional aboriginal musicians they encountered in the outback and in the city areas where most aboriginal heritage people came to live. And, to complete that circle, many Australian Americana artists feel drawn to Nashville,

9

Austin, or other US centres of Roots music in order to further their professional careers. Australian descendants of immigrants also have their music influenced by Indigenous Australians, who, in turn, have been influenced by American music.

Yes, the trail of Americana has many forks and byways. And it's unlikely to be leading in any one particular musical direction. On the contrary, today's musicians who acknowledge American Roots are taking their music in more directions than (say) Country or Rock musicians of the past, because they are less constrained by the commercial control of the late 20th century recording industry. Ironically, the system that is now depriving all but a tiny percentage of the very most popular musicians of a living wage through royalties is offering those not wholly committed to commercial art to benefit by exploring new musical fusions and directions we would have been unlikely to discover in the pre-internet age. It falls to a handful of advocate curators and trade organisations to help ensure that those fine artists in that field don't completely wither through lack of financial irrigation. The Covid-19 pandemic has decimated most musicians' revenues from live performance and merchandising. It falls to all of us in society to ensure that 'good', i.e. skilfully executed, inventive, original music (including Americana) does not wither away completely as a result.

Our actions to preserve the making of new music by talented people should be as autonomic and visceral as the instinctive response to music that 99%+ of our species shares. Who of us can say we have never been moved emotionally or physically by some piece of music? Americana music remains closer than many contemporary musical cultures to the mature human emotions of relationship and family, by virtue of its individuality and honesty. Allowing the diversity and authenticity of our music to diminish has the same impact upon human culture as the programmatic extinction of species has upon our environment.

THE HISTORY OF AMERICANA MUSIC

"Country taught me how to sing, it put me on a path. But I was never going to be locked into a formula. I don't want to be considered a current country artist."
– Emmylou Harris

Emmylou Harris, Ahoy, Rotterdam, The Netherlands. Photo C.Kuhl

THE AMA: WHO, HOW, AND WHY?

It's a quiet September evening in Nashville, 2017. We're privileged to have Brent Cobb with us on camera for a little private gig and a chat. He shares with us the following:

> I remember when we were putting an EP out in 2012 here. Someone that I was working with said, 'Well, you don't want to be considered Americana, you know… nobody wants to be considered Americana. It doesn't really get a whole lot of attention… a sort of dead-end road'. And then it started infiltrating, and so now you have all these major labels seeing the success of these independent artists such as [Jason] Isbell. And they go, 'Wow, I guess there's some money to be made here!'. And so now there are all these major labels have their little side Americana labels, and I don't know whether to be happy about that or pissed off, you know? So, I guess it's good. It's a double-edged sword, but it's good because it helps the music get to a wider audience.

Brent is a distant Georgia cousin of Dave Cobb, top-Nashville-producer via a stint in LA. Dave produces some of the biggest names in Americana: the Highwomen, Jason Isbell, Brandi Carlile, Chris Stapleton, and the late John Prine. Dave, and his 'extended family' Shooter Jennings, kickstarted Brent's

Brent Cobb, Nashville. Photo Brumby Media

career – having never met him – when he sent them a demo. A couple of days after Brent's interview, it's a rainy night in Nashville and we are talking to the man himself. Dave cut his musical teeth on Rock.

Q: Why the change of genre?

So, I grew up in a Pentecostal family and we did have gospel music in our house and in our church, you know, we had pedal steel, bass guitar, acoustic guitar, and piano. So... all the foundations of country, and old hymnal-based gospel, and my parents listened to Kenny Rogers and Barbara Mandrell, so for me I wanted to rebel. I was sneaking Ozzy records into the back room, listening to Black Sabbath and Van Halen and then AC/DC, and I wanted everything but [Gospel]. I think when I was a kid, you know, we had southern food every day for every meal and the first time I had pizza I think I was probably about 11 or 12 and I was like 'Screw this! This is way better than collard greens!'

I think it was the same with music. I think I ran away from the music that was around me and I ran to California to make Rock records and when I got there, I met this guy Shooter Jennings, and we made this record which was called 'Put the 'O' Back in Country', which is the first Country record I ever made. [I] didn't really listen to Country very much and [Shooter] put me onto all the good Country: that's where I learnt about Waylon [Jennings, Shooter's dad] and [Jimmie] Reed, and all the greats that now I love. It took me a long time to appreciate... the music that was around me...

Dave was emerging from a busy round of press work to support the recent release of Jason Isbell and the 400 Unit's *Nashville Sound* album. Reviewers were beginning to credit Cobb, D., and colleagues with 'reinventing the Nashville sound.'[1]

Q: What did they mean, Dave?

I don't know if we reinvented shit, really. Historically the 'Nashville Sound' really started out with RCA [Records Nashville] and the quads [producers Chet Atkins, Steve Sholes, Owen Bradley and Bob Ferguson], here in Nashville, and they realised Sinatra and Dean Martin and all these people were making tons of money with these lush arrangements and these beautiful pop songs. Well, they just decided 'let's just put that in Country music.' So, if you think of Patsy Cline's [version of] 'Crazy', it's a beautiful pop song with beautiful arrangements, and she has a beautiful country voice and I think they realized there was a lot of money to be made… I think they thought it was more universal than the hillbilly roots of Country music, you know.

Q: So, how did you get back to those roots?

I don't know if we moved away from the roots. I think we just make music that makes us happy, you know. A lot of the times, when I'm doing a country record, I'm hearing the Rolling Stones' 'Wild Horses' in my head [laughs]. Obviously, I'll hear some of the roots I listen to now, but I don't think we reinvented the roots at all. I think we just make music that's honest, and maybe if honesty is the root then that's what we're doing, but it's definitely not trying to angle, or go 'okay, we've got to put down that… phaser pedal, and got to put a mandolin on that, to get back to the roots.' That's not us.

In a 2019 interview for Relix,[2] Americana Music Association (AMA) Executive Director Jed Hilly reflects on the progress he has made since taking the lead role in 2007. Hilly is a canny businessman: a former Sony executive, a native New Yorker who cut his teeth on the thrills and shills of deal-making in the music business. After 9/11, Hilly had something of a philosophical epiphany, moving his children from the big city down to Nashville before he took up his new role. But let's let Jed Hilly start the story at the beginning: "The AMA began back in 1999 at a meeting during the South by Southwest festival with thirty-three people in a room trying to define a word that wasn't in the dictionary."

Hilly's first significant action heading the AMA was to persuade the National Academy of Recording Arts and Sciences (now named The Recording Academy, RA) to introduce a Best Americana Album category into the industry's ultimate accolades, the Grammy Awards. His second, he jokes in the interview, was to ask the RA to remove the word 'twang' that they had used in their own definition of the category. The reason for this was to differentiate Americana from Country, where twang had been a talisman word forever. Hilly points out that by the noughties, Country was an avowed 100% commercial artform. Whereas Americana is a fine art:

Ansel Adams was not engaged to take photographs for real estate brochures… Country songwriters are hired by labels to write hits. An Americana artist writes a song to tell a story.

In 2011, Hilly was "thrilled" to discover that no less an authority than J Merriam-Webster's Collegiate Dictionary had added a musical definition to the word: "A genre of American music having roots in early folk and country music."[3] No 'twang', there, either. Instead, Hilly is enthused by the word 'roots.' He describes the music as a "horizontal genre" incorporating the "American Roots music traditions of Gospel, Country, Blues, and Rock 'n' Roll." Hilly illustrates this concept with a list of some major artists featured in the 2010 AMA annual AmericanaFest programme: Candi Staton, out of Muscle Shoals, whom most would term a Soul artist; the late Dr John, voodoo 'night tripper' out of New Orleans; the legendary Booker T Jones of Stax out of Memphis; and Chicago Bluesman Buddy Guy. "The beauty and the strength of Americana is in its diversity," explains Hilly.

The twang-less Americana Album Grammy survived a major reshuffle of award categories by its guardians the RA in 2011/12. In 2014, the RA (in close correspondence with the AMA) went on to introduce awards for Best American Roots Song, followed in 2015 by Best American Roots Performance. Hilly is justly proud of his achievement in bringing Americana music to the attention of the wider public, but he is particularly proud of what the AMA's own annual awards mean to the musical community he helps to support.

In May 2016, *Billboard* magazine announced that their Folk Albums Chart would be renamed the Americana/Folk Albums

Chart. Perhaps a subtle change for anyone not connected with the industry, but an important one for Larry Murray, the manager of Green River Ordinance, an independent-label band whose February 2016 album *Fifteen* was not included by *Billboard* in its Country Albums Chart. *Fifteen* would have come in at #7 on the *Billboard* Country Albums Chart in its week of release and would have been declared the top-charting debut for the week. Instead, the album debuted at #1 in the Folk Albums Chart. Murray explains why being #7 in the Country Chart would have been a better result for the band:

> In the country world they're still being identified... It would have a huge impact on their ability to play country festivals and support other country acts. And it's the story they deserve.[4]

After some wrangling involving Jed Hilly and AMA, *Billboard's* co-director of charts, Gary Trust, announced the name change effective June 4. Green River Ordinance are now retrospectively listed as #1 Americana/Folk album artists.[5]

The name change had a favourable reception from record executives, who were respectful of the progress the AMA and its international partners had made in raising the profile of the movement in the previous few years. *The Tennessean* issued a terminologically confused quote from Larry Murray: "When you say 'Americana' it gives different weight to an artist's stature."[6] But his sentiment was clear. By 2016, the term could add stature to an artist's reputation in the market. Hilly's AMA were accomplishing their marketing strategy of differentiating Americana as 'fine art' – equally valuable but, of course, quite *different* from the 'commercial' art form of Country music.

Hilly sees the formation of the AMA as a reaction to artistic choices being made by Country music radio in the 1990s, with the implicit backing of the Country Music Association (CMA). The Telecommunications Act of 1996 allowed media cross-ownership, with radio's regulator the Federal Communications Commission stating that this was to allow free-market competition. The actual result, notes Hilly, was the reduction of a diverse and competitive radio industry: "From 10,000 radio stations down to ten companies owning 10,000 radio stations. The opportunities for artists of integrity were gone."

A dramatic reduction in operators also reduced competition and niche marketing opportunities. On Country music radio, the playlists became blander and more formulaic, focussing obsessively on big-selling artists like Shania Twain and Garth Brooks. In the recording industry, major labels were dropping artists as well-known as Rosanne Cash, Emmylou Harris, Joe Ely, and Dwight Yoakam because their output did not fit the CMA/Country music radio mould.

But Hilly saw a strategic marketing opportunity from his experience with the nascent Americana movement: in 2007, when he took over direction of the AMA, there were but 790 members, and no major record labels represented. Today, there are over 3,000 members including representatives across the US recording industry. The annual AMA conference and music festival, AmericanaFest in Nashville, has gone from an attendance of 5,000 in 14 venues in 2008 to 29,000 over 70

Jed Hilly, SXSW, Austin, Texas. Photo Brumby Media

venues in 2019. Hilly is clear that the AMA's mission remains not to maximise revenues, but "to advocate for the authentic voice of American Roots Music around the world".

A workable definition of 'Roots Music' in the context of Americana is music that existed before the advent of commercial recording. Music that became captured on those field recordings and 78rpm shellac records of the 1920s. Music that was practised in households and small communities, disseminated through participation in churches, back stoops of cabins, and dancehalls; made popular with millions of radio listeners all over the USA in the early 1930s. The 21st century AMA's reference to 'Roots' mirrors the folk revival movement of the late 1950s and early 1960s, when a backlash against the industrial maturation of pop music brought folk out from the underground, driven by the ever-recurring artistic quest for 'purity.' Roots artists published on the earliest commercial records, like Skip James, the Stanley Brothers, and Mississippi John Hurt, were 'rediscovered' and given international currency on modern vinyl by a new generation of young (often northern, urban, educated) musical explorers, starting with Harry Smith,[7] and continuing with many others, notably Richard Spottswood and John Fahey.[8]

Those early recordings. Sometimes it's hard to put a modern label on them. When Dock Boggs performs 'Pretty Polly' or 'Sugar Baby', is he playing Kentucky mountain Folk or Blues? It's easy to forget, as a 21st century consumer of carefully marketed and labelled musical product, that the labels don't really matter: how does the music make you feel? That's what was, is, and will remain, important.

AmericanaFest, unlike most other festivals featuring Americana music, remains a not-for-profit enterprise. All venues – bar the Ryman Auditorium (former home of CMA's Grand Ole Opry) – donate their space in return for drinks sales revenue. Performers receive a *very* modest honorarium.

So, how is this a marketing strategy? Hilly explains: "Commercial realities are based on the artist and the community that supports them."

The AMA's primary mission is to help artists find a degree of protection from the demands of purely commercial art, reducing the constraints on artistic expression. Using one of his favourite artists as an example, Hilly asks: "Is it my role to help Rosanne Cash sell more records? No, it's to help Rosanne protect her inspiration."

In return, the AMA find themselves promoting a movement that has a really diverse range of high-quality product, appealing to an equally diverse and rapidly expanding customer base who are loyal because they take their music seriously and expect a high degree of artistic integrity. And that, friends, is smart marketing. Hilly's final word on the strategy: "Come to [AmericanaFest]. You will see someone you have never heard before and you will follow them for the rest of your life."

HOW DOES IT DIFFER FROM COUNTRY MUSIC?

The cultural schism of what was to become Americana from the mainstream of Country music is inextricably linked with the complex history of American politics. No single song epitomizes this complexity better then Merle Haggard's 'Okie from Muskogee'. In 1969, Haggard, an ex-convict from Bakersfield, California, was struggling to come to terms with protests against the Vietnam War by young people whom he considered unqualified to disrespect the sacrifice of freedom made by American service personnel. Haggard's own experience of loss of freedom (he served two years for robbery in the notorious San Quentin Penitentiary) led him to reject the protests against the war as a mark of personal sympathy with the plight of the conscripts and volunteers who were fighting it. Haggard's family were dustbowl migrants from near Muskogee, Oklahoma. A journey through Oklahoma at the height of the war gave Haggard reflection on how it seemed to him at the time that small towns in the rural South were relatively unaffected by the unrest that was highly visible in the cities. Haggard wrote with his drummer Roy Edward Burris, trading lines that build the character of a small-town 'square' in song:

We don't smoke marijuana in Muskogee;

We don't take our trips on LSD

We don't burn no draft cards down on Main Street;

We like livin' right, and bein' free.

The song became an immediate hit, live and on record, reaching #1 in the *Billboard* Country Charts. Biographer David Cantwell writes that Merle had come upon a song "that expressed previously inchoate fears, spoke out loud gripes and anxieties otherwise only whispered… now people were using [Okie] to connect to these larger concerns."[9]

The political reality in Muskogee in 1969 was somewhat different to the picture painted by 'Okie'. Muskogee has a large population of black people, who in 1969 were faced with vicious inequality. Historian Peter La Chapelle notes:

Haggard bought into the conception that [smaller Southern cities] were free from racial strife, while invoking an equally salient stereotype that urban blacks instigated social disorder.[10]

But in 1969, the 'silent majority' of white America were fearful of the violence that had erupted in Watts, LA and in other big cities; organisations like the Black Panther Party and their support of the anti-Vietnam protests were linked, giving a racist connotation to the diverse groups of young Americans who were protesting the war. The US two-party political system was turning itself inside out and upside down since the election of President John F Kennedy in 1960 and the adoption of Lyndon Johnson's Great Society reforms in 1965. This triggered the end of the chasm within the Democratic Party along the Mason-Dixon line. Northern liberals like Franklin D Roosevelt had been at ideological odds with a coalition of Midwestern Republicans and segregationist Southern Democrats who moderated their ambitions in Congress. Black voters in the South had traditionally favoured the Republican Party since the days of Abraham Lincoln; now they were backing Johnson. White working class voters shifted Republican, especially during the Cold War presidencies of Dwight Eisenhower. By the time Ronald Reagan was elected in 1980, the ideological chasm had become realigned more or less on party lines: Republicans were conservative, Democrats liberal.

In 1972, with Republican President Richard Nixon's approval rating at its highest (67%) despite his appalling escalation of the war in Vietnam and Cambodia, the US CMA presented him with a unique recording (only two copies exist) entitled *Thank You Mr President*. Prominent on the album was Merle Haggard's 'Okie from Muskogee', a song that Nixon liked so much he had asked Johnny Cash to play it for him when Cash first visited the White House in 1970 (Cash refused).

Also on President Nixon's gift from the CMA was a message from CMA past president and failed Republican senatorial candidate, Tex Ritter:

> Country music, which in reality is the voice of your silent majority, can sing about the troubles of the present with as much love of country as in the past. [It] can break the enormity of war down to the very personal.[11]

On St Patrick's Day 1973, a couple of months after Nixon finally bowed to domestic and international pressure by signing the Paris Peace Accord withdrawing US troops from the Vietnam War, the President invited Merle Haggard to sing 'Okie' at a White House party. The occasion was recorded on film. Haggard's performance is reverential, bordering on sycophantic, concluding with a sentimental poem composed to celebrate the First Lady's birthday which fell upon that same day.

According to music historian J Lester Feder the CMA and Nixon had a "mutual self-interest" in Country music, as a cultural vehicle to which they could harness America's conservative heartlands. Feder records that by 1970:

Over two-thirds of country record sales were made outside the South. What largely united listeners from coast to coast was a longing for a more simple, more stable, and more wholesome time than the present.[12]

For Nixon, the record and concert sales that energised the CMA demonstrated Ritter's assertion about Country music being a direct emotional mainline into the soul of white middle America.

Historian Bill Malone opines that Country music has always had socially conservative tendencies, arising with the Southern Democrat populist traditions of the 1880s and 1890s. Until the 1950s, populism was, by the standards of American politics, a left-wing concept. Malone cites Slim Smith's 'Breadline Blues' as an early example of a popular Country song expressing populist reaction to the Great Depression. Both Malone and Feder are quick to qualify that 'political' songs have always formed a small minority of Country hits, emphasising the socially conservative ethos of family, love, hard work, and endurance of personal tragedy that forms the core of the Country canon. Malone cites the Cold War era of the 1950s as the context for the growth of reactionary conservative themes in Country music. By the 1960s, Country music radio was playing a "conservative anthem every minute."[13]

In the early 1960s, the Democratic Party in the South was

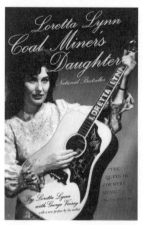

traditional, segregationist. George Wallace, Democrat Governor of Alabama, used Country music in his campaign for the 1968 presidential nomination. Nixon "used Wallace's playbook" to appeal to white, working class, socially conservative voters across the nation. Songs like Loretta Lynn's 'Coal Miner's Daughter' were used by conservative politicians as a counter to the popular culture of black pride embodied simultaneously in the popularity of James Brown and other African American artists.[14]

During the post-Nixon era, when the Republican Party had taken over as the voice of reactionary America, the strong links between the CMA and the Republican establishment surfaced in media and marketing. When the Dixie Chicks made public statements against President Bush's Iraq war in 2003, their records were dropped from CMA-affiliated Country radio stations' playlists. So strong remains the perceived link between Southern working class culture and redneck politics, that in 2020 the band felt it necessary to drop the word 'Dixie' from their name.

A favourite saying around Nashville – home of both the CMA and the AMA – is that Americana is 'Country music for Democrats.' Whilst neither music organisation would seek to limit their congregation to a particular stratum of voters, it is fair to say that today's CMA retains a more conservative (with a small c) outlook than its youthful cousin the AMA. Time will tell whether irresistible market forces will see the Americana umbrella furl into a rigid commercial enterprise like the CMA. Ironically, the CMA was founded in 1958 for some surprisingly similar reasons to those that gave birth to the AMA. Bill Malone explains in his history, *Southern Music/American Music*, that the CMA was founded to promote Country in reaction to the overwhelming popularity of Rock 'n' Roll in the late 1950s:

> One of the CMA's main strategies was to persuade radio stations to play Country music exclusively… Most Country stations developed their own versions of the Top 40 formats pioneered by Rock stations.[15]

The 'top 40' format naturally leads to the tight playlist mentality, especially as the younger DJs brought in to give Country a competitive edge were often recruited from Rock stations, where this was already the norm. Malone notes:

> Led by Chet Atkins, the country music industry reacted to the Rock 'n' Roll threat by attempting to create a product that

would appeal to the broadest spectrum of listeners… a music shorn of its rural characteristics[16].

Ultimately it was this strategy that led the AMA to be formed in reaction to the sleek, tightly controlled and playlisted product that Country became under the auspices of the CMA.

Today's popular music culture, where consumers expect recorded music on tap for free, monetised only by advertising or subscription to the carrier, favours the differentiation of major label music from the rest. The Americana umbrella still covers relatively few major-label acts within a diverse population of niche-label and independent artists. Whilst the Americana industry is unlikely to undergo the rapid metamorphosis of Rap/Hip Hop music from outlaw/underground to celebrity culture, it still may need to adapt to commercial reality. If, as Jed Hilly maintains, Americana is a fine art form, it must find ways of attracting elite patronage (and dwindling subsidy) that is the mainstay of other fine arts.

If Americana is to remain true to its working class roots, it must rely on finding a medium of distribution that generates a reasonable income even for entry-level artists, such as existed in the early days of the recording and radio industries during the 1920s and 1930s. The nearest equivalent we have today are the channels and pages of social media influencers, which provide exposure without monetisation for the artist. It will take government intervention in response to lobbying by representational bodies such as the AMA and musicians' unions to ensure that market forces come to favour artists who wish to retain a degree of individual expression.

THE UMBRELLA

Out of Buddy Holly's native town of Lubbock, TX comes Colin Gilmore, son of veteran songwriter James Gilmore. When we interviewed Colin after his Victoria Room show at SXSW 2018, he defined Americana thus:

Americana. I mean, it's, kinda hard to describe, because it can be anything that started in America. I remember when somebody first described it to me, they started saying like, Jerry Lee [Lewis] or John Cougar Mellencamp. I kinda got it. I was like: 'All right, so, it's something that is Roots-based, but has some traditional in it and then some Rock 'n' Roll in it.'

Q: So, do you think similar music in Australia could be described as Americana?

Yeah, I think so… I think the influences have gone back and forth quite a bit. So, I remember when the [Australian/UK immigrant band] The Greencards came over. I'm a huge fan. At the time, a whole lot of people [were] coming from [Australia] playing what sounded to me like traditional American music, but kind of doing it like better in some cases!

THE STREETS OF LAREDO

Here is a song that illustrates in microcosm the multi-threaded trail that leads with a single tune through many nations and traditions:

'The Unfortunate Rake' (trad.)

As I was a-walking down by St James' Hospital,
I was a-walking down by there one day,
What should I spy but one of my comrades
All wrapped up in flannel though warm was the day.

I asked him what ailed him,
I asked him what failed him,
I asked him the cause of all his complaint.
'It's all on account of some handsome young woman,'
Tis she that has caused me to weep and lament.

And had she but told me before she disordered me,
Had she but told me of it in tire,
I might have got pills and salts of white mercury,
But now I'm cut down in the height of my prime.

Get six young soldiers to carry my coffin,
Six young girls to sing me a song,
And each of them carry a bunch of green laurel
So they don't smell me as they bear me along.

Don't muffle your drums and play your fifes merrily,
Play a quick march as you carry me along,
And fire your bright muskets all over my coffin,
Saying: There goes an unfortunate lad to his home.

Familiar lyric? *The Unfortunate Rake*[17] is an album that traces the folk process operating on a single song. The liner notes record that:

The oldest text we can find for any member of the 'Rake' cycle of songs … had been collected … from a singer who had learned it in Dublin in 1790. The singer… could remember only a single chorus. Which goes:

My jewel, my joy, don't trouble me with the drum,
Sound the dead march as my corpse goes along
And over my body throw handfuls of laurel,
And let them all know that I'm going to my rest.

Johnny Cash's version of the cowboy classic 'Streets of Laredo' features the following refrain, delivered in Cash's unmistakable gravelled basso:

Then beat the drum slowly, play the Fife lowly.
Play the dead march as you carry me along.
Take me to the green valley, lay the sod o'er me,
I'm a young cowboy and I know I've done wrong.

Marty Robbins was one of the most successful country singers of his generation, with 17 #1 US Country chart singles in a nearly 40-year career. Robbins was born in Glendale, a suburb of Phoenix in Maricopa County, Arizona. His mother was mostly of Paiute Indian heritage.[18]

In 1960, Robbins published one of the most famous versions of the song on his album *More Gunfighter Ballads and Trail Songs*. Here is a singer of Native American heritage singing a ballad originating, as far as anyone can tell, somewhere in

18th-century Dublin, using an arrangement drenched with Mexican American guitar motifs.

Fast-forward to 2012 when New Zealand band Streets of Laredo emerged into the Brooklyn Indie-Folk scene, using Americana as a visual and audible theme, if not exactly recognised by the industry as an Americana act.

DO YOU NEED TO BE PRO-AMERICAN MUSIC TO LOVE AMERICANA?

Remember hipsters? Heavily bearded young chaps dressed as lumberjacks, patronizing ridiculously expensive artisan food and drinks outlets? The short-lived fad that swept first-world Caucasian communities in the mid-2010s has been journalistically linked to Americana music, possibly because of the fashion aesthetic.[19] True, if one were to visit any of the major Americana music events two or three years back, there would be a large contingent of such folk in the audience. But do you need to fit the fashion stereotype to love the music? It's as ridiculous as insisting that you must sport a Mohican to love Punk Rock!

The Atlantic, a 'witty' magazine, predominantly read by older males[20] correctly pointed out in 2013 that since Jed Hilly and the AMA had persuaded the RA to hand out a Grammy for Best Americana Album in 2009, nobody under 60 had won.[21] The same article sought to convince readers that music labelled as Americana was "dad rock" – old, white, and male – despite the fact that of those five Grammys, three were won by women (the other two by the same man – Levon Helm). True, only one of the awards went to an African American (Mavis Staples), but less than 20% of the population of the US is African American, so that does not seem anomalous. *The Atlantic* article chose rightly to take to task a breed of American music that is Caucasian, male, and conservative in outlook:

> If an art form is going to name itself after this country, it should probably stop weatherproofing itself against America's present-day developments. [You can't claim] the

legacies of black Gospel and Blues if the performers and listeners venerating them are almost all white.

What it fails to do is acknowledge the much wider inclusive element that Americana brings to the party. Perhaps in 2013 this was less apparent to a writer embedded in US culture and focusing on the elite, rather than the grassroots level.

The Atlantic depicts Amanda Petrusich's book, *It Still Moves*, as a "loving depiction of Americana's roots," continuing:

> It sometimes seems like the Delta's legacy is most present in modern Hip Hop [rather than Americana] where its basic tenets are still being perpetuated, even if the form has altered dramatically.[22]

It is widely agreed that Hip Hop derives more directly from African musical culture than Americana,[23] but the style of music that most informs what we now think of as Americana derives from an amalgam of historic rural American music that existed in the era often dubbed the 'melting pot' before the technology for recording and publishing sound. In the earliest recorded examples of this music, it is difficult to separate the African American influences from those of European Folk music. The stereotypical analysis also negates completely the contribution of musicians of indigenous American heritage to American Roots music. Rather, the Delta's legacy persists in both forms in different aspects. The US music festival South by Southwest (SXSW), one of the biggest platforms outside of Nashville for live Americana music, is also listed as the "#1 Hip Hop festival in the US."[24] The SXSW audience is a diverse gathering of music lovers who typically enjoy the event by taking in every genre on offer.

Musicians will inevitably blend forms and styles to create new musical expression. Arising from contemporary cultural influences this new music says more – and touches more hearts – than its ancestral forms, by virtue of combining elements from different traditions and speaking to today's generation. It's this process of continual innovation that has made American music stand out in international popular culture. American 'Roots' music, the music that existed before the media-industrial complex started silo-ing everything, was culturally mixed in its players and styles, as evidenced by those very earliest recordings.

The dominant musical culture in contemporary American popular music is Rap and Hip Hop. "Hip Hop is as old as outlaw country," says Charles Hughes, author of *Country Soul: Making Music and Making Race in the American South.*[25] "The black music incorporated by Americana stops at about 1972." Hughes maybe hadn't heard the Dead South's record 'In Hell I'll be in Good Company' with its macabre murder rap chorus set to banjo and bull fiddle by young dudes sporting Civil War whiskers and Stetsons.

On the other side of the coin, Kyshona Armstrong's latest single 'Fear' is a moody swamp thing by an African American Roots artist embracing the joys of Heavy Rock, a genre that originated in the UK. Americana is as near as one can get in the heavily siloed world of commercial music to all things for all people.

And then there is Southern Rock. Listen to Drive by Truckers circa 2003[26] and you have the vocal mannerisms and suspended majors of the Rolling Stones in their 70s heyday, spiced with three howlin' geetars straight outa Lynyrd Skynyrd–actually, Hughes is maybe right with that one.

But if you want an indisputable illustration of how Americana really drives a 16-wheel truck through the conventions of redneck Country music, listen to Mavis Staples running through 'The Weight' with the band Wilco and Nick Lowe backstage in Chicago.[27]

The roots of Rock are with the marginalised communities of America in the 1940s and 1950s. Interviewed in 1997, Link Wray from North Carolina, who identified as half Cherokee, half Shawnee, said:

We played Western swing, but [my brother] Doug had this real loud drum style. I guess we were playing Rock 'n' Roll in the 1940s. We were playing real heavy music on Tex Davis' country show.[28]

By the way, Davis went on to co-write Gene Vincent's Rock 'n' Roll classic, 'Be-Bop-a-Lula'.

Music historians credit Wray with the invention of the power chord, an essential tool of electric guitarists such as Pete Townshend, Jimmy Page, and Jimi Hendrix, who brought Heavy Rock into being in the UK in the 1960s. But back in 1957, Wray would have heard records of the time by electric bluesmen like Sam Maghett (Magic Sam) and Muddy Waters.

Wray's big break came when he and his brothers cast off their hillbilly costumes in favour of rocker attire. Fredericksburg, Virginia, 1957: Wray and his brothers were the house band for Milt Grant, whose *Record Hop* TV show out of Washington, DC was a barometer of hot music across the nation. Grant would bring stars from his show to perform to a dancehall audience in Fredericksburg after the show. One night the star attraction was The Diamonds, a somewhat polite besuited mainstream harmony vocal quartet who had scored a hit with 'Strolling' – a characteristic four-triplets-to-the-bar rhythm that had inspired yet another teen dance craze. Grant asked if Wray's band could play a stroll. Wray admitted he didn't know how. But his brother, drummer Doug, jumped onto the kit and started up a slow, brooding stroll rhythm. His other brother, vocalist Vernon, hooked up Wray's tiny guitar amp to the vocal mic to give it more power over Doug's heavy drums. Wray launched into his wild Chicago-inspired power-chord riff, the tiny PA speakers rattled with distortion, and 'Rumble' was born.

The kids started screaming and came up to the stage. They was hollerin' 'We want that song!'. They didn't care about the Diamonds no more… I had to play it about four times before we left.[29]

The song had no catchy name at the time. Grant saw profits to be made and had Wray's band make a recording, which he took to Archie Bleyer at Cadence records, whose teenage daughter said it made her think of the gang fight scenes in the latest Broadway hit *West Side Story*. Bleyer, who was more used to the gentler music of his star artists the Everly Brothers, was horrified when, persuaded by his daughter's reaction, of the single's commercial potential, he released the record to have it banned in Boston and New York because of fears it would incite further violence. Wray confessed, "I wasn't thinking of gang fights; it was a Southern thing... Elvis, Jerry Lee, we all wore shades and leather jackets."

But the controversy generated by the contemporary media frenzy with teenage gang violence did no harm to the record's sales, and Wray quickly moved labels to produce a further canon of work until, in Link's words, "The Beatles' invasion and assassination of President Kennedy killed my music".[30]

Link Wray, The Village Underground NYC. Photo Anthony Pepitone

By the 90s, Wray had moved to Denmark. By then he had acquired 'heritage' status, his 1971 Polydor-released collected works receiving solid Americana credentials from *MOJO* magazine: "The sort of backwoods, Bluesy-Folky-Gospel-Country-Rocky organic old America beloved of Creedence Clearwater Revival and The Band."[31]

A man of spiritual rather than religious beliefs, Wray passed into the spirit world in 2005, leaving 23 grandchildren from three marriages.

The fusion of African American and Native American literally gave birth to the father of Rock 'n' Roll, Chuck Berry. Berry's autobiography[32] traces his ancestry to African slaves, Chihuahua and Oklahoma Native Americans, and a rich immigrant lady from Leeds, UK. His 1955 debut hit 'Maybellene' is acknowledged as one of the most truly representative slices of Americana. Berry had written the song as 'Ida Mae', but his label boss Leonard Chess didn't like the name. "It was too rural, and he thought its similarity to [Bob Wills' Western swing hit] 'Ida Red' might pose copyright hassles."[33] Berry's American melting-pot genes brought to a Western swing song the urgency and irresistible *joie de vivre* that was to inform a generation of musicians all over the world. Of all the musical forms so far to come out of that continent, only Hip Hop has had greater commercial impact and longevity in worldwide popular music.

I am talking with North Mississippian singer/songwriter John Murry (now an Irish resident) about Native American heritage and its influence on Americana. Of his biological parents, Murry says:

> If you have an ancestor in the United States before 1850 you have an even chance of having native blood… I should have been offered to the [Cherokee] Nation, in that more than 50% [of my ancestry]: there's a bit on my mother's side, but my father… he was Cherokee, with a bit of Comanche there too. [Comanche chief] Quanah Parker was one of my

great-grandfathers. But here's a thing: Quanah's mother was Cynthia Ann Parker of Scottish descent, who was kidnapped by the Comanche as a child, but refused to return to marry into her former [European American] community.

From an early age, Murry was familiar with an important part of his local musical culture, and its diverse heritage. He recalls a conversation with Irish musician Jim Lockhart, of Celtic Rock band Horselips:

> I played him some Othar Turner from the Rising Star Fife and Drum Band from where I was growing up. He just went 'John, this is black people playing Orange Order music!' They were making these [fifes] out of canes.

Turner's music, known as 'Hill Country Blues', is an amalgam of Native American drumming with Scots Irish fife and drum melodies, to a West African proto-Blues groove. A local tradition in North Mississippi started by Turner is the Labor Day picnic, at which a goat would be butchered and cooked while the band entertained the guests. Murry remembers: "I used to go to the goat roast where they would open up an 18-wheeler and cut the goat's throat. Then they'd make the roast, but they'd also use the skin for the drums."

Murry notes that the Native American contribution to American music has been "largely whitewashed out" of the historical commentary. There are relatively few historical sources that note the indigenous connections to the Blues through the fusion of Native American and African drumming traditions and patterns.[34] "People like [the late Native American activist] John Trudell and [Mohican multiple-Grammy-winning flautist] Bill Miller are integral parts of this Americana story," says Murry.

Owing to the complex genealogy of the American South, Murry can claim kin with Nobel Laureate William Faulkner, both through his adoptive parents, and biologically via a connection with the Murrays of Dunmore that was revealed to him in an NPR radio interview.[35] The eloquence and erudition of his discourse is a testament to the literary streak that informs his brilliance as a songwriter. But his musical strength, as with all the greatest songsmiths, is the atmosphere he conveys in his delivery: in Murry's case the brooding menace in the dark shadows of the South.

Kasey Chambers is probably Australia's most widely known female Americana artist. Just after the release of her 2018 album *Campfire*, she talked to us about her experience of pulling in strands of music from around the world:

> I wanted to put all of that into this album and I guess bring people in, to sit around our campfire while we jam. You know, that's what the whole album is about. I think a lot of this record was about stripping everything back and going back to the roots of music for me… growing up in the Australian Outback, and then also drawing from all these different places around the world that have influenced my life. I spent a few years living on Norfolk Island, which is where I made [debut album] *The Captain*… I spent a lot of time in America touring, and a lot of the music that I've grown up listening to is American music; John Prine and Emmylou Harris, this sort of music sounds beautiful around the campfire… I spent a bit of time travelling in Africa over the years and have been really influenced by the music over there, even though it's very different to mine. I love the way that they create so many beautiful sounds with just voices… that was a real inspiration… So, all of that sort of ended up on this record.

Audio reproduction technology has only been available as a commercial medium, with the advent of mass-market record players and commercial radio broadcasting, from about 1920. Music evolved and was disseminated much faster as the technology became available in homes. Eventually, music from all over the world was spread globally through more compact recording and audio reproduction equipment until we arrive at the incredible streaming technologies of today.

Paradoxically, music marketing practices, which began with demographic targeting of records (for example, the 'race records' market established from the mid 1920s)[36] and continued with playlist-related content selection in radio programming, still tend to silo music audiences heavily by genre. US Media executives assumed from the start that only African Americans would want to listen to Blues, Jazz, (and later, Rap and Hip Hop), and that Caucasians would mainly be interested in Country; all this, despite the way that the ancestors of these musical styles had cross-fertilized with each other and with Indigenous American music in the 'melting pot' era prior to 1920. This assumption may have been as much to do with the marketing notion of targeting a particular 'community' of customers (even though most actual communities in the US are racially diverse, despite a history of racial segregation). The use of radio shows to sell specific products to specific demographics is endemic in commercial radio, particularly in the US.

Recent academic research shows that the advent of 'disruptive' technologies via the internet – through internet protocol (IP) streaming music and video – are loosening that stereotypical marketing stranglehold somewhat by putting more power into the customers' hands to programme the music they prefer. For example, a 2019 paper crunching the content of 400,000 playlists concludes:

> We have found a more balanced situation in [streaming playlist] datasets [than radio playlists] in terms of popularity, although they contain playlists with a high level of diversity in terms of semantic tags.[37]

Before IP streaming, the disruptive technology was cassette tapes. "Home taping is killing music," complained the record industry, but mixtapes allowed fans to do what they now do with playlists: select music they enjoyed from diverse genres in a single package. The industry solved the home taping issue by making streaming effectively free (monetizing with intrusive advertising and other restrictions), and by clamping down on illegal downloads using digital rights management

(DRM) technology. This was bad news for musicians, who had previously derived respectable 'mechanical' royalties from sales of tangible recording media (records, CDs, and high-quality pre-recorded cassettes), and from broadcast radio and video plays. With the advent of IP streaming, music became a free commodity: in the last ten years customer expectations have changed radically to a world where their favourite music streams on-tap. Streaming royalties are so low that all but multiple-million-stream musicians now have to derive practically all their income from live performance and merchandise, notably the current resurgence of vinyl as a collectors' item. The Covid-19 pandemic effectively cut off live performance and retail merchandising at gigs, leaving musicians with at most a feeble revenue stream from royalties.

One of the few bright spots on the horizon is that the major streaming outlets are now making their advertising intrusive enough to drive more consumers to their preferred business model of ad-free subscription services. Subscription services lock in customer loyalty so they're good for the streamers, but are they good for the musicians? Well, the way that streaming services work is that their total revenues (mainly advertising and subscriptions) are pooled, and artists (or the labels who represent them) receive a share of the pot based on their streaming figures. More subscriptions should mean more revenue, right? But groups advocating for musicians, like Keep Music Alive, say the shared-pool system is unfairly weighted towards ultra-popular artists who net vast numbers of plays. It is also vulnerable to 'bot fraud', whereby pluggers seek to inflate artists' stream numbers artificially by using software to make automated plays. Mark Taylor of the UK Keep Music Alive Alliance explains:

> The price of a subscription has stayed static for a number of years, but frankly, given where we are economically right now, and pressure on peoples' wallets, that's probably not the route to go down as a campaign.[38]

Pressure groups such as Taylor's are advocating an alternative, 'user-centric' algorithm for dividing up the streaming pot. How would this work? For subscribed users, the algorithm apportions the subscription fee from each user to the artists they actually listened to that month. Artists argue that this system more fairly rewards them for the investment that their listeners are making in them, without affecting the market for giga-streams of pop acts. And this would benefit Americana artists, who tend to have dedicated and discerning fan bases.

Time will tell whether all the major streamers will adopt user-centric royalty models. The good news is that French streamer Deezer recently deployed a "user-centric payment system" (UCPS) for its premium subscribers.[39] Market leader Spotify has so far resisted calls to change its system, despite recent revelations about a Bulgarian scam where allegedly over 1,000 fake subscriptions were set up, auto-repeating a single artist's track and netting far more in streaming royalties than the cost of the subscription.[40] Music Managers Forum UK CEO Annabella Coldrick wrote at the time the scam was discovered:

> Our members increasingly believe that, despite the complexities of introducing a user-centric model, it is inherently fairer to reconnect the fan to the artist along with the additional benefits of greater transparency and accountability throughout the streaming value chain.[41]

Some of today's Americana artists are avoiding Spotify in favour of Deezer in order to illustrate the relative iniquity of the Spotify revenue model for smaller artists. An example is Australia's Harry Hookey, whose 2014 Nash Chambers-produced album *Misdiagnosed* is not available on Spotify. Interviewed on tour in Austin, TX, Harry told us about his priorities:

> I've basically been just touring around as much as I can… I've built up a small but loyal following. I find people always turn out to [my] shows when I come back to their towns… they're kind of like friends. For me, having loyal fans is more important than having lots of them.

In October 2020 the UK Government announced that their Department of Culture, Media, and Sport Select Committee would examine the "Economics of Music Streaming". The investigative committee of MPs took evidence from major labels, UK rights management regulator PRS, and musicians and writers including the hit-making producer Nile Rodgers and Fiona Bevan, a successful songwriter who has worked with Ed Sheeran and Canadian artist Hawksley Workman, among many others. Although the major labels defended the total-streams model of Spotify as a fair representation of popularity, this ignores the fact that a large proportion of streams are played algorithmically (akin to radio playlist programming), rather than by request from active listeners. Rodgers identified perhaps the most important issue with the current situation, which is opacity on the value to the streaming service operators of each stream played. This means that, unlike the major label corporations, creators and performers of music are unable to negotiate equitable revenue deals with streamers.[42] If there was ever a positive to be taken from the pandemic, it is that a lack of touring has allowed musicians to focus on achieving fairer returns from their recorded music. UK music journalist Paul Sexton told me: "The complete absence of touring revenue has meant that anyone who has ever put a record on a streaming service thinks in more detail about how that works – or dare I say it? – how that *doesn't* work... [In light of] these recent hearings, I don't think there is anywhere for [the streaming services] to hide."

Another problem posed by IP technology that particularly affects Americana artists is discovery. IP has diminished consumer time with old-school broadcast radio and TV, so despite the efforts of dedicated aficionados around the world, like Bob Harris in the UK, Bob Boilen in the US, and Paul Kelly in Australia, IP streamers find it harder to see the wood for the trees when seeking out the best in Americana music. Enter the internet radio station. Internet radio has lowered the bar to entry for genuine music enthusiasts to spread their love internationally, in many cases from the comfort of their own home studios. Internet radio particularly benefits grassroots and emerging musicians by giving them a small space on a big international platform. I am speaking with Mandolin Jack, who from Southwest London curates online his songwriter show for the illustrious Country Music Radio (CMR) Nashville. He tells me about how he started his popular show:

> CMR is a highly respected radio station over here and in the USA. Lee Williams [CMR CEO] is the driving force. He's just won another award to add to his collection.[ii] Lee gave me a songwriter show a while back when I was the UK co-ordinator for the Nashville Songwriters' Association. I took a break for a while to teach, but when I retired, I asked Lee if I could do another show: he had me straight back!

Jack keeps his focus on the quality of individual songs, selecting tracks and artists that will keep his audience's attention.

> I spread my net wide. I find just Country is too close a network. I remember Bob Harris playing a song on his show once and saying 'This is a standout song for me because it was written by the singer. On his own. Without five other people joining in.' And it certainly had a lot more heart and soul in it than something written by five people: you get a great hit line, but it has no soul.

As a frequent visitor to Nashville, Mandolin Jack has some experience of the system with the Nashville Songwriters Association, who are "proud to point out that they foster co-writing," but he refutes the idea that Nashville is all about big teams writing Country pop hits. He says:

> Nashville has never been exclusively about Country. It's a true music town. All the great Louisiana Blues were recorded there – Slim Harpo, Lightning Slim. There is this great funky,

---

i. Williams won the Country Music Association's award for International Country Music Broadcaster in 2013; his latest is a Media Innovator award in September 2020 for his promotions company Django.

bluesy scene there. Walk down Church Street and you will hear industry folks and musicians talking music, music, music!

I know loads of writers who work solo in Nashville. Mean Mary, who is featured on my show this week, has written half of her new album – which is called *Alone* – alone; the other half she wrote with her mother.[ii]

Until the Covid-19 pandemic, there were plenty of small venues supporting solo singer-songwriters in Nashville, such as the Bluebird and Brown's Diner. Jack's not been over since 2019 but says, "I don't know what it's like now, but I hear that it may be terminal for some of them."

One of the greatest pioneers of internet radio was the late Barry Everitt. Barry was a highly respected promoter for the Borderline club in London from 1999 until 2007 when new owners "terminated his contract". Interviewed in 2012,[43] Everitt describes how he took over, given six months to turn the Borderline around as a "failed BritPop venue":

I said, 'we're closing for two months while I re-book' … just frantically got on the phone to all my Americana friends… brought everything to the Borderline… great location, lovely sound… very 'woody'. Within a year we were voted 'Venue of the Year'.[44]

Back in psychedelic 1970, Everitt had made his radio debut on *Radio Geronimo*, a barely legal station broadcasting out of Harley Street (cheekily just around the corner from the BBC in London) via a massive transmitter in the French Alpes Maritimes operated by Radio Monaco, just to the right on the dial from Radio Luxembourg. Geronimo was owned by Rock 'n' Roll characters Jimmy Miller and Tony Secunda, who allowed its somewhat chaotic presenters totally free artistic rein, but (possibly because of this) failed to attract advertising revenue. In its short existence, Geronimo became a legend amongst music enthusiasts of the period, already tuned into John Peel's output on 'pirate', and later BBC, radio.

---

i. ii   Novelist Jean James

After the 2008 financial crash, Everitt focussed again on radio. He had already begun the internet radio station originally called Radio Borderline, but swiftly renamed the station House of Mercy Radio when he left, after discovering that the site of the Borderline had once been a shelter for prostitutes by that name, set up by nearby St Barnabas' Church. Everitt described his programming strategy (and remember, this was before streaming really caught on) as:

> People don't want to gamble on buying recordings they don't know about… they want to buy what they know is ok… tuning into the Roots stations… going 'I really like that one!' That's why we feature an album… play 5 or 6 tracks on one show, so you don't find out there was only one great track… We're a bunch of underground hippies really, with cowboy hats this time.

As Everitt succumbed to the cancer that would kill him a few weeks later, his 2017 benefit gig featured musical tributes by UK Roots music greats Wily Bo Walker, Stick in the Wheel, and Danny and the Champions.

Another contemporary aid to discovery for aspiring Americana musicians is the market created by curated or algorithmic streaming playlists. Several platforms implement this market online, best-known probably being SubmitHub, where for a modest fee, artists or labels can get a guaranteed airing of their music to their selected group of curators and influencers. The near future is likely to see a raft of meta-business around music discovery and distribution, as streaming business models become fully mature. In a cyberspace of relentlessly vast choice, it is vital for artists to know how to navigate these meta-businesses to ensure they are given a fair hearing. Mandolin Jack compares YouTube to the broadcast radio shows he grew up on:

> I do a lot of discovery on YouTube. It operates more like an old-fashioned radio station. The algorithms work on what you just watched, but will pick from anywhere, across many channels. You play Mean Mary, then you hear the Grateful Dead.

Danny and the Champions of the World. Truck Festival 2015,
Slippery Saddle Saloon. Photo John Morgan

DIFFERENT STRANDS IN
US AMERICANA MUSIC

*Three chords and the truth – that's what
a country song is.*
–Willie Nelson

Americana is a trail you follow, and you pick things up on the way. It's a trail followed by musicians who want to reconnect with their ancestral roots. It's a trail followed by listeners who want to discover how those musicians have wrought input from many cultures into something of their own. It's a trail where musicians from outside America are contributing their own take on American culture with a twist from their own backyards.

THE COUNTRY MUSIC INDUSTRY

On a cool February evening in 1939, Sara Carter stepped up to the mic at XERA, the giant radio transmitter just across the Texas border from Del Rio, Mexico. Sara's nickname was 'Jake' and she held herself proud, "like a man" – unconventional in that time and place. Her voice and body were strong from years of felling lumber for the paper mills in the mountains, until the hot August 1927 day in Bristol, Tennessee, that changed her, and her family's, lives for ever. The Carter Family had been hired, for a truly handsome fee in those days, by the station's owner 'Dr' John R Brinkley, to use their music to sell his products over half a million watts of signal, reaching right across the US from California to New York City.

But Sara had other matters on her mind. In 1936 she had quietly divorced Alvin Pleasant Delaney ('AP') Carter, the man who, in 1915 had discovered 16-year-old Sara singing to her autoharp on the porch of a shack clinging to the Clinch Mountain ridge, the spine of Appalachia. Sara's love for AP had died through a combination of AP's Methodist "coldness"; his frequent absences to collect songs and market the family singing group; and with Sara's growing love for Coy Bayes, AP's young blue-eyed cousin, whom AP had engaged to help run the family smallholding in his absence. To help preserve the biblical family values enshrined in the Carters' brand, Coy's extended family had taken him off to California, and in nearly three years, despite sending many letters, Sara had heard nothing from him. Sara had reluctantly agreed to accept Brinkley's money for the sake of the Carter family business, but six months over the Rio Grande cooped up with her ex-husband had left her desperate.

The Carters broadcast two live shows per day on XERA, featuring tunes made popular in working class homes and more genteel parlours all over the nation from their Victor recordings, starting with the seminal Bristol Sessions in 1927. The morning show featured cheery tunes like 'Keep on the Sunny Side', while the evening show would take a more mellow form, with ballads of love and loss; both shows were frequently interspersed with commercial messages advocating Brinkley's patent medicines and other franchised commodities. That night, in front of the mic that would take her voice across the continent, Sara's lonesomeness got the better of her when she proclaimed, "I'm gonna dedicate this next song to Coy Bayes in California." With that, Maybelle started strumming her guitar, and Sara began singing one of their earliest songs, 'I'm Thinking Tonight of my Blue Eyes.'[45]

More than 1,500 miles across the Sierra Nevada, the Bayes family were gathered around their radio set, as were a great multitude of American families in the pre-TV era. Coy's mother had kept Sara's letters from him, and he thought that fame had

Maybelle, AP and Sara Carter

erased Sara's memories of him. But when he heard her message crackling over the ether he drove clear across the country, down to Texas, where the reunited lovers soon married.[46]

Forlorn and still in love with Sara, AP never recovered his voice, leaving XERA to resume life as a carpenter and occasional general storekeeper on Clinch Mountain. Sara continued to perform with the Carter Family until the early 1940s, when she relocated permanently to California with Coy.

*

The birth of Country Music on record occurred, according to most musicologists, in 1927, at a hat factory warehouse in East

Tennessee. The midwife was one Ralph Peer, who in return for a $1 annual salary, kept the rights for all the recordings he collected for his employers, the Victor Talking Machine Company. Peer had taken his mobile recording equipment to the South in search of music that might be popular with working people. In nine sweltering Appalachian summer days, Peer recorded 76 songs by 19 different groups. The Bristol Sessions, as they became known, were the recording debut of two artists that emerged to take key roles in the history of Country music, and by inheritance, the history of Americana: The Carter Family and Jimmie Rodgers.

The Carter Family represented the 'churchhouse/ schoolhouse' Folky strand of Roots music that emerged from Peer's legendary recordings in Bristol, Tennessee. Jimmie Rodgers ('the Singing Brakeman') came out of the 'barroom/ barndance' honky-tonk tradition in the more secular strands of live Country music. The records sold from the Bristol Sessions made Rodgers and the Carters national stars, and put East Tennessee, and its capital Nashville, at the plumb centre of the Country music map of the US.

It was the Great Depression that really formed the next phase of the evolution of Country music. By the early 1930s working class people had little spare cash with which to buy records. And many of these people were leaving the country heartlands of the South to head for the Golden State of California, seeking escape from the Dust Bowl to a kinder climate. And at this time working people all over the US were turning from expensive records to the airwaves of the burgeoning radio network as a way to hear the most talented exponents of their own homegrown music for free.

Radio created a symbiotic connection between the Country music industry and the wider business community. Station owners used popular music over the new medium to promote more prosaic products (often from their own businesses) right into the humble homes of fans who formed their mass market across the nation. The Dust Bowl migration brought musicians from the South into the big cities, notably the vast conurbations of Los Angeles and the San Francisco Bay Area. The Maddox Brothers and Rose (the 'sweetheart of hillbilly swing'), Buck Owens, Bob Wills, Woody Guthrie, and Merle Haggard all helped to create what became known as the 'Bakersfield sound', bringing rhythmic elements of swing Jazz (then also exploding on radio as a cross-culture dance form), amplified steel guitars, and radio-friendly drums into the broadcast mix. Chicago's mighty WLS transmitter spread West coast and Nashville Country music right across the heart of the US, notably through the Saturday night Barn Dance shows live from the 8th St. Theatre.

The movies also played a huge role in making Country music popular in the 1930s. Orvon Grover ('Gene') Autry was a not-very-successful recording artist with budget labels attempting to produce cheaper recordings that would compete with radio, on which he imitated the yodelling style of Jimmie Rodgers. Given a chance to appear on WLS, Autry toned down the yodelling. Billed as the 'Oklahoma Cowboy', he had a massive radio hit with 'Home on the Range' (President Roosevelt's self-confessed favourite song). In 1934, Oklahoma farm boy turned singing cowboy Autry landed a contract with Mascot Pictures, taking riding lessons in order to fill the lead role in a bizarre cowboy/sci-fi B movie, *The Phantom Empire*. Autry basically plays the radio star he now was, breaking off from fighting mysterious subterranean beings clad in silver pharaoh outfits, just in time to perform on his radio show. Despite critical indifference, the movie was a popular hit, spawning a vast genre of singing cowboy pictures. Soon every studio except MGM had a singing cowboy under contract. Country music took on a certain Hollywood aura as the movies exposed it to a wider audience. Rose Maddox and her brothers were one of the first Country acts to secure the services of tailor to the stars Nathan Turk, who supplied the iconic rhinestone cowboy outfits that were to become *de rigueur* during the coming age of the televised Saturday night barn dance shows out of Nashville's Grand Ole Opry.

Radio and the movies were responsible for the growth of Country music as an industry until after WWII, when commercial television began its bid for dominance as a mass medium. TV entertainment shows in the 1940s followed closely the radio tradition of barn dances and 'Oprys'. Country musicians often found themselves spots on variety shows that derived directly from live radio broadcasts of live shows in big-city venues. The business connection with music became cemented with mergers and acquisitions. The purchase of the Victor Talking Machine Company by the Radio Corporation of America in 1929 made RCA for a time the biggest producer of phonograph records in the US. In 1941, RCA launched one of the first commercial TV networks through its subsidiary NBC.

Music fans could watch an hour of *The Grand Ole Opry* live from Nashville every week on NBC, or *The Ed Sullivan Show* from New York, featuring live music of every popular genre. The now-defunct DuMont network even aired the first music show to be hosted by an African American, Hazel Scott, a Jazz show pianist. Despite her popularity, Hazel's show was canned by the network when her name appeared in a publication connected with the Communist Party. Hazel made a voluntary appearance at Senator McCarthy's House Unamerican Activities Committee hearings to clear her name, but even the most libellous smear was enough to make US business owners take their money and run in the opposite direction.

The point of divergence of the Americana community from the mainstream of the Country music industry can be traced right back to that early 1950s Cold War period. Nashville, home of the CMA, became particularly conservative in its approach, both politically through figures like Tex Ritter, and musically through producers like Chet Atkins and his 'smooth Nashville sound'. Knocking some of the honky-tonk swagger and 'rootsyness' out of Country music became perceived as a necessity to give it wider advertising-sales appeal.

Atkins and other Nashville producers from the late 1950s onwards looked to adapt Country to a broader audience on 'top 40' radio and commercial TV-show formats by reducing 'rural' elements (banjo, steel guitar) from the orchestration, and seeking out smooth-voiced Country singers like Jim Reeves and Glen Campbell who could make the crossover into pop. Pop singers had already become hip to Country songwriters. For instance, Hank Williams Jr, Jerry Lee Lewis, and Andy Williams all famously covered Hank Williams Sr's 'I'm So Lonesome I Could Cry'. From the early 1960s, popular musicians of many stripes were flocking to Nashville, whose City Fathers had adopted the epithet 'Music City' in recognition of the songwriting, production, and Country industry talent that had raised its national profile.

In early 1966, Bob Dylan was struggling with his seventh

studio album, *Blonde on Blonde*, in Columbia's New York studios. Dylan's producer Bob Johnston was a Texan, whose mother had written for Gene Autry, and who had performed as a Nashville Rockabilly artist in the early 1960s. Johnston suggested that Dylan and his Hawks musicians Al Kooper (Hammond organ) and Robbie Robertson (guitar, harmony vocals) relocate to Columbia's Studio A in Nashville's music row, much to the ire of Dylan's manager Albert Grossman.[47]

Bob Dylan, St Lawrence University 1963

But the move was made, and the Nashville ensemble setup used by Johnston and his session players worked so well that Dylan and his Hawks were able to complete some mighty works, culminating in the 11-minute-plus 'Sad-Eyed Lady of the Lowlands'.

Dylan was to return to Nashville for two more classic albums, *John Wesley Harding* and *Nashville Skyline,* during the reclusive phase of his career that followed his mysterious 1966 motorcycle accident. 1967's *John Wesley Harding* has a western gospel feel with short songs: most notable is 'All Along the Watchtower', made internationally famous by Jimi Hendrix's cover. *Nashville Skyline* is an out-and-out Country album, featuring a duet with Johnny Cash on 'Girl from the North Country', and 'Lay Lady Lay,' one of Dylan's most popular singles, replete with steel guitar and twang. Having temporarily given up smoking for some of this period, Dylan sings in an uncharacteristically affected smooth tone, no doubt influenced by the prevailing Nashville mode. This somewhat weird strangulated style is most evident on 'Girl from the North Country', in contrast to Cash, who is clearly having none of the rough edges knocked off his glorious tonsils to suit the crossover trend. Their ensemble vocal work is, to be polite, 'spontaneous' – unkind critics might say 'ragged' – a far cry from the family harmonies that feature in so many of the great Americana acts from the Carters on down.

But Dylan certainly qualifies as an early member of the Americana family under today's criteria: his storytelling in song without condescension to the 'Moon-June-Spoon' school of commercial songwriting; his deep love and respect for the traditional music of his homeland; his refusal to be pigeon-holed into radio-friendly formats. At the time he was recording in Nashville, there was already a nascent 'outlaw Country' movement kicking over the traces that harnessed Country musicians to the commercial bandwagon that was the Nashville sound.

OUTLAW COUNTRY

Willie Nelson came to Nashville from his native Texas in 1960. His origins were unpromising: his mother ("three-quarters Cherokee")[48] and father split when he was a baby, leaving him in the loving care of his paternal grandparents. But he recalls his mother as "a beautiful singer" and his father as "a fine fiddler". And those musical genes have served him well, even as he passes his 88th year on this planet.

Nelson got his first break with Pamper Records' Ray Price at Tootsie's Orchid Lounge, just next to the Grand Ole Opry's Ryman Auditorium. By 1969, he was earning a fortune, knocking out smooth Western swing-time numbers – including, bizarrely, a cover of Morecambe & Wise's 'Bring me Sunshine', but also iconic tunes of his own like 'Crazy' – for Chet Atkins at RCA Victor. In 1970, he lost much of his fortune on bad touring ventures, got divorced, and had his Nashville ranch burn down. Not surprisingly, Nelson interpreted these events as signs that a change was required. He left Nashville for Austin, Texas, let his hair grow, started smoking dope in public, and continued songwriting, now in an unconstrained, honest, idiosyncratic direction. Austin became a gathering place for Country artists disillusioned with the Nashville industry. The famous Armadillo World Headquarters venue was the centre of the Austin 'hippie' music scene.

Austin remains a centre for contemporary Americana and continues to welcome musicians from all over the world with a unique hospitality. Israeli musician Mark Smulian recalls to me his first impressions in 1989:

> A day or two after the installation of my answering machine I returned home in the afternoon to my first message; 'Hi my name is Paul and I understand that you are a bass player. I have a gig tonight and my bass player can't make it, so if you don't get back to me, I will pick you up at eight o'clock. See ya then.' Good that I didn't have another gig, as he didn't leave me a number to call back.

At eight more or less there is a knock on my door and Paul is standing there. My first impression is of a lanky guy, very long straight hair and an intense energy that is bubbling over all the time. He grabs my amp, I grab my bass, and we bundle into his van ... The drive to San Marcus takes about an hour, no distance at all in Texan terms, but long enough to become acquainted. San Marcus is a small town and driving into the town as darkness was descending felt a bit surreal. I had never been in a town like this before, but I had seen similar-looking places in hundreds of Hollywood movies. This place had clearly been here a long time and had simply adapted over the years to the prevailing fashion. Inside there was, of course, a healthy bar, and the other side of the bar a stage which had clearly been turned into a disco dance floor fifteen years earlier, as there were big, silver, light-reflecting balls hanging from the ceiling and an enormous mirror running along the back... I was tempted to look for spandex but was distracted by the drummer setting up on the stage.

Tonight's gig was a trio – guitar, bass and drums – that is a very tight-knit kind of affair. A very naked affair, one could say. Trios develop a unique sound that can take time and practice in order to realize their full potential. I was coming into a trio gig, had never met the musicians before. I had no idea what music we were going to play, and it apparently covered quite a few genres. The audience don't know this – it's not their problem either. They are paying money to see an artist they really like, in this case Paul, a highly respected and successful guitar player, and expect to get their money's worth.

Put it another way: we couldn't fake it; or think of it as a fun way to pass the evening. This was work and needed to be delivered at the highest standard. Very few professions demand this kind of real-time group expertise. Musicians do it all the time, and often the audience has no idea that this is going on. The drummer wasn't happy to see me. Paul had failed to tell him that the regular bass player was not coming, and he was understandably pissed off.

I decided to wait for him to chill a bit. As I was waiting, fiddling with my equipment, Paul came out of the back room dragging this enormous bass amp... 'I think you're gonna need this...'

He was right, my little amp was way too small for that venue. As I am setting up the big amp, Richard starts to play a more straightforward, funky type of groove and I get really excited, it is clear that he is a wonderful drummer, with a driving groove that really makes you want to get up and dance. I pick up my bass and lay down a simple riff over his drums and – in less than a second – we both have these ridiculous grins on our faces. Sometimes, but not too often, I am lucky enough to work with a musician who is totally in sync with me from the first second. Strange as it may seem, musicians don't have to be completely locked in together to make great music, but when they are – Wow! The magic flows. There is no effort, no need to talk and work stuff out, we simply become one voice. This is what happened with Richard.

From that moment all fear, worry, anger at what could be, simply melted away: we knew that we were going to be just fine. We played the first set, it was great; we felt like we had been playing together for twenty years, the club was packed, and the audience loved the music.

We took a break between sets, and that is when [owing to accidently being too close to a scuffle at the bar] I ended up on my back with a black eye. So, I played the second set with a black eye and a mild concussion, I think.

And then I was given a lift home to Austin by barmaid Stephanie who, having adopted the position of Florence Nightingale, decided to nurse me back to health.

I knew during and after the gig that we were making amazing music, but it was only a year later that I really began to appreciate how special that night had been and how deeply music can leave an everlasting impression on people.

We all are aware of the nostalgic powers of music to trigger memories and we have all become addicted to some great songs, but what happened that night in San Marcus is different from this.

…A year later I was back in Israel and during the Iraqi war I received a package from someone in the US whom I had never met. This woman had asked Richard the drummer for my address and had sent me a present. In the package was a wonderful very high-quality sweatshirt – so good that I wear it to this day – and a note.

'Dear Mark, you don't know me but I was at the San Marcus gig, the music you guys made still resonates with me and I feel that if the world could learn from the extraordinary way that you guys communicated that night, then maybe you wouldn't be sitting under the missiles now being fired into Tel Aviv. I hope this sweatshirt keeps you warm during these cold winter nights. Be safe, Jennifer'.

I remember thinking, 'Wow! ...Let music lead.'

*

Willie Nelson's old friend and fellow RCA artist Waylon Jennings was one of many Country artists of an independent disposition who played in Austin. In 1972, Jennings, having hired Neil Reshen to negotiate him a new contract with RCA giving him full creative control, introduced Reshen to Nelson. Reshen became Nelson's manager on the spot. Reshen negotiated Nelson's release from his RCA contract, and got him less restrictive contracts first with Atlantic, and then Columbia, where he recorded the seminal proto-Americana album *Red-Headed Stranger*. The album features stripped-down production, totally atypical for mainstream Country of that period; infinitely closer to Dylan than the 'Nashville sound' artists of the period. The songs tell a long story of a fugitive from the passionate murders of his wife and lover.

Red-Headed Stranger is 33.5 minutes of pure double-platinum. Columbia Records were less than impressed when Willie turned in what they thought was a demo, but with full artistic control in Nelson's contract they begrudgingly had to release it. Luckily, they did. The album remained 28 weeks in *Billboard*'s general chart, eventually spawning movie tie-ins and a place in the National Recordings Registry. But before all that, its sales success cemented the credibility of the 'Outlaw Country' movement with the industry.

Kris Kristofferson, Willie Nelson, Waylon Jennings at Dripping Springs reunion, 1972. Photo Bozotexino

Waylon Jennings' RCA release *Wanted! The Outlaws* featured Nelson, Jennings' wife, Jessi Colter, and Tompall Glaser, owner of the now-revered 'Hillbilly Central' studios in Nashville, which became Jennings' musical headquarters. The record was an immediate mainstream hit, with its iconic cover in the form of a tattered reward poster out of a Western movie. Jennings comments in his autobiography:

> For us, 'outlaw' meant standing up for your rights, your own way of doing things… and outlaw was as good a description as any. We mostly thought it was funny; Tompall immediately made up outlaw membership certificates... RCA was delighted... At last, an image![49]

Nelson continues to perform, as the elder statesman of Americana, along with his faithful instrument Trigger, the venerable Spanish-style guitar he acquired back in 1969.

As well as the Nashville/Austin outlaws, there was, like the Bakersfield Country sound of the previous generation, a California Outlaw Country sound developing at the same time. But California being California, they called it 'Cosmic American Music'.

Gram Parsons came to Americana from 'Country Rock', a genre epitomised by his former band, The Byrds. Son of WWII flying ace Ingram Connor II, Parsons took his surname from his stepfather after his father's suicide when he was 12. Both of his biological parents were alcoholics; something which cast a shadow over his brief but musically luminous existence.

Parsons and his harmony vocal partner Chris Hillman, who had brought him into The Byrds as a salaried employee, were influential in the creation of the iconic Byrds album *Sweetheart of the Rodeo* (1968), part of which Parsons, an avid Country fan, persuaded the band to record in Nashville. When Parsons left the band in 1968 in a dispute over a proposed tour of Apartheid South Africa, he spent the summer hanging out with his pals from the Rolling Stones, before heading back to LA to form, with Hillman, his next band, the Flying Burrito Brothers. The Burritos were short-lived but influential in the Country Rock scene. Critic Robert Christgau famously described the Burritos' *Gilded Palace of Sin* as "an ominous, obsessive, tongue-in-cheek country-rock synthesis, absorbing rural and urban, traditional and contemporary, at point of impact".[50]

During the brief life of the Burritos, Parsons' songwriting and performance became increasingly erratic through massive drug and alcohol consumption. He was eventually fired from his own band.[51] Gram's trust fund income enabled him to bankroll a solo venture with a young singer that Hillman had urged him to see performing in a New York Folk club.

In his book, *The Americana Revolution*,[52] Michael Scott Cain traces the history of Americana from the formation of the Americana Music Association by radio and industry figures including Rob Bleetstein, Brad Paul, and Dennis Lord. But the trail of Americana leads from early Roots recordings, into outlaw Country, through rebellion against the constraints embodied by the Country Music establishment in the mid 1960s. When long-haired psychedelic artists like The Byrds embraced country in their music, the backlash from the

Nashville royalty of the time was fierce.[53] And then out of The Byrds came Gram Parsons, and Gram Parsons met Emmylou Harris, and the rest became history.

Lucinda Williams, Filmore NYC. Photo Dina Regine

ALT-COUNTRY

Approaching the 21st century, the next generation of outlaw country musicians became labelled 'alt-Country'. Raiding their parents' record collections for Parsons, Harris, and Jennings – and injecting a squirt of Punk – came artists like Uncle Tupelo/ Son Volt, Wilco, and the Drive by Truckers. To balance the testosterone-laced tendency of some of this music, Lucinda Williams, Neko Case, and Gillian Welch emerged, to help to create the refreshingly gender-neutral community of 21st century Americana musicians.

Lucinda Williams currently ranks #79 in *Rolling Stone*'s "100 Greatest Songwriters of All time"[54] By the end of the 20th Century, she had become recognised as one of America's leading songwriters. Her father, the poet Stanley Miller Williams, was also riding high, chosen to read his poem *Of History and Hope* at the second inauguration of President Clinton in 1997. But literary success had come relatively late in the lives of both father and daughter. Miller Williams was a professor of biology before switching chairs at the University of Arkansas to English Literature on the strength of his poetic work. His daughter only came to public notice as a songwriter at the age of 35 when she released her third album *Lucinda Williams* in 1988. But it took Williams Jr another 10 years to achieve commercial success with her fifth album 'Car Wheels on a Gravel Road'. The album took the Grammy for Best Contemporary Folk Album in 1998. By this time, the critics had recognised the strength of Williams' writing. In 1994 'Passionate Kisses', a song from her eponymous debut album, had won Mary Chapin Carpenter a Grammy for Best Country Vocal Performance. *Rolling Stone* summed up Williams' gift:

> Few songwriters use repetition as skilfully as Williams: on 1988's 'I Just Wanted to See You So Bad', she ramped up the song's sexual obsession by restating the title after every other line.

Quoting Williams' acknowledgement of her father's help in achieving her trademark concision: "Dad stressed the importance of the economics of writing".[55]

Williams continued to release a string of charting albums, and to perform and record with the cream of Americana, notably a series of shows in Los Angeles and New York in 2007 featuring guest appearances from a widely-cast net of musical styles, including Steve Earle, Emmylou Harris, writer-producer Chuck Prophet, and David Byrne. In 2020 she released *Good Souls Better Angels*, an album featuring the single 'Man Without a Soul', alluding to disgraced US President Donald Trump.[56]

Amanda Petrusich references "Y'alternative" as her favourite tag pinned to the American Roots movement of the late 1990s. Music journalism of the period frequently tried to identify this type of music as a 'next big thing', using the pigeon-hole to classify a style "for the most part commercially unviable".[57] The tongue-in-cheek approach to Country music adopted by the Y'alternative crowd was the butt of much ire from many a Nashville musician in the noughties. Petrusich quotes fulsomely Th' Legendary Shack-Shakers' frontman JD Wilkes as he spills venom over alt-C for "its mostly indistinct flavour…precious and boring, exclusively and tediously practised by longhaired, overestimated singer-songwriters".[58] Wilkes is entitled to his opinion by virtue of his band's relentlessly truthful and uncompromising onslaught on swamp classics such as Slim Harpo's 'Shake your Hips'.

At the turn of the millennium, no cultural artefact did more to raise public consciousness of Americana than the hit movie *O Brother Where Art Thou?* Music producer T Bone Burnett had collaborated with Joel and Ethan Coen on their 1998 hit cult movie *The Big Lebowski*. Not long after, Burnett recalled: "Ethan Coen called me and asked, 'How would you like to make a movie about the history of American music? I mean, that's one hell of an elevator pitch.[59]"' The idea that became *O Brother Where Art Thou?* began with the Coens' concept of setting Homer's classic *Odyssey* in the Depression-era Southern USA, with a rich backdrop of the music of that time. For his new soundtrack, recorded before shooting began in 1999, Burnett picked songs from the dawn of recorded Roots music. The movie's theme, 'Man of Constant Sorrow,' was first recorded in 1928. It was composed (as 'Farewell Song') in 1913 by Burnett's namesake, one Richard Burnett, a blind banjo player from Kentucky. T Bone Burnett re-recorded the song, using a combination of vintage techniques and modern digital processing, with Dan Tyminski from Alison Krauss' band on lead vocal. In the movie, the song became a centrepiece fictional re-creation of an early recording session, with escaped convicts Ulysses Everett McGill (George Clooney) and his companions answering a local radio station advertisement offering $50 for any song recorded. Other musical highlights include Ralph Stanley's *a cappella* re-recording of Appalachian classic *O Death*, the vocal trio Alison Krauss, Gillian Welch and Emmylou Harris for the song of the Sirens 'Didn't Leave Nobody but the Baby', and Chris Thomas King's performance of the Skip James tune 'Hard Time Killing Floor Blues'.

O Brother Where Art Thou? dropped into a market perfectly poised to popularise American Roots music with a new generation. When the film hit US theatres in December 2000, the internet was still a novel medium. As Jed Hilly mentioned earlier in this book, FCC changes to the US radio industry had recently consolidated niche local stations into corporate giants with greatly restricted playlists. 90s grunge had blown over. The charts were full of teen pop and tunes from artists who had been fashionable with young audiences in the 1980s. Theatrical cinema was at a peak of popularity for young adult audiences. The Cinemagoers could exit the auditoriums into shopping malls where they could buy authentic music fresh to young ears in the form of a movie soundtrack CD. Burnett comments:

> The more records that sold, the more theaters the studio would put the movie in; it just kept growing together like that. …Every time the movie went to a new format — cable, broadcast TV, DVD — there would be another wave of interest.[60]

The soundtrack album is one of the most popular Americana albums to date, with five Grammy awards and eight-times Platinum RIAA sales certification. It's probably fair to say that this movie did more than any other work to put the musical concept of Americana on our cultural maps. Songsmiths like Ralph Stanley and James Carter ('Po' Lazarus') were finally rewarded with substantial royalties for a lifetime of effort.

One of the alt-Country generation of artists who benefitted from *O Brother…* was Gillian Welch. The movie was a "mass media bomb," she said. "All these people hear it and say, 'I like folk music.' No one's feeding it to them. The truth is, it's really good for your soul."[61] Welch, who had worked with T Bone Burnett prior to the movie, gained an assistant production credit in addition to contributing lyrics to her sirens' trio with Harris and Krauss. Welch, who grew up in Los Angeles, has a connection with the American South that is almost mythological. The *New Yorker* reported that her adoptive parents (musicians and entertainers) told Welch that her biological mother may have been raised in North Carolina. Welch described an overpowering force of attraction the first time she heard Bluegrass music as a student in California.[62] Welch and her long-term musical partner Dave Rawlings were living and performing 'writer nights' at small venues in Nashville in 1994 when she secured a publishing deal. A year later Welch signed with Jerry Moss for LA label Almo Sounds. Welch's manager Denise Stiff recalled:

> Welch played for him in his office. Behind his desk, Moss began quietly singing harmony with her. When I heard him, I thought, 'Those are David's parts. Jerry's heard them on the tapes, and if he's singing them, he's missing them.'

From that point there was never a doubt in Stiff's mind that Rawlings would be a permanent part of Welch's deal. In Welch's words, they remain "a two-piece band called Gillian Welch."[63] Welch and Rawlings had the further good fortune to have their uncanny harmonies faithfully recorded by T Bone Burnett, after he had heard them live at Nashville's Station Inn. Welch recalled of those session: "[Burnett] always worked from the angle that he loved what he heard the first night — just Dave and myself. That was always the core."[64]

Welch made two albums with Burnett before *O Brother…* came along. The first, *Revival* (1996) was nominated for a Best Folk Album Grammy (before the Americana category was added). At the time – and possibly influenced by the album's visual packaging without fully acknowledging that – some reviewers took a purist view, singling out Welch's perceived lack of Roots writing credentials.[65] The critical theme continued for Welch's second T Bone album *Hell Among the Yearlings*. But a couple of years later the landslide that was *O Brother Where Art Thou?* helped to modify opinion on American Roots music from a niche for connoisseurs to a hip revival spearheaded by a new generation of musicians. Welch crowned the flash of fame generated by the movie with her 2003 album *Soul Journey,* which features the remarkable 'Look at Miss Ohio', a song which encapsulates the provincial American female psyche in so few well-chosen words. Some critics remained envious, *Pitchfork*'s review damning Welch as "the most relevant of the 'O Brother Pluck Art Thou' gang of neo-yodelers".[66] But by then the movie soundtrack sync had secured Welch's ability to acquire lucrative work as a writer and performer.

Eight years in gestation, Welch's 2011 album *The Harrow and the Harvest* was widely praised and popular, making #20 in the US *Billboard* main album chart.[67] By 2015 the AMA were proud to bestow Welch and Rawlings with a Lifetime Achievement Award for Songwriting, a vindication that Welch celebrated the following year by releasing *Boots No 1: The Official Revival*

Bootleg on the occasion of the 20th anniversary of the release of *Revival*. The duo's 2020 album *All the Good Times* won the 2021 Grammy for Best Folk Album.

Welch is a self-confessed admirer of Haight-Ashbury-turned Americana icons The Grateful Dead, most notably in the refrain of 'Wrecking Ball', the final track of *Soul Journey*:

I'm just a little deadhead...

Welch and Rawlings have covered many Dead tunes, and performed live[68] with founder member Bob Weir, who had helped to keep the Dead in touch with American Roots music during the drug-laden early 1970s on the albums *Workingman's Dead* and *American Beauty*.[69]

Dave Rawlings and Gillian Welch, Seattle. Photo furtwangl

THE MODERN FAMILY

In June of 2015, Rosanne Cash performed at Dockery Farms, site of an early 20th century Mississippi sharecropping cotton plantation. The place is rightly held to be one of the birthplaces of the Delta Blues by virtue of its past illustrious residents: Charley Patton, Robert Johnson, and Chester ('Howlin' Wolf') Burnett.

After her headlining performance, Cash spoke with 'Cadillac' John Nolden, a local 88-year-old Blues harmonica player who had been enlisted to perform at Cash's afterparty. He told her:

> When I was behind the mule in the cotton fields back in the 50s, we had a radio on the porch and whenever your daddy [Johnny Cash] came on the radio we all ran out of the fields to gather around and listen.

The encounter was emotional for Cash: it revealed graphically for her the debt she and her family owe to the musicians who came before.

> This man has been playing the Blues harp his whole life and I owe what I'm doing to him and, yet, I'm getting all the attention. It just struck me so profoundly how much we need to honor him and his tradition.[70]

Americana has not always been a popular label with musicians through fear of being pigeonholed. The late John Prine's manager once famously remarked that Americana was "the only genre with more artists than fans".[71]

Australia's venerated songwriter and unofficial poet laureate Paul Kelly[72] describes his relationship to the genre:

> Americana doesn't seem that old to me. I've been around a long time but – I don't know – I'm not the one to define it. The definition keeps changing like most labels – maybe useful to some extent… I was heavily influenced by Hank Williams and Jimmy Rogers, Bill Monroe and the Stanley Brothers so I've got a lot of Americana influences as well as British ones,

Australian ones, so I don't think I fit in to one tent, I certainly can go from tent to tent.

Catherine Britt is an established artist in Australian Americana, with an impressive eight studio albums spanning a 14-year career. She views the whole story of the Outlaw Country movement as part of a continuous cycle in the development of American music:

> I think, to me the Outlaws and that whole movement that happened... if you look back through the history of Country music, it's happened continuously. There's always been this outbreak of somebody's fighting against the mainstream and trying to compete with Rock 'n' Roll and Pop music to get on the radio, because all of a sudden Country wasn't on the radio anymore. And I think there were always these people going, 'No, we've got to stick to what we do best.' It pops up in every, almost every decade. You know, like the Bakersfield sound, when Buck Owens and everyone went to California and said, 'Well, stuff Nashville, then. We're going to go do this!' And then the outlaw movement happened. There's always these sorts of things where people hop back and take it back again. Dwight Yoakam and people like that have hits. I think that will keep happening. Today you've got the Chris Stapletons... people who are still trying to honour that sort of traditional music.

Sturgill Simpson personifies the Outlaw tradition in American Roots music. Born into generations of Kentucky miners on his mother's side, son of a state policeman who had worked as an undercover narcotics officer, Simpson broke from family traditions:

> My parents divorced when I was in seventh grade, and I numbed out. I worked at McDonald's but saw a better opportunity selling pot and pills. I also chose to eat acid during my junior year...[73]

A disingenuously self-confessed "poor student", Simpson "barely graduated", and enlisted in the US Navy in his senior year of high school. Three years on a US frigate and some time after hanging out in Tokyo with an ex-Navy buddy led indirectly to the title of Simpson's self-produced 2016 album *A Sailor's Guide to Earth*. Simpson recounts how upon entering Canada from the US some time later (early 2000s), he and his buddy were asked the purpose of their visit by a female border official. Both men suffering from the after-effects of a recent heavy evening, Simpson's friend replied flippantly that they were off to research his next book, *A Sailor's Guide to the Pacific Northwest*. "And what was your previous book called?" Asked the officer. "*A Sailor's Guide to Tokyo,*" came the prompt reply.[74] It took nearly ten more years for Simpson to find his place on Earth as a professional musician. During which, he had risen from train conductor to managing a Union Pacific Railroad yard in Salt Lake City. He had also met and married his wife Sarah, whose comment, "you're really quite good at this," finally persuaded Simpson that he could support his family as a full-time musician.[75]

After an abortive move to Nashville, where Simpson became disenchanted with the factory system of songwriting which he encountered, he eventually met up with Dave Cobb, who was to produce Simpson's first two albums. The second of these was the iconic *Metamodern Sounds in Country Music,* which received a Grammy nomination for Best Americana Album in 2014. Cobb told us a few years later:

> Simpson…. when we recorded Metamodern… just the fun that we had, laughing our ass off, just playing with old tape machines and making them do crazy effects and breaking stuff. We were in a room about the size of a closet making that. But just, cutting up thinking like, 'boy we've really ruined our careers on this one.' We looked at each other and we were like, 'man, we've really' (holds up his hands) 'Sorry, sorry! You've lost your fans now'. Because the record we made before was more traditional Country.

Metamodern Sounds… brings a psychedelic dimension to Country music not previously explored even by long-haired bands like The Byrds. The valedictory track 'It Ain't Flowers' moves way beyond flower power, into the darkest reaches of the clever mind of a man who has lived his life wrestling with demons. By "breaking stuff", Simpson and Cobb have made a piece of music that I can imagine the great John Lennon in his more adventurous moments being proud of.

On the face of it, *A Sailor's Guide to Earth* may seem to have led Simpson back more towards mainstream territory. Gone are the psychedelic tape effects and songs about DMT and turtles. But wait, sandwiched by Simpson's perceptive and mature writing comes track 5 'In Bloom', a sensitive treatment of a song by Kurt Cobain, a man whose own demons vanquished him fifteen years or so before Simpson mastered his by achieving success as a recording artist. Despite the self-destructive elements of his early years, Simpson's perennial work ethic has seen him through to a ready-made musical confidence that allowed him to follow *Sailor's Guide* in with 2019's *SOUND AND FURY* an album nominated for the postponed 2020 Best Rock Album Grammy. Simpson's lockdown output now has reverted to an exquisitely rebellious Bluegrass-inspired collection in two volumes: *Cuttin' Grass (1 & 2)*. Mere genre rightly cannot hold this outlaw.

When we interviewed him in Austin back in 2017, Executive Director of the Americana Music Association Jed Hilly put it this way:

> Everyone's sort of felt a little bit like musical outcasts for a while… we feel like we look after our own, I guess, in this style we're using… I struggle sometimes and talk out of both sides of my mouth. On the one hand, I'm fighting the recording Academy and I want to get the Grammys to recognize the genre and create a Best Americana Album of the Year category. What I told them was this is a genre of music. It's not just a category or a format. This is a bona-fide genre of music. It is fine art compared to commercial art. It is inspired from the traditions of Gospel and Country and Blues that came before us, made contemporary by artists like Kasey Chambers, Lucinda Williams, Emmylou Harris, Bob Dylan.

Hilly is conflicted because, as an industry insider, he was successful earlier in his tenure at the AMA in persuading the American musical establishment to recognise and reward the genre that he acknowledges is rebellious and non-commercial in its ethos. As a former Sony Corporation executive, Hilly knows only too well how the balance between units sold and artistic integrity works… or doesn't. The brief, incandescent, collaboration of Gram Parsons and Emmylou Harris on the album *Grievous Angel*, and its critical and commercial reception illustrates this unstable see-saw perfectly.

A GRIEVOUS ANGEL BRANDED

Just before Parsons' untimely death from an overdose of morphine and alcohol in a motel room[76] at the Joshua Tree National Monument, Emmylou and Gram repaired to the Wally Heider Studio 4 in Hollywood to record songs they had worked up on a chaotic tour earlier in 1973. An *Uncut* magazine article carries Harris's recollections of the recording and her admiration for the ease with which Parsons used his voice and this pulled Harris "into his world":

> When we started… I didn't know what I was doing, but I did understand that he was the lead singer … [watching] him [told] me what he was going to do with his mouth, and because it seemed to work right away, I went with it.[77]

Parsons introduced her to the music of the Louvin Brothers, who had come to Nashville Country music out of the Gospel tradition of Alabama. In his review of Charlie Louvin's biography, *Satan is Real*, Alex Abramovich described the brothers' performance: volatile, often drunk and violent, Ira on mandolin, who sang, to Charlie Louvin's lower register, an impossibly stratospheric version of the 'high lonesome' style popularised in the 1930s by Bill Monroe. Abramovich writes:

> But every so often, in the middle of a song, some hidden signal flashed and the brothers switched places… even the most careful listeners would lose track… This was more

than close harmony singing; each instance was an act of transubstantiation.[78]

Harris had met Parsons with no preconceptions about becoming a Country singer, but learning with him to be a duet partner, and being inculcated into his vast love and knowledge of Country, concentrated her commitment to the genre. She says:

> When I heard Ira.... They say certain stimuli make your chakras vibrate, and my chakras were vibrating when I heard 'Born Again', with Ira's voice going up into the stratosphere. And I'd always loved The Everly Brothers.

Another article records less hagiographic observations on Parsons' capabilities at the session:

> He came in late. Emmy brought him to the studio. She was kind of minding him. We'd already tracked four or five tunes, and he was not in any kind of shape to record with us. He was generally out of it for the most part.[79]

What transpired – however it was achieved by their joint efforts – is a masterpiece of musical empathy, and a seminal work in the history of the genre. It's notable that Harris references two truly great sets of duetting brothers in her quote: the Louvin Brothers are full-on C&W mainstream (their Nudie suits may have also influenced Parsons' sartorial style) and the Everly Brothers successfully straddled Pop and Country, but the magical sincerity of their vocal blend is very much true to the spirit of Americana music.

Arguably the best example of the Parsons/Harris magic on *Grievous Angel* is a cover of the Everly Brothers' 1960 hit, 'Love Hurts', a song that epitomises Cosmic American Music, Parsons' own alternative terminology to the Country Rock pigeonhole to which he was assigned by the industry. An industry that in 1974, despite overwhelming posthumous critical acclaim, was not capable of finding a way to market the album to commercial success. A peak position at #195 in the *Billboard 200* should be regarded as signal failure for an industry that has shown itself capable of playing the untimely death card mercilessly for popular artists in both Rock and Country genres (Janis Joplin and Patsy Cline, to name but two).

Reprise, Parsons' label, could not find a peg to hang it on in 1974; *Grievous Angel* slipped between Rock and Country. After Gram's death, Mrs Parsons asked Reprise to replace the planned cover and billing featuring Emmylou Harris. Had Parsons not let life slip through his fingers with the trust fund money, *Grievous Angel* by Gram Parsons and Emmylou Harris would have been the breakthrough album for Harris. As ever, Robert Christgau sums it up perfectly:

> On [Parsons' previous album] *GP*, Emmylou Harris was a backup musician; here she cuts Parsons's soulfully dilettantish quaver with dry, dulcet mountain spirituality…The best Gram Parsons album… since *Gilded Palace of Sin,* with all that irony and mystery translated from metaphor into narrative.[80]

Thankfully, Harris enjoyed more substantial success later. Record labels Reprise, and latterly Warner, were able to market her music across the Country-Rock-Pop divide, partly because of her less rebellious stance towards the industry. And by the time Harris became publicly active as a feminist and for animal

Gram Parsons, 1972 courtesy Reprise Records

rights in the 1990s, the world was ready to square that away with her music as a commercial commodity. Partly this readiness was due to the efforts of Jed Hilly and his colleagues in delineating the genre of Americana to the international music market over the last three decades. Americana existed – and was cool – under other names in the years prior to the formation of the AMA, but it took the efforts of the AMA, and of sister organisations around the world, to make it a brand.

Americana in the US is by no means wholly rooted in the Southern Country/Outlaw/Y'alternative scene. Out of Long Beach, California came the Nitty Gritty Dirt Band (NGDB), whose 1972 album *Will the Circle be Unbroken* introduced Roots artists such as Maybelle Carter, Earl Scruggs, Roy Acuff, and Doc Watson to a new generation of rock music fans. After an earlier false start in 1967, the band was set firmly on track late in 1969 by founder members Jeff Hanna, a singer-guitarist fresh out of Linda Ronstadt's band, and multi-instrumentalist John McEuen, under the management of McEuen's brother Bill. By 1971, the McEuens had persuaded banjo master Earl Scruggs and flatpicker *par excellence* Doc Watson, with other Roots legends, to join the band at a week-long recording session in Nashville[81,82]. The resulting three-LP vinyl album was certified Platinum by the RIAA in 1997, indicating over a million sales in all formats.[83] *Will the Circle be Unbroken* has become an iconic artefact of the Americana movement, a major historic source of American Roots music for younger ears. The NGDB have continued to develop their role as Roots ambassadors over many years of albums and live performances. In 2017, the band celebrated their 50th Anniversary tour, after which McEuen finally announced a solo departure[84].

The late great John Prine was raised a Yankee in Illinois, although his parents were Southern folk from Kentucky.[85] Prine honed his early songs – the songs that brought him to the immediate attention of Kris Kristofferson, Paul Anka, and Jerry Wexler (Atlantic Records) – walking the streets of

Maywood, Illinois as a mailman. When his friend and fellow songwriter Steve Goodman persuaded Prine to give up the mail round and move to New York, Prine was initially doubtful: "I got a job in a club, I'd sing three nights a week then sleep all week. To me it was the perfect job." But the breaks just kept plopping into his lap. On November 4, 1971, Prine's first night in New York, Wexler heard him opening for Kristofferson at the Bitter End club in Greenwich Village; he offered Prine a $25,000 contract the very next day.

At the time, the Atlantic roster was short on singer-songwriters, and Prine's contract called upon him to generate ten albums' worth of material over the coming five years – not uncommon for an early 1970s recording deal. Prine's set list for the Bitter End show reveals he already had a dozen strong tunes under his belt, notably the Vietnam veteran ballad 'Sam Stone', and the song for his grandfather, 'Hello in There'.[86] His earliest recordings for Atlantic capture Prine's accentuated southern twang, a vocal trait he toned down later in his career as he became more confident in his standing amongst his musical peers. Prine was always noted for his humility, which is an important factor in his songwriting and in the popularity of his work within the culture of artistic integrity that runs through the Americana movement. It is the inspiration his songs have given to other artists that have really shaped Americana.

Bonnie Raitt's cover of Prine's 'Angel from Montgomery' is an Americana artefact of iconic status. Interviewed in 2000, Raitt said:

> I think that Angel from Montgomery probably has meant more to my fans and my body of work than any other song, and it will historically be considered one of the most important ones I've ever recorded.[87]

The song has been covered by over 30 different major recording artists, including John Denver, Emmylou Harris, Old Crow Medicine Show, Brandi Carlile, Maren Morris, and Maggie Rogers.

On Prine's untimely death from the Covid-19 virus, online tributes heartfelt and wide-ranging poured in, notably from *Late Show* host Stephen Colbert, a beautiful version of 'Hello in There' from Carlile, a whole set from East Nashville's Todd Snider, and even a sincere but somewhat strange rendition of 'Paradise' by Pink Floyd's Roger Waters.[88]

John Prine, Yellowstone National Park. Photo YNP Matt Ludin

Bonnie Raitt, Grand Park Pavilion, Chicago. Photo Jennifer Noble

AMERICANA MUSIC IN THE US TODAY

"I never saw music in terms of men and women or black and white. There was just cool and uncool."
– Bonnie Raitt

Apart from Jed Hilly and the AMA, one of the key discoverers and publishers of Americana in the US has to be Bob Boilen. Boilen's Tiny Desk Concerts has become an online go-to for anyone seeking high-quality new music. Americana acts from the highest echelons have made it their pleasure to squeeze in behind Boilen's office desk over the years, including John Prine, Steve Earle, Neko Case, and Yola. But the beauty of Tiny Desk is in Boilen and his team's diligence in seeking out the best new music. By 2014, playing a Tiny Desk Concert had become an enormous deal for any aspiring musician, and Boilen instigated the Tiny Desk Contest as an opportunity for unsigned musicians to win a place behind the desk.

Boilen joined National Public Radio (NPR) in Washington DC in 1988, through the simple method of "showing up on NPR's doorstep every day".[89] By 1989, he was directing NPR's news flagship, *All Things Considered*. As well as being a passionate radio enthusiast, Boilen had been in a band (Tiny Desk Unit), a theatre composer (Baltimore's *Impossible Theatre*), and was a pioneer of digital audio sampling. Boilen's introduction of snippets of music into *All Things Considered* was popular with listeners, and by 1999 he was ready to curate a major music show for NPR, which he christened *All Songs Considered*.

In 2008, Boilen was attending the South by Southwest festival (SXSW) with NPR music's Stephen Thompson. One night they were trying to listen to Laura Gibson from Oregon, then a lesser-known singer-songwriter. Boilen recalls:

> It was this awful bar… [Gibson] had a quiet voice, and we could barely hear her at all… Stephen jokingly said [to Gibson], 'You should just come play in our office.' I just lit up. I thought that would be so cool.

Tiny Desk Concerts was born three weeks later, when Gibson showed up at NPR's DC office. Boilen and some colleagues cleared some space off a desk, grabbed a couple of microphones and a camera, filmed a completely unadulterated, raw performance, and put it online.[90] Fast forward 11 years and Boilen and Thompson are still listening to over a hundred different acts at SXSW.[91]

Two weeks before the 2020 SXSW the City of Austin issued a Covid-19 order that effectively cancelled the festival, which in 2019 had made over half a million dollars for the city.[92] Boilen responded in typically positive fashion:

> I'm sad that SXSW was cancelled, though it was the smart thing to do given the circumstances. It's such a remarkable place to discover new artists. So, we asked artists who had been planning to perform there to enter the [NPR Tiny Desk] Contest.[93]

The Tiny Desk Contest 2020 was won by New Yorker Linda Diaz with a dreamy R&B number, 'Green Tea Ice Cream', which looks like it was shot in her local college or high school classroom, but nevertheless conveys with crystal clarity and musicianship Diaz's message:

> I am recognizing the things in my life that are good, and many of those things are coming from my community. I think in that way, it's super radical to love yourself as a black person in this time.[94]

Aaron Vance is a singer-writer out of Mooreville, Mississippi, who records with Nashville-based independent label Windy Holler Music. We caught up with him after a performance at AmericanaFest 2017. Vance traces his musical roots to Country and Gospel:

> My granddaddy was a farmer and also, he was a truck driver. And my dad then came up. It was four brothers and four sisters. My dad was the oldest boy and I'm the only grandson. So, when I was coming up, I was around them all the time. And my grandfather, his name was R William Vance and he was a big fan of Waylon Jennings, Hank Sr, George Jones, and Jimmy Dean. And so… I would come up and over his house, by the weekend, pretty much every weekend… I remember these songs he would play, and he would ride me on the tractor. And I came up, just listened to it, you know… and my dad's a preacher, so I was always in church. So, every now and then he called me up and come sing or whatever. So, it was pretty much instilled in me at that time.

Vance considers himself a natural performer, but his decision to make a career of music came relatively late:

> Well, me being the oldest, I got two sisters. And with me being the oldest… I was by myself for the first four years, so I didn't have nobody else, you know, to talk to. So, I had to do something to entertain myself, so when we go to church, call me up and I'll just [sing]… no fear at all.

> Being a preacher's son, I played basketball in high school and daddy kept a tight rope… My granddaddy, he died when I was a four-year-old. And a lot of things we did together, I remember it… like… how you remember that… You know, I was there when he died, the day he died and everything… So, at the age of 23, I pretty much knew I wanted to sing, but it was a late age because of what I went through in my life. You know, 'cause when I left high school with a basketball scholarship… I went to college on that scholarship. So, I didn't get to do a lot of [other] things. And so, after all that, I ended up transferring to Old Miss and I didn't play any sports. So, I pretty much got there, and I got a chance to do my… music. And I started out doing karaoke and uh, it went from there to band and then went from there to playing my own stuff, and boom!

Being of African American heritage and Southern in upbringing, Vance brings forward a charmingly diplomatic response to our questions about African American performers in Americana and Country:

> You can count them on one hand, you count on one hand, just put it like that. I think the reason is because of the way some of us are raised, you know, I was blessed to ... have the blood of a family that had land to farm. A lot of blacks don't have the land to farm because [it's] not out there for them to buy or they're not able to buy it or somebody has taken it from their family, or whatever. So... a lot of us pretty much moved towards the city and [black people] are not raised like that [there]. I was blessed to be raised that way.

Q: But isn't Americana more diverse than Country?

> With me being a black country artist, it never has been bad. It's a plus because, like I said, it's only a few of us out there... So, it's a good thing because people are scared of what's new, but people are very curious of what's new. So, they hear you and they see that you stand out... It's a different ballgame, but it's been good for me, though, because of what I stand for and how was raised.

Aaron Vance captured in a Nashville Studio. Photo Brumby Media

Let's take a quick helicopter ride over the dizzying heights of the AMA's Spotify charts now. According to the AMA, #1 to #3 are the holy trinity of Americana, Nathaniel Rateliff, Marcus King, and Jason Isbell's 400 Unit. These three white male artists account for around three million monthly streams on this one platform alone. Add in streams for Isbell's former bandmates, Drive by Truckers, and the other top fivers, The Wood Brothers and The Lone Bellow, and you have yourselves another three million-plus. Of these acts, only two prominently feature women, and none features black frontline performers. To put the numbers on the spectrum, Aaron Vance is currently pulling less than 1,000 monthly streams, whilst at the top end, African Canadian R&B artist The Weekend pulls 60 million-plus.

Elsewhere in this book I take a quick look at the distribution of streaming revenues across that spectrum, but just to say here that the tens-of-million-streamers each benefit way more than ten times each of what million-streamers makes, who benefit way more than ten times each of what 100,000-streamers… You get the idea.

So, in bald commercial terms, it would seem the AMA has a direction still to take in terms of addressing racial diversity and gender bias within the commercial arena. Except that the AMA says that, unlike major labels, it advocates for the artistic integrity of the musicians, rather than just the revenue they generate. But then every artist needs to make a living.

During the pandemic, when revenue from live performance all but dried up, there is an urgent need to ensure that all who shelter under the umbrella receive streaming revenue opportunities, not just the elite. Isbell makes clear his appreciation of his relative good fortune in some comments of a recent episode in the popular NPR *Tiny Desk* livestream concert series, with his wife, Amanda Shires. Shires says, "I'm just grateful that we have a home", to which Isbell replies,

"Yeah, we are very fortunate. We have a nice place here and an awesome daughter who is learning how to yodel."[95]

Michael Jason Isbell is a native of North Alabama, raised in a family who participated fully in Gospel, Bluegrass, and the music of the Grand Ole Opry.[96] But at 21, with a publishing deal from Muscle Shoals' FAME Studio under his arm, Isbell wanted to play Southern Rock. In 2001 he was invited to join the Athens, Georgia, band Drive By Truckers by founder member Patterson Hood, whose father David Hood had been a musical mentor to young Isbell back in Alabama. By 2001 Athens was a cultural beacon of contemporary music, home to bands including the B52's and R.E.M. Isbell spent six years with the Truckers, contributing songs to three studio albums which worked their way progressively into the middle reaches of the US charts.

In 2007, impending divorce with his first wife, Truckers bassist Shonna Tucker, contributed to Isbell's departure from the band.[97] Isbell and Tucker had known each other since they were teenagers, and the split hit hard. Isbell re-centred back to Alabama to form the band "The 400 Unit", named after the popular designation for the psychiatric ward of Eliza Coffee Memorial Hospital in Florence, Alabama. Perhaps the choice of name reflected Isbell's deteriorating mental health post-divorce: early in 2012, Isbell's closest friends and colleagues, including future wife Amanda Shires, instigated an intervention which led to Isbell undergoing rehabilitation at Cumberland Heights in Nashville.[98] By May 2013, Isbell was sober, living in Nashville, happily married to Shires, and recording *Southeastern* with Dave Cobb. Cobb told us about how he approached the making of this masterpiece:

> I'd read about the making of *Bridge Over Troubled Water* by Simon and Garfunkel, [whom] I adore, and they were talking about working early on 'Mrs Robinson'. They cut just acoustic. It was just those two, and they went away, and the band came in and played on it later and that's the sound of that song. They were able to preserve the same feel as

with them playing acoustic guitar, but there was a full band around it. So, when we did Jason's record, I totally stole a lot of their stuff, I put it in my kitchen. [Isbell] recorded just the way he wrote it and then we added the band to it. And I think we were able to make it feel as if it was just him playing the acoustic guitar even though it was strings and big band around it. Just that whole record was fun because I'd never tried that before, and I remember getting goosebumps several times, but specifically that song 'Elephant'.

The resultant song, 'Elephant', is one of the saddest songs I have ever heard: a story about a friend dying from cancer redeemed from unutterable misery only by the refreshing directness of its lyric.

Southeastern won Isbell Best Album, Artist, and Song at 2014's Americana Music Honors and Awards. Cobb and Isbell have continued their winning collaboration with three more studio albums. *The Nashville Sound* (2018) is the most successful to date, making #1 in both *Billboard*'s Rock and Country charts. Isbell's latest, *Reunions,* was released early exclusively to independent distribution, intended to aid small businesses affected by the pandemic.

One of the top streaming US female Americana artists of the 21st century has to be Brandi Carlile (2.9m monthly streams). Carlile admits to "rednecky" enthusiasms, having been born and raised in the rural Pacific Northwest. She has the distinction of being the only Americana artist I know of to have a restaurant named after her. The Carlile Room in downtown Seattle specialises in 'duck-fat hush puppies' – redneck food *par excellence*.[99]

Carlile grew up in the woods, nearly an hour's drive from the nearest freeway. She explains, "My great-grandmother was a country singer who passed it on to my grandfather, who passed it to my mother, who passed the torch to me."[100] While the city kids were immersed in grunge music, the Carliles played country in "elaborate family jams" and at Seattle Country music venues like the Paragon. She soon hooked up with twins Tim and Phil Hanseroth, who became her core band. The Hanseroth brothers produced several name bands on the Northwest music scene, and Carlile would often share a club stage with a diverse selection of their clients, including Canadian Rockers Nickelback. Signed to Columbia Records in 2004, Carlile released her eponymous debut album, based on home demos of her own songs. The album was enthusiastically received by the press, and Carlile quickly began the touring life of a successful major-label artist.

By 2007, Carlile had piqued the attention of the great T Bone Burnett. Burnett produced her second album, *The Story*, which captures her live band sound subtly packaged in the rich tremolo that is signature Burnett magic. On the title track, Carlile's voice begins to falter as she moves into the climax and then rips apart, ragged, as the band powers up behind her. Some producers would consign this take to oblivion. Burnett chose it for the final version.

By 2008, music from *The Story* was featuring on hit TV show *Grey's Anatomy* and Carlile was touring the world. For her 2009 album *Give Up the Ghost*, Columbia engaged none other than apex producer Rick Rubin, who has the skill to coax the finest elements out of Carlile's vocal range, and the reputation to pull in guests such as Carlile's childhood idol Elton John to play jaunty piano and cameo vocal on 'Caroline'.[101]

After ten years and four albums with Columbia, Carlile moved to New York Indie ATO Records[102] and thence to Elektra/Low Country. As her career matured – and having learned her craft from the best in the industry – she found the confidence to assert a more collective and egalitarian approach to her work. And this has proved itself by yielding greater chart success. Her 'Indie' albums *The Firewatcher's Daughter* and *By the Way, I Forgive You* made single-digit peaks in the main US Billboard charts (her best performing Columbia album made #10), although *The Story* remains her top-selling release.[103] The detail in these figures is more reflective of the changes in music distribution technology, coinciding with the rise of streaming and the decline of physical sales. But overall, they show that Carlile continues to enhance her popularity without the backing of a major label.

In 2012, Carlile married UK actor Catherine Shepherd, and they share two daughters. Carlile, her long-time bandmates the Hanseroth brothers, and Shepherd are active in the cause of using music to help disadvantaged people.[104] In 2019, Carlile's supergroup project The Highwomen released their self-titled #1 Billboard Country album (see chapter Women call the shots). In 2020, Carlile paid tribute to the late John Prine with a lockdown cover of 'Hello in There'.[105]

Chris Stapleton is another major contemporary US Americana musician, an eight-million-plus monthly streamer on Spotify. Born into a Kentucky coal mining family, Stapleton began his musical career as a fan of Georgia Country singer Travis Tritt, who acknowledges the tribute:

> I love him. I think he's the future of country music… Any time you hear about new artists that grew up listening to your music as part of [their] influence, that's always a great honor.[106]

In 2001, Stapleton moved to Nashville where he worked as a writer with Sea Gayle Music, before joining Bluegrass ensemble The Steeldrivers on lead vocals and guitar in 2007. The band's debut album reached #57 in the US Country charts. 'If It Hadn't Been For Love', written by Stapleton and bandmate Mike Henderson, scores over 16 million streams to date on Spotify, and has been famously covered by UK star singer Adele as a bonus track on her album *21*.[107] Another Stapleton/Henderson song, 'Angel of the Night', is a favourite of the grassroots Americana community worldwide.[108] The band, which features Tennessee fiddle virtuoso Tammy Rogers, continues to be a major influence in today's Americana[iii].

---

i. iii. In 2015, while performing at the Swanage Blues Festival, I heard a performance of the Stapleton/Henderson song 'You Put the Hurt on Me', which inspired me to write and record the one-off live Country demo 'That is All' in response to my father's last year on Earth fighting Alzheimer's disease.

Stapleton took a back-step from touring in 2010 to raise his family with songwriter wife, Morgane Stapleton. Morgane worked in a neighbouring Nashville writers' office and describes how they got together in an interview for *Paste* magazine: "Chris asked me to write a song with him for the first time one Friday night at six o'clock. We just spent most of the night making out!" To which Stapleton replies, "We did go to dinner though…"[109]

Stapleton's breakthrough as a solo artist came when he heard Dave Cobb's production on Sturgill Simpson's *High Top Mountain*, which won the Grammy for Best Americana Album in 2014. Stapleton sought out Cobb and persuaded him to produce *Traveller*. Released in 2015, the album went to #1 in the main US *Billboard* chart with support from a live performance with Tennessee native Justin Timberlake at the CMA Awards that year. Popping up front row at that star-studded Nashville performance was none other than Americana celebrity Keith Urban.[110] By 2018 Stapleton too was gliding through A-list territory, with two more charting albums by Cobb under his belt, writing for Timberlake, and raising five children with Morgane, who sings backing vocals in many of his live shows. Stapleton has always sounded most comfortable live harmonising with great Country female voices, notably Morgane and, from earlier days, Rogers. In August 2020, Stapleton announced the forthcoming release of *Starting Over*, his fourth Cobb-produced solo album featuring Mike Campbell and Benmont Tench from the late Tom Petty's Heartbreakers.[111]

Elsewhere on the great spectrum of Americana comes Robert Randolph, pedal steel player and master of Gospel Funk. Randolph is a native of New Jersey, who cut his musical teeth in the Sacred Steel tradition of the African American Pentecostal Church. A teen tragedy – his best friend was shot to death – caused Randolph to take up serious music study. "It kept me off the streets," he says in an early interview. In

2000, Randolph, who was working as a paralegal while playing in church, appeared at the Sacred Steel Convention in Florida, where his talent received notice, and he was advised to take his music to a wider audience. Randolph says his father, the Deacon of the church,

> "...was a little shaky about it at first, like a lot of other church folks were, but as time went on, they've seen what I've done and the songs I sing and the lives I've touched through the music."[112]

Randolph took his 'Family Band' – cousins Danyel Morgan (bass and vocals) and Marcus Randolph (drums) with Hammond B-3 player John Ginty – out of the church and into local venues, where they were spotted by Southern Rockers North Mississippi Allstars, who set up a joint project, The Word, with members of both bands. The exposure led to Randolph's band being signed with Warner in 2003. Randolph evolved a vibrant stage show touring all over North America, where dance (band and audience participation) plays a major part. His third (2010) album with Warner, *We Walk This Road*, was produced by the one-and-only T Bone Burnett, who shares Randolph's Christian upbringing. The album hit a #74 in the US Billboard 200 and #4 in the US Christian Rock charts. Randolph says:

> We wanted to get the band and a bunch of great artists together and really help me capture a vision of 100 years of American Roots music. This is the original library of music that made American music what it is today. [113]

In 2011, Randolph was interviewed in London by Paul Jones for his BBC show, where we captured on camera a moment of his infectious enthusiasm.

In 2013, Randolph switched to Blue Note Records, and out came *Lickety Split*, a Funk-Soul mother of an album that fuses audible shades of Lenny Kravitz, with Carlos Santana (in person on two tracks), with Randolph's increasingly confident songwriting and co-production, backed by absolute muscular

Paul Jones and Robert Randolph. Photo Al Stuart

groove from the Family Band cousins' rhythm section. Randolph's latest offering, *Brighter Days* (2019), produced by the ubiquitous Dave Cobb, returns to the Sacred Steel tradition, rooted in Gospel, sung and played with feeling that Cobb's production fully realises on a mixture of funky tunes and spiritual ballads.

From the other side of the spiritual tradition emerges Hannah Aldridge out of Muscle Shoals, Alabama. Daughter of Nashville writer, producer, and Muscle Shoals music royalty, Walt Aldridge, she mines a dark Southern Gothic lode. Aldridge is popular in Europe, and frequently plays in the UK at the Maverick Festival. When we spoke to her she was heading for Sweden and hoping to perform there, subject to Covid restrictions.[114]

Her debut album *Razor Wire* was recorded in Nashville with help from Jason Isbell's 400 Unit, who back her on the one cover track, Isbell's song 'Try'. *American Roots Music UK* designated this "a classy album", noting:

> This lady has a huge talent that enables her to roam at will through just about any emotion she chooses and on this terrific album she gives an exhibition on just how multifaceted she and her music are.[115]

Aldridge's song stories may be a bit 'out there' to garner massive commercial success, but that's not the point. The Americana umbrella is there to shelter honest artistry of all stripes and moods, even exposing the "scars from the lashes of the bible belt" that she confesses in her biography.[116] Her 2020 collection of live recordings, *Live in Black and White*, includes earworm duets with notable UK Americana artists Robbie Cavanagh and Danni Nicholls.

Veteran Nashville producer Will Kimbrough has had a distinguished career as a guitarist, winning the AMA's Instrumentalist of the Year in 2004. In 2017, after six years working with California-raised Nashville-based singer/writer Brigitte DeMeyer, he released *Mockingbird Soul*, an album of

Brigitte DeMeyer and Will Kimbrough. Photo Al Stuart

duets penned by DeMeyer. We caught their performance at the London's Gibson Studios in March 2017, a preview to their Maverick Festival appearance and UK tour.[117]

Kimbrough's expressive bluesy acoustic guitar work is, indeed, in a class by itself. The title track features Kimbrough on electric slide, a performance of taste and restraint that vignettes DeMeyer's velvet voice to perfection.

Kamara Thomas lives and works in Durham, NC. Back in 2013, she uprooted from Brooklyn to de-stress, with her husband and young daughter Cherokee, to a district already familiar to her from visits, with her former bandmate, Martin Whyte, to Whyte's parents' home in Chapel Hill.

From 2003 until Cherokee was born in 2011, Thomas' bass had oiled the churning engine of indie rockers Earl Greyhound. This engine, fired by drummer Ricc Sheridan, stirring the grunge-laden guitars of Whyte, a vortex into which Whyte's vocal was brought into sharp relief by Thomas' acerbic harmonies like a stripe of cream spiralling into a fresh cup of espresso. Just after her move to Durham, *Indy Week* caught up with Thomas sipping a more relaxing beverage (wine) at Bull McCabe's pub while she told of her immediate post-Greyhound projects: her 2013 album *Earth Hero* "travels in gently melancholic, acoustic-based Americana and allegorical storytelling".[118]

The startlingly vivid album and its sophisticated performance videos were created in New York while Thomas and her husband negotiated the stairs of their small apartment with their baby daughter, her stroller, and all the assorted paraphernalia and exhaustion of a start-up family.

Thomas describes herself as "a singer, songspeller, mythology fanatic, and multidisciplinary storyteller."

"I was definitely the tension creator in Earl Greyhound because I was always doing this," she tells *Indy Week*, of her relationship to the more instrumentalist approach taken by her former band. Thomas' brand of visual storytelling often uses body painting and ornament that appears to borrow from native American tradition. The figures that appear in her videos are often masked or wear the painted faces of indigenous storytellers.

Thomas' holistic approach to her art has occasionally led, as such things frequently do, to inappropriate criticism. In 2017, *Paste* magazine included Thomas in its list of "14 artists proving black Americana is real," if, indeed, such proof were required. In 2018, Thomas released the track 'Good Luck America', a surprisingly uplifting six-minute testimony on the fate of her country under President Trump.

In recent years Thomas has developed Country Soul Songbook, an artistic community and convention that explores aspects of contemporary American Roots art and music. The 2020 convention was themed as "I Am Your Mama's Country Music"[119], a passing reference to Thomas' own childhood soundscape of Loretta Lynn, The Outlaws, and Emmylou Harris. The convention included performances from indigenous musician Pura Fé, of the Tuscarora Deer Clan of North Carolina, and from Ulali, the *à capella* group that Fé helped to found. Thomas is currently preparing the 2021 convention (viruses permitting), while keeping her chops in with a series of lockdown performances. Like many artists who do not go gently into pigeonholing, Thomas distributes her music independently via Bandcamp and streaming services.

The contribution of Mexico to today's US Americana is embodied in the veteran band Calexico, named after their border home town, which is sliced from the top of the larger community of Mexicali by the border wall (actually at this point a monumentally stern fence of iron girders – worthy of the sculptor Antony Gormley – rusting in the desert sun).

Calexico was founded back in 1994 by Joey Burns (guitar, bass, vocal) and John Convertino (drums), who have been making consistently high-quality music ever since. With an ensemble including Mariachi trumpets supplied by Jacob Valenzuela and multi-instrumentalist Martin Wenk, the band fuse Country, Indie, and Mexican Folk styles with a gentle touch that has led to high placings in *Billboard*'s US Americana/ Folk Chart[120]. The band made their 2015 album *Edge of the Sun* with contributions from Virginia-born genre-buster and sometime Tuscon, Arizona resident Neko Case and South Carolina's Iron and Wine (aka Sam Beam). The collaboration with Beam grew into a full-length album, *Years to Burn* (Sub Pop, 2019), which contains the experimental little gems 'Outside El Paso' and 'Bitter Suite' (Pajero), which together form a sort of Mexican-tinged Miles Davis trip. In 2020, the Calexico's lockdown contribution was the commercial Winter Holiday album *Seasonal Shift*.

It's impossible to survey modern US Americana without a mention for its undisputed guitar hero Billy Strings out of Michigan. Strings is a flatpicker *par excellence*, a disciple of the late Doc Watson, the blind musician from North Carolina who put guitar on the map as a Bluegrass lead instrument.[121] He learned from his stepfather Terry Barber, with whom he occasionally performs as a duo.[122] In 2018, Strings was playing a set of Doc Watson tunes at the High Sierra Music Festival. He recounts his memory of learning the tune 'Beaumont Rag' with Barber as a seven-year-old:

> I started really listening to what he was doing with the melody instead of counting [the chords] … then I just nailed it! He reached over and squeezed my little hand… One of the proudest moments in my life and the reason I do this.[123]

Before the pandemic, Strings could be found performing all over the country, with his regular touring Bluegrass band and as a guest of the cream of Americana. We captured Billy Strings on camera live in Asheville NC just before the lockdown,[124] where he also displayed his electric guitar skills on a version of the Hendrix classic 'Voodoo Chile' with Indiana musical explorers Umphrey's McGee.[125]

The development of the Americana music family in the US over the last three decades reflects all the most positive aspects of the evolution of US culture in the same period: towards gender and racial equality, liberal capitalism, and a sensitive analysis of social issues including substance abuse, domestic abuse, and mental health. Despite the retrograde cultural pressures on the US of the last five years, the spirit guiding Americana music has survived, even unto the pandemic. How fully it will re-emerge remains to be seen.

Billy Strings. Photo Al Stuart

Harry Hookey being interviewed in Austin, Texas. Photo Brumby Media

AMERICANA MUSIC IN AUSTRALIA

*"That's the way music's always worked for me, songs
come along or pieces of music at different times and just
stop you in your tracks, transform you. And it's why
I started to make music, because I wanted to grab
a little bit of that power."*

– Paul Kelly

Australia is a big country. Large cities with music venues and
the population density to fill them ring the coasts, but typically
separated by a short-haul flight or a multi-day drive. The states
of Western Australia and the Northern Territory are extreme
examples: from Perth's Astor Theatre, the next nearest stop for
a top-selling artist's tour would be, say, Adelaide's Thebarton
Theatre, more than a 1,000-mile flight or an over 40-hour drive.
Even in the less populated parts of the US, there is a network
of big-city venues within a day's drive from one another: Salt
Lake City, Denver, Albuquerque, Las Vegas. And in the US, a
smaller-budget artist can sustain a tour through small venues
dotted along the route. The big empty spaces between western
and northern Australian cities may inspire romantic notions of
campfires and endless red-dirt highways in Australian Americana
music – and believe me, they truly are bigger than the Wild West
of the USA – but it's no surprise that Australia's music industry
is centred on the southern and eastern seaboard conurbations.
Australian artist Harry Hookey put it to us this way:

> That's the thing, the population density, makes touring an
> infinite loop. It takes ten hours to drive from Melbourne to

Sydney, and there's towns in between but mainly small country towns, whereas you go from Nashville to Memphis, so many big cities, there is just so many people, so many places to play.

It seems that the closure of the music industry during the pandemic has put paid to Hookey's musical ambitions. Like many other young musicians, he has made the decision to leave the industry for a more certain career path elsewhere.

Historically, Australia's 'music city' is Melbourne, Victoria, home to diva Dame Nellie Melba, and more recently, to Paul Kelly, Nick Cave, Missy Higgins, Kylie Minogue, and Jason Donovan, just to name a few. Popular culture twins Melbourne with Austin, Texas, as a national home for rebel Roots music. But the Americana Music Association of Australia began life at an industry conference in Sydney, New South Wales, in 2016.[126] The epicentre of Country music in Australia lies just 400km further north – nearby by Australian standards – at Tamworth, New South Wales.

Why Tamworth? Well, according to Max Ellis (one of the founders of the Golden Guitar Awards and Tamworth Festival and Awards Chief Executive 1973–84 and 1992–2003), that's mainly down to the town's radio station, 2TM, which in 1965 hit back at the newly arrived TV service by airing "specialist programs such as drama, Jazz, Folk music and even the supposedly despised 'Country & Western' music, in night-time slots".[127]

So clear was 2TM's signal on the uncrowded Australian airwaves, it could be heard all over the East Coast. As a result of the unexpectedly massive popularity of 2TM's Country music programme *Hoedown*, the station started staging concerts, some featuring national stars who lived within reach, like Slim Dusty. A group including Ellis and Hadley Records label owner Eric Scott decided to market Tamworth consistently on-air and in other promotional material as Australia's 'Country Music Capital'. Ellis explains in his contribution to Australia's country music archive that promotion of local business and tourism, rather than bringing the music to a wider audience, were the primary reasons for the move.

The music enthusiasts from the founding group established a local association (eventually named the Capital Country Music Association, CCMA), to channel the marketing power of the music and the nascent festival for the benefit of the Australian music industry. From the CCMA's introduction of Australia's first national Country Music Awards (the Golden Guitar Awards) in 1973, the festival grew into an event of national renown and importance, spanning ten days of diverse attractions including concerts by top Australian Country artists, rodeo, bluegrass and talent competitions, and the famous Peel Street busking sessions.

By 1992, though, cracks were appearing: 2TM and its marketing subsidiary BAL introduced unpopular changes without consulting the Golden Guitar brand owners CCMA. CCMA members, including one of the original festival founders Max Ellis and star couple Slim Dusty and Joy McKean, decided to incorporate a new national association, the Country Music Association of Australia. The new 18-strong CMAA board of music industry members made it their mission to regain control of the awards, and with that, the festival. In January 1992, a vast concert in Tamworth's rodeo arena generated substantial funding for the new organization. 2TM had been out-marketed by the musicians who had made the event the success it had become. The CMAA's history page puts it this way:

> By June 1992, the CMAA had achieved its first of many achievements. After lengthy negotiations, Radio 2TM generously agreed to hand over the Awards without charge to the new body.[128]

Today Tamworth is internationally acknowledged as Australia's Capital of Country Music, thanks to the continued efforts of the CMAA. A mere 288 miles to the northeast of Tamworth lies Byron Bay, home to surfers and Bluesfest, the largest Blues 'n' Roots music festival in Australia.

On Easter weekend 1990, Keven Oxford and Dan Doeppel staged a five-day event at the Arts Factory in Byron Bay, a former piggery that Doeppel had purchased as a music venue to entertain the influx of hippies into the area[129]. By 1994 the festival had outgrown the piggery: Doeppel handed over to current festival director Peter Noble, who with Oxford, developed the festival into an event eventually finding a permanent home at the 120-hectare Tyagarah Tea Tree farm. From 2004 to 2008, the festival was run by Noble and a consortium of Melbourne and Sydney promoters including Michael Chugg, but in 2008 Noble bought out the consortium to become sole owner of Bluesfest.

Michael Chugg, owner of international festival promoters Chugg Entertainment, had never expected a good return on Americana at Australian festivals. Speaking in 2017, Chugg told us: "Well, Americana's probably even the poorer, poorer, poorer relation [of Australian Country music]."

What is noticeable about the line-ups for Bluesfest is that 2007 was the first year in which artists now identified as Americana – like Bonnie Raitt, Missy Higgins, and Kasey Chambers – featured heavily on the bill. That trend continued under Peter Noble's sole proprietorship to 2020's postponed festival announcement.

Brian Taranto is another Australian promoter whose commercial expectations were low when he started Melbourne's Out on the Weekend Americana festival in 2014. When we interviewed him at the 2017 Americana Music Awards, in Melbourne, Neil Young fan Taranto joked: "I lose money on Americana – I can afford to help as I have made my money selling tee-shirts!" But Taranto's Americana festival continues to expand. Of the 2019 event, he enthused:

> Wow, what a day! I think it may have been the best yet. It just felt like a great community of like-minded good-time people enjoying quality music.[130]

Bluesfest and Out on the Weekend were casualties of 2020 but due to the Australian government's stringent handling of the pandemic Bluesfest is now up and running again. In past years, promoters have traditionally monetised festival appearances from international stars by booking in short tours of large Australian venues during their visit. For the logistical reasons I've already mentioned, these tours tend to focus on the Southeastern seaboard.

Grizzly Bear frontman Ed Droste reportedly expressed his frustration with this in some 2018 social media posts:

> People always ask, 'Why aren't you coming to Perth?'... and I'm trying to explain there is no value put on live music anymore. We feel it's important to bring with us the fullest show we can... But now... we literally lose money.[131]

For Indie stars The Grizzlys, the audience expectations of money spent on the show will match their million-plus monthly Spotify streams. With a few notable exceptions (did somebody say Keith Urban?), Australian Americana artists will be performing to a lower budget. But that doesn't make it easier. On a low budget you are in smaller venues, yielding lower door money. If the door money in Perth doesn't cover the cost of getting from Melbourne to Perth – even via Adelaide, notorious amongst bands for a lack of midsize and large venues where a decent ticket revenue is at least mathematically possible – you don't play Perth!

WHAT IS AUSTRALIANA?

In December 2013, the Australian Country music world was rocked by the surprise resignation of its president, Australian national treasurer John Williamson. On December 10, 2013, just prior to the Golden Guitar Awards of January 2014, Williamson went public in the Australian press, citing as reason for his departure the CMAA's "obsession with American Country music... hell-bent on creating more Keith Urbans".[132]

In his resignation letter, Williamson reportedly singled out (without naming names) a nomination for the upcoming Golden Guitar Awards for *The Great Country Songbook,* an album of "90% American covers", by Troy Cassar-Daley and Adam Harvey. Cassar-Daley and Harvey responded two days later by withdrawing from their nomination for the award.[133]

Incoming CMAA president, Bushwackers frontman Dobe Newton, was quick to pour oil on troubled waters, issuing a statement in which he regretted "unedifying soundbite exchanges" and "dragging Keith Urban into the debate". In the concluding paragraphs he notes:

> [Cassar-Daley's and Harvey's] joint statement that they will attend the Awards ceremony to support their colleagues is a testament to their professionalism and an example of a generosity of spirit that we hope others will follow.[134]

Williamson's stance against the Americanization of the CMAA awards was supported by Tamworth star Felicity Urquhart and Queensland songwriter Graeme Connors, who supported a preference for original Australian material in the Golden Guitar nominations. However, CMAA board member Graham Thompson was quick to defend Newton, pointing out that it is not the CMAA's role to determine "what type of Country music an artist shall play".

Ironically, on its release in June 2013, *The Great Country Songbook* had been narrowly knocked off the top spot to #2 in the Australian Recording Industry Association (ARIA) charts by American artist Kanye West's *Yeezus,*[135] but nevertheless achieved ARIA-certified sales of 70,000 and platinum status. Did Cassar-Daley and Harvey consider their reputation tarnished by Williamson's public comments? They had won four Golden Guitars the previous year, and their social media at the time reflected deep disappointment at what they saw as a necessary withdrawal from the chance to see their 2013 work rewarded. When we spoke with Cassar-Daley in 2018 he was philosophical:

Slim Dusty used to say to me "run your own race". And it's an incredible bit of advice because you can be looking around you all the time going 'Oh Jesus, do I have to keep up with them, or am I trying to do this, or should I sound like that?' You just gotta write what comes out. And if you can be your own person and run your own race, I reckon you're on the right path.

The rift of 2013 sparked a wider discussion about what Australian Country music means and how it relates to other Australian Roots music. Enter the AMA. In spring 2014, Jed Hilly's AMA announced the formation of an Australia Advisory Group. This small (100% male) group included promoter and label owner Brian Taranto and the incoming CMAA president, Dobe Newton. Nashville-based Australian producer and the then AMA Board President Mark Moffatt was appointed chair of the group. The inclusion of Dobe Newton was significant: neither the AMA, under Jed Hilly's direction, nor the CMAA, wanted to see any wide industry rift developing between Country and Americana in Australia, as had occurred in the US. Newton's own band, the Bushwackers, were, during the late 1970s and early 1980s, Australia's contribution to the post-Punk hillbilly backlash spearheaded by UK/Irish bands like The Pogues and The Men They Couldn't Hang.

So well has Newton papered over the cracks that Australian Americana remains embraced by the CMAA. Golden Guitar entry requirements were changed to limit entries to artists who are "permanent residents" of Australia.[136] The controversial 2014 awards were the last to feature international artist categories.[137] By 2016, Troy Cassar-Daley was fully rehabilitated as a Golden Guitar winner, bagging Album of the Year, Single of the Year, Producer of the Year, and both of the two Song of the Year awards then on offer. Australian Country, as represented by the CMAA, has become much more of an Australian national genre, with less direct reference to, and influence from, US Country Music. But Australian Americana has maintained a trunk-line connection to Nashville, represented at industry level by the Australia Advisory Group of the AMA.

DO YOU HAVE TO GO TO NASHVILLE?

The selection of Australian Nashville-resident writer/producer Mark Moffatt as AMA Australia group chair was a shrewd move on several levels. Moffatt had originally made his name producing what he can legitimately claim as the world's first non-US Punk Rock hit single, 'I'm Stranded' by Queenslander Housing Commission kids The Saints, released September 1976, over a month before Dave Robinson's Stiff Records launched the iconic 'New Rose' by UK Punks The Damned. In 1991 Moffatt produced the album *Tribal Voice* by Indigenous/ European Australian band Yothu Yindi. Hired in 1992 to help with Keith Urban's transition from Australian band rocker to Nashville Country star, Moffatt recalls:

> The publishing company that brought me [to Nashville] had signed Keith Urban. And after a while I realized that's why I was here. They wanted someone to kind of work with him behind the scenes, transitioning him from his band to his solo career.

Here we have Moffatt, an Australian with serious musical credentials across multiple genres serving the world-wide culture-sharing umbrella of Americana as AMA Past President, heading up the AMA Australia Advisory Group, which includes Dobe Newton the president of Australia's CMAA: an organisation which has moved to defend and promote Australian Country Music culture against US incursion. Somehow the alliance is working. Moffatt now serves the AMA as an International Board Member[138].

Having lived in Nashville long enough to be considered a pillar of that musical community, Moffatt takes a dim view of the space that Country (and, by association, Americana) occupies within Australian culture:

> There's no country radio format really like there is in the States. It's just, that perception that's been so deeply ingrained, [of Country] being hokey has kind of marginalized Country and Roots music out there.

But it's Moffatt's Australian roots outside of Country that make him an effective advocate for Americana in Australia. Working with the Australia Council for the Arts, Moffatt facilitates a three-month residency grant worth AUD $15,000[139] that allows young Australian artists to get immersed and absorb the Nashville professional experience. To achieve this, Moffatt admits "I spend a few months before just prepping them to hit the ground running." Increasingly, the recipients are producing music that is not in the traditional Country mainstream. Moffatt told us:

> There's a young Melbourne singer-songwriter called Ben Wright Smith… Ben was the 2015 Australia Council Nashville residency winner and got to spend three months in town, put a great band together and played most of the major Nashville Rock venues. We recorded some great tracks including 'No One', which he finished with Oscar Dawson back in Australia.

2017's residency winner Larissa Tandy from Melbourne relocated to Vancouver, "taking a break from the rise and grind of Nashville's Music Row". Her latest release, 'Don't Steal My Bounce', is "a joyful three-minute snapshot of 2am in a Nashville nightclub – a banjo peels off, the bass drops, and cowboy boots dance on a discarded Bridesmaid sash".[140] Many of Tandy's songs share obsession/disaffection with the internet and psychosexual identity. Oh, and they are craftily constructed and taste of Americana!

Queenslander Josh Rennie-Hynes' 2018 residency gave birth to his third solo album, *Patterns*, which *Americana UK* sums up as: "A set of well-crafted Nashville-influenced songs which show great promise for Josh Rennie-Hynes's future. 7/10."[141] Rennie-Hynes' latest release, *Summertime*, is a collaboration with

Nashville writer Dylan Smucker, full of Chet Atkins smooth strings and George-Jones-sings-Sinatra vocal.

Back in 2016, Sydney-sider Sinead Burgess was a major-label signing, recording her well-penned songs to the then-prevailing London Grammar-style of sparse Indie Pop beats. Having signed off from a Universal subsidiary, 2019 Nashville residency winner Burgess supplemented her income with a sponsor deal from guitar-makers Gibson. To a sparse and overwhelmingly male audience of music-gear geeks at the monumental NAMM tradeshow: she quipped in introduction to her song 'Mamma Raised a Ramblin' Man':

> I wrote this after going into a lot of guitar stores where [clerks would tell me things like] 'you're a good girlfriend for putting up with all this guitar stuff.' And I was, like, 'Well I kinda play too!'[142]

And she does. Her self-released 2018 album *Damaged Goods* is full of sweet, woody guitar and pure no-nonsense Country sentiment. Burgess is an interesting exception: while many unsigned artists go to Nashville to seek fame and fortune with a major-label contract at the end of the yellow brick road, the former Pop teen has decided to use her adopted city as an opportunity to get grown-up as an artist. When Jed Hilly talks of Americana as fine art compared with the commercial art of Pop, Sinead Burgess is a good illustration.

It's September 2018. We are talking to Nash Chambers, musician, producer (brother of Australian Americana star Kasey Chambers) and his wife Veronica, who have just relocated from Sydney to work in Nashville.

> Well, we are literally in music city, so I mean that speaks for itself, I don't think there's any city on the planet that is as concentrated with music studios, musicians, song artists... So that part is very exciting, there are a lot of people here and a lot of them wanting the same thing, fighting for the same thing. People are very open but, you know, it's going to take a while to sort of carve out our place... But, look, just the sheer possibilities... not only in Nashville... it's such a central

location in all America as well. It's sort of an adventure, and so far, we're heading in the right direction, but those things have been known to change very quickly!

Veronica: I think you're up for the challenge actually.

Nash: Well, there's so many opportunities here. I guess in some ways I'm starting, but you know... We've had business with Kasey's career here for close to twenty years, so we do have relationships, people we know... so we're just gonna try to build on them... You know, the music industry can take a long time, but it can also happen very quickly too. I think the main thing is to be amongst them, to present ourselves, give ourselves a chance, an opportunity to be involved... You never know where things will lead and that's the excitement of the music industry.

Flash back a year to South by Southwest 2017, Austin, Texas, Nash Chambers and AMA chief, Jed Hilly, are chatting in a hotel room before the evening's entertainment kicks off. Hilly mentions a talk Jason Isbell gave about the community that is Americana, and Chambers hops onto the love and passion behind the music. Hilly comes back:

Nash Chambers, Hunter Valley, NSW. Photo Brumby Media

Yeah… you grew up [with music] in your family. I mean your sister has no choice but to make music. She could never not make [it]. She could be waiting tables or cleaning houses – she's still gonna be playing music no matter what she does. Emmylou Harris, you know, for all the millions of records she sold, I guarantee you if she was working at a bank, she would be coming home and playing music 'cause she has to, because it's in her blood.

Later that night, Kasey Chambers was to unleash her new album *Dragonfly* on that Austin audience. The record, co-produced by Nash Chambers and Paul Kelly, was her 11th studio album. It made #1 in the Australian ARIA chart but failed to chart in the US. Reviewers picked Chambers' set as a highlight for the evening but noted it was: "[A] rare state-side appearance (the veteran singer is happy with her life in Australia) … Her voice remains an extraordinarily powerful vehicle."[143]

Kasey Chambers had bitten into the US charts with her second album *Barricades and Brickbats*, produced by brother Nash and featuring hit single 'Not Pretty Enough'. The album and single gave Chambers a double #1 in the Australian charts and went seven-times platinum in Australia with certified sales of 490,000, following her 1999 Australian hit debut album, *The Captain*. Kasey's later work has focussed on her Australian roots, without losing the American Roots music she picked up playing country covers all over her home continent with Nash and their parents in family band Dead Ringers. Her latest album, *Campfire*, features Alan Pigram, a Yawuru Australian indigenous musician from Kimberley/Broome.[144] Today, Nash Chambers is the proprietor of Essence Music Group and Troubadour House Studios in Nashville.

For many emerging Australian Americana acts Nashville remains the ultimate goal. Ashleigh Mannix, one half of duo Little Georgia told us "We went there [in 2016] for AmericanaFest… Awesome….Can't wait to go back… I would love to move to Nashville." On reflection, the duo told us they worry that the sound that they have struggled to create may be changed by being away from their Australian roots. But then again:

> I mean there are more people in California than the whole of Australia. So, in reality if you wanna make a career out of music it's really where [to be]. We're an island a long way from anywhere, so it's hard to make a career out of music in Australia.

Ruby Boots moved to Nashville from Western Australia in 2016, after a warm reception for her first album *Solitude* (2015), distributed by Universal Australia. Back in Perth, Boots (aka Bex Chilcott) had used her time wisely to gain qualifications in business, which allowed her to self-manage her early career effectively. A frequent visitor to Nashville since 2012, Boots hit town with her eyes wide open. "I faced this thing where I was either going to sink or swim… and I don't like f***ing sinking."[145] Chilcott hasn't released any music since her 2019 single 'Might be Losing my Mind', but she continues to maintain her social media profile. Let's hope she can hold it together through to the end of the pandemic.

Other musicians who have been on the Australian Americana scene for longer have a different take. When we interviewed Catherine Britt, she had this to say:

> You know, I did the Nashville thing and I realized that it was totally not for me, but I'm so glad I did it. But it is really a different world. It is a machine and the music is for a very different world from what we're doing here in the Americana world. And, from what any singer-songwriter is doing. They're not working in that treadmill world, I guess, or making music for radio for an audience, [thinking] 'I'm going to write this song because I know housewives listen to country radio from this time to this time and they're between 25 and 42.'

Troy Cassar-Daley gave us this advice:

> Australian artists need to use Nashville, I suppose, as a stepping stone if they want that whole career thing. You've got someone like [Country artist] Morgan Evans who had done what he had to do here, he had a record deal here, but

Troy Cassar-Daley Brisbane, Queensland. Photo Brumby Media

he wanted to have a crack at diving into the big pools, and Nashville was a natural progression for Morgan and I think that's what you have to do.

I think that if you go and listen to some of the singer-songwriter nights it's very, very inspiring. I'm not talking about just the ones at The Bluebird with the people that have written hits for radio, I'm talking about the ones in the little bars where it's an open mic or it's in the round with a few writers that you really, really enjoy.

Anne Kirkpatrick, daughter of Australian Roots icon Slim Dusty, told us:

I feel protective of our industry here in Australia, our producers and our musicians who are world class. And I do sometimes feel a bit sad about the trend to race over to the States and always record there and take the work away from some really good producers and musicians here. Having said that, obviously I know that it's a great experience and it's good in a lot of ways, but I think we do have a great industry here in Australia, and also I just like to see younger artists explore all the avenues here in Australia as well as incorporating the American avenues. They just dash off when they've missed some great stuff here and there's a lot for them to write about here to make it a bit more unique.

Having said that, I totally get that it's a big world out there and I'm all for embracing new musical things, which I did when I was younger. Obviously, Keith [Urban] is probably the most successful [example of that] experiment. A lot of [people] think he's American. I bet the perception is mainly because [he] stuck at it. I think: 'Oh, we're just so proud of Keith. I mean, he went over there; it was like taking ice to the Eskimos.' Really, wasn't it? I mean, he went over there, and he hung in there and did the hard bloody yards. And he had his band, the Ranch, there for a while, and obviously his style of writing and music fitted in very well with the scene over there. And he embraced that and made it work for him. But he learned his chops back here in Australia and took it over there and we're just really proud of him. Good on him!

Do you think it's a shame, that people think he's American and don't realise he's Australian?

Anne Kirkpatrick, Sydney, NSW. Photo Brumby Media

I think it's awful that people think he's American, and we definitely want everyone to know he's Australian. But I can understand that because he has made his musical career and name in America – I mean he's enormous over there! I can understand that people would think he's probably American, but it should be further up in his biography – right at the top – that he comes from Australia, 'cause we're proud of him!

Kirkpatrick will doubtless take comfort that although the Australian press reported[146] that Urban and his Australian-born wife Nicole Kidman voted in the 2016 US Presidential Elections, as they hold dual Australian-American citizenship[147], most biographical sources continue to give prominence to Urban's Australian nationality.

Urban was actually born in New Zealand, but raised in Queensland, Australia, from an early age. He moved to Nashville in 1992. His rise to international celebrity has inevitably resulted in both countries expressing national pride in his achievements[148], with Urban featured in Nashville's Country Music Hall of Fame and Museum.

But by the time Urban released his 2018 *Billboard 200* #2 album *Graffiti U,* music critics were treating him as a celebrity rather than as a musician. Trigger Coroneos in *Saving Country Music* blog was merciless:

> …He's doing an about face from his biological clock. Starting with the stupid cover where he's trying to portray some angsty 20-something club rat ripped on designer drugs, you can tell that Keith who recently turned 50 is far from ready to embrace the onset of maturing adulthood.

This is the type of analysis more usually employed for female artists, many of whom will have read this with a knowing sigh. True, Urban has become a huge pop star, which automatically renders him fair game as a celebrity, but Coroneos' ire at Urban's inclusion in *Graffiti U* of modern forms of American music by working with younger artists from different genres overflowed into denigration:

There's a song on here called 'Drop Top' featuring Kassi Ashton who is quite literally half of Keith Urban's age, which unfurls like a police report transcription of a date rape at Coachella.

Fortunately for Urban, such stuff does not appear to have damaged his reputation to the extent that it affects his sales.

TODAY'S AUSTRALIAN AMERICANA MUSIC SCENE

Like many of his generation, Paul Kelly's musical projects have ranged over his long career from Pub Rock (*The High Rise Bombers*), to Ska (*The Dots*), to 80s jangly Pop (the unfortunately named *Paul Kelly and the Coloured Girls,* soon changed to *the Messengers* for international releases) through to some rather finely produced lounge dub (*Professor Ratbaggy*) and some heavily Crowded House-influenced adult-oriented-Rock solo records, including the Christmas hit 'How to Make Gravy'. In 1990, Kelly encouraged Australian Indigenous musician Archie Roach to create *Charcoal Lane*, an album featuring the elegiac Americana-framed 'Took the Children Away', a song that recounts the forcible removal of Indigenous children (including Roach) to orphanages and foster homes in the years before 1969. This album won Roach a Human Rights Achievement Award the following year[149]. In 2020, after several nominations Roach was awarded ARIA recognition for Best Male Artist and Best Adult Contemporary Album.

But Kelly has always had a special place in his heart for American Roots music, which emerged in the noughties, beginning with a support slot for Dylan's 2001 tour of Australia. Following tours of the US and UK, 2004's double album, *Ways and Means*, is Americana to the core. From the opening instrumental 'Guannamata', replete with surf twang and Link Wray swagger; the honest narrative lyrics of songs like 'The Oldest Story in the Book'; redneck metal strip mining slide ('Heavy Thing'). Song subjects that come easily to the experience and perception to a man then approaching

Paul Kelly, Melbourne, Vic. Photo Brumby Media

his fiftieth-year mould effortlessly into Americana's musical format: grit and shimmer in the guitars, slack slick slippers-on Levon Helm percussion. Although not the most commercially successful of Kelly's albums, *Ways and Means* is his *Exile on Main Street*, a testament of fine songwriting born on the road in the US. Not all of the material works perfectly: 'Sure Got Me', for example, is a 'Rebel Rebel' riff with an unwise falsetto introduced in the bridge and lingering to the end like an unwelcome uncle at the family barbecue. 'To Be Good Takes a Long Time' contains some delightfully anarchic drumming behind an outback pub piano solo. Lyrically, though, the album remains solidly top-drawer, with little Dylanesque gems like 'Can't Help You Now':

> I gave you all the sweetest meat / I was happy just to lick the bone / Now I don't even pick up the phone.

Interviewed in Melbourne, 2018, Paul Kelly had this to tell us about working with Kasey and Nash Chambers:

> Well, I've known Kasey and Nash for a long, long time. We toured together when Kasey was starting; we did a duet [Hey!]

pretty early on we still play… We've just hung out a lot. I love playing music with them; just playing lots and lots of country songs – we do that sometimes – and a year before last I was lucky enough to produce half of *Dragonfly*. She was – she probably still is – on this rich vein of songwriting at that time and she would send me these songs on her phone she'd been asking me for a couple years to produce. I'm not that keen on producing other people – I find it probably a bit stressful – but… She sent me these little recordings on the phone and the songs were undeniable: OK, we've got to record these songs! … Producing Kasey was pretty much pick the right band and step back and let her record the songs …. Producing in that sense is don't touch it and don't try and put your hands all over it; let her unfold what's going on 'cause she brings it, you know, [when] she starts singing the band better be ready!

By this time, Kasey felt the need to answer her #1 single 'Not Pretty Enough' with a song released on EP in advance of the *Dragonfly* album. Kelly notes: "[When we] started off she was trying to get out 'Ain't no Little Girl' for someone else, but she wasn't quite happy with it."

Kelly's hands-off production let loose this juggernaut of a song, originally released on an EP. Even with a track featuring US multi-platinum fellow antipodean Keith Urban,[150] the EP only made #99 in the ARIA chart. But the *Dragonfly* album, including the entire EP, made it to #1, Kasey's first Australian chart-topper for nearly nine years.

Kasey Chambers grew up spending a lot of time with her family in the Australian bush, living a nomadic lifestyle. It's been a good preparation for life on the road as a musician. She tells us:

I think going to school was the biggest culture shock that I had in my life because I'd spent a lot of my early childhood sitting around a campfire, doing correspondence schooling with my mom, my brother and I… That was our classroom. And then when I ended up going to high school… I just did not feel like I fit in at all. It was like such a massive shock and I didn't last there very long; I just didn't really connect with it at all. I think in a lot of other ways, I have connected really well to general society. I love people, I love being around lots of people all the time. So, I think my job now is perfect, because I think I would get bored if I spent too much time on my own.

Her father, Bill Chambers, worked as a fox hunter on the vast Nullaboor Plain. He tells us about growing up with American music:

> When I was about ten or 11, I got obsessed with Buddy Holly and the early Rock 'n' Roll stuff, Elvis... but Country music has always been my first love. But I love Bob Dylan and the fringe of Country music has always influenced me, anything that was a bit left of centre, or dark songs, murder ballads, anything like that. I'm not so big on the 'positive' Nashville songs that are coming out these days, I like the darker side of country music... Johnny Cash... what a character, I saw him with the Carter Family and the Statler Brothers in the late 60s in Adelaide, it was just an experience I'll never forget. Mother Maybelle Carter was still alive then, and she was one of my heroes.

Bill Chambers recalls the aboriginal Australians he met appreciating the music of pioneering bush balladeer Slim Dusty:

> I remember giving groups of Aboriginals a ride in the land cruiser at different times and they'd hop in the front and say, 'Hey, you've got Slim Dusty tapes, do you wanna swap for a boomerang?'

As Kasey and Nash Chambers grew their own musical skills, Bill and wife Diane formed a family band, which eventually became the Dead Ringer Band, to supplement their income playing tiny bar venues scattered across the Outback. It became clear that Kasey's voice and writing were leading the band into greater recognition and bigger venues. By 1997, the band's final studio album *Living in the Circle* had made it clear that "Kasey was the Dead Ringer Band's most valuable asset."[151] By 1998, the band had split, Bill and Diane had divorced, and Kasey Chambers had embarked on her solo career. By 2005, she was the "International Ambassador of Australia's Roots music scene".[152]

Paul Kelly's own output hit a peak of success, beginning in 2017 with back-to-back ARIA #1 albums of music by Kelly and Bill McDonald. The first, *Life is Fine*, from EMI Australia, features a distinctly creepy video for single 'Firewood and Candles', in which Kelly cooks a trout with sauce made from a large red plastic diamond excised from its belly. Perhaps Kelly wished to continue the humorous vein of earlier videos such as 'Song of the Old Rake' (2012), but this offering doesn't quite hit the spot. Staying with EMI Australia, *Nature* (2018) features five 20th century classic poems and had mixed reviews after hitting #1 on launch, but in 2019 was awarded ARIA's Best Adult Contemporary Album.

Kelly's musical journey from Pub Rock to Americana appears as a maturation process, bringing his music into that 'adult contemporary' category in which the industry places many Americana musicians. But much of Kelly's earlier music is also of that category: not teen Pop, but also not Americana either. Although Americana artists, young and old, are often rewarded with an 'adult' label for the honesty and maturity of their lyrics, many acts appeal also to younger audiences. As an Australian National Treasure, Kelly reaches a young audience too. Like the classical pantheon of Americana – Cash, Carter, Parsons, Harris, Nelson, Jennings, Parton – the ageless appeal is the inner strength of Americana.

Mick Thomas is another veteran Melbourne musician who has a shelter beneath the Americana umbrella. Thomas began his career playing Folk clubs in Geelong. He moved to Melbourne as a student and fronted a number of Pub Rock bands before forming Folk Rock outfit Weddings, Parties Anything (affectionately known by Australians as 'the Weddos'), a band that "uniquely combined the 'bush' music which came to Australia with its original white settlers, and the Punk Rock attitude of the 70s," in 1984.[153] Along with Perth band the Triffids, these musicians helped to bring Australian Roots music up to date. In 1989, the Weddos recorded their third studio album with Muscle Shoals veteran Jim Dickinson in Memphis, Tennessee. Their 1991 single 'Father's Day' was a top 30 Australian hit. In 2017, Thomas duetted with Australian singer Ruby Boots on a cover of Bob Dylan's 'Most of the Time'.[154]

Unlike the Triffids, Thomas is indirect about acknowledging his place in Americana. Of a recent fan-requested covers recording project he blogs about the absence of:

> The whole modern idea of 'classic songwriting'. Not a Townes Van Zandt or John Prine tune in sight. The one Bob Dylan tune requested was... 'Winterlude', surely one of his more idiosyncratic and plain oddball ditties.[155]

This probably says as much about Thomas' respect for some of Americana's venerable wordsmiths as it does about his fans' uniquely Australian rebellious tastes. Much of Thomas' recent output illustrates the complex kinship between Australian bush ballads and Americana. His most enduring current project is Roving Commission, which he formed in 2011 with former Weddos bandmate Mark 'Squeeze-box Wally' Wallace. Roving Commission acknowledge the Wurundjeri indigenous people in Thomas-illustrated video for the song 'Anything you Recognise'.[156] Coincidentally, in a bizarre ARIA senior moment, the Weddos were awarded the Best Indigenous Album Award two years running, even though the band protested no connection whatsoever with Australian indigenous music.[157]

For her work of 2016, Blue Mountain Sydney-sider Julia Jacklin was FBi Radio's 'Next Big Thing' at their 2017 SMAC Awards.[158] How is she doing now? Her 2019 album *Crushing* is helping her to generate a very respectable 888,000+ monthly Spotifies and reached #8 in the ARIA album charts. It's full of slow-burning music that she credits to Art Rocker Fiona Apple as her biggest influence. Certainly, one can hear shades of Velvet Underground in their gentler moments in these tunes, which Jacklin says are about:

My growing confidence, but also growing fear of introducing boundaries in my life and then having to reinforce them continuously… I'm kind of looking at myself in a mirror and giving myself a pep talk.[159]

UK *Guardian* critic Emily Mackay opines that Jacklin's second album "ruminates on infatuations turned millstones over haunted Americana and garage rock".[160] Whilst MacKay's meaning may be obscure, *Crushing* is definitely haunted by Neil Young's Crazy Horse ('Don't Know How to Keep Loving You') and Nico ('Body') in equal proportions.

Like her mentor Apple, Jacklin is taking Americana in just exactly the direction *she* wants to go. According to most reviewers, the album made it to #1 in the UK Americana Music Association charts primarily on the quality of its lyrics: "Jacklin has an ability to mine minuscule details from immensely complex situations and package them in searing couplets."[161] But the melody lines are pretty memorable too, as is the emotion in their delivery.

Queensland-based Grunge-Folk duo Little Georgia are at the stage of their career where the pandemic could really bite hardest. Ashleigh Mannix began her career performing at open mic nights in Canberra and moved on to supporting a lesser-known Ed Sheeran at the Slaughtered Lamb in London, to showcasing at Folk Alliance in Memphis, Tennessee, and playing solo sets at BluesFest Byron Bay and Fuji Rock Festival in Japan. Justin Carter toured extensively throughout Australia and Japan as part of Surf Rock band CarterRollins. A chance duet at a Sydney open mic led to their current collaboration.[162]

We caught up with Mannix and Carter at October 2018's Australian Americana Music Honours show in Melbourne. It was clear at that stage that they were honoured to be invited, even at the cost of getting there:

We love playing music together. So, who cares about the rest? Doesn't matter as long as long as we can support our family… I mean we both work during the week…so that we can come here tonight to play music, [although we've] got to pay for our flights.

In November 2018, the duo released their debut studio album *All the While*, recorded and produced by Grammy-winning producer Nick DiDia. The album features 'Texas', a song of Southern loss delivered as a stadium-rousing tour de force climaxing with Ash's ad-libs in the vein of Pink Floyd's 'Great Gig in the Sky'. The band showed their live chops at 2019's low-key Hay Mate festival in Melbourne.[163]

Booked in for the Byron Bay BluesFest 2021, Little Georgia are laying low on social media, just waiting to see if they can pick up their career where it so promisingly left off.

Meanwhile, contemporary indigenous Australian artists are completing their own musical cycles of assimilation/ enhancement by branching into many fields of American Roots-influenced music, including Rock (Bad//Dreems), Soul/Rap (Baker Boy), and American/Pacific Island Folk (Emily Wurramara).

AMERICANA MUSIC IN BRITAIN

"Since I was a kid, I've had an absolute obsession with particular kinds of American music. Mississippi Delta blues of the 30s, Chicago blues of the 50s, West Coast music of the mid-60s, but I'd never really touched on dark Americana."
−**Robert Plant**

We are backstage with Bristol-born singer Yola at AmericanaFest 2017 in Nashville. She describes how it felt as a young woman growing up in a family where music was not regarded as a viable choice of career:

> Feeling my way. There was no order to it at all. One thing I knew is that I had to make it make sense, look sustainable, look like a real job thing. 'Cause I was banned from pursuing music as a job. So, anything I had to do, I had to do it right. If I screwed it up or looked suspect or swag in any way… I couldn't ever really come out of the musical closet to my mum and say, 'Mummy, I'm a musician.'

Most of the historical heroes of Americana grew up poor and achieved fame and fortune because of the burgeoning recording music industry and big-audience radio and TV shows. For the current generation of young musicians in the UK, that kind of musical fairy tale has become less accessible apart from the few that gain success through reality TV or win the lottery of lucrative soundtrack 'sync' deals. Yola explains:

> When you grow up in a poor household, you don't have the luxury of [saying], 'I'm going to go and travel to India to find myself.' And then after I do that then maybe like I'll go into a degree in, like, 'philosophy of yoga pants' [laughs].

You don't have the luxury of doing classics or something that you have no idea how you're going to apply it… If you grew up with no money, you become very aware – by the time you're done with school, by the time you're done being in the place where they feed you all day – of having to get your life sorted. You need that earlier.

Yola's passion and intelligence acted as a spur to work harder to prove her choice to go into music was a good one:

So, the kind of, I suppose, decadent choice of being a musician seemed insane… I had to prove that it was a natural thing for me to do, that it was going to make sense, that the reason that I wanted to [recover] from each fall was because I was supposed to do it and I was going to be the thing I was best at …a little war that was happening: I was about passion and [mum] was about like the logic of things. So, I had to sell it hard. And I think that's how I got into like music younger than many maybe would have. I started earlier because I had to.

At the time we spoke, we had no idea that Yola was being watched by scouts from Black Keys' guitarist and producer Dan Auerbach's label Easy Eye Sound. Interviewed by Ricky Ross for the BBC. Yola recalled: "They asked me to send over

Yola and band, Nashville AmericanaFest. Photo Brumby Media

some recordings of my recent songs to Dan. He came back saying 'Can we get her into the studio, like, NOW?'"[164]

Yola returned to the UK from AmericanaFest in October 2017. By December that year she was back in Nashville to write and record with Auerbach at his Easy Eye studio. Yola describes working with Auerbach and one of his trusted writers – "the man with the best bar band in Nashville" – Pat McLaughlin as "not an easy guy to forget. He has amazing… dreamy… energy. He was sat in that chair, almost dowsing it out, eyes closed, aloft, pulling it out of the ether."[165]

The album that Yola made with Auerbach, *Walk Through Fire,* was finally released in February 2019, to a storm of critical acclaim. The whole Easy Eye process enabled Yola to give herself an outlet for songs that reference, from her twin mainstays of classic Country and classic Soul, the heyday of classic 1960s Pop. The opening track, the Carter/Auerbach/McLaughlin composition 'Faraway Look', is a masterpiece in that gilded frame, decorated with harpsichord and bells; a passing homage to George Martin's work with Liverpool 1960s Pop sensation Cilla Black.

After that AmericanaFest gig, before *Walk Through Fire* was even a gleam in Yola's eye, she told us a story she has repeated often in subsequent interviews, a personal tragedy in 2015 that was the inspiration for the first song on her earlier self-produced debut EP and went on to inform the album's title. Yola's relationship with her family had deteriorated to the point where she was alone:

> I felt as though I was nobody's number one situation. You know, I wasn't my mother's number one situation. I wasn't my sister's number one situation. I was an orphan for all intents and purposes.

Then came the moment:

> Where I realised I was in a house fire… so I was a human torch, and I was wearing a maxi dress. The funnel for my [table centrepiece burner] was faulty and while I was filling

it the thing was just dripping, dripping… So, when I came to light it the fire spread from the reservoir over the floor to my dress… I was on fire and immediately, I was like, 'What does fire need? Fire needs oxygen, right? Stop, drop, and roll!' And so, I stopped, dropped into my rug, and just patted down. And that moment… Oh, it was horrible. It was being on fire just now and I would have to put out the rest of the fire round here. [And I was saying to myself], 'It's a lot better than my previous situation!'

After the fire, the experience of being temporarily homeless, having to camp out with friends for a week or so at a time, gave her the support network she had lacked in her "last situation".

I would have never been able to have the strength to write, produce myself, pick up guitar, just to get all the ideas out of [my] head. 'Cause if you fall you need someone to catch you. It's not really the catching: I'd always catch myself. I've had to, it's more just not being alone. It's… a little faith maybe.

Yola's determination to use adversity positively has led to four Grammy nominations for *Walk Through Fire* plus a total of three UK Americana Award wins, one in 2017 and two in 2020. On February 21, 2020, *Variety* announced that she had been cast to play "the Godmother of Rock and Roll" Sister Rosetta Tharpe in Australian director Baz Luhrmann's forthcoming film drama on the life of Elvis Presley.[166] Yola spent lockdown in Nashville, where she performed in a special Grammy online show at the Ryman Auditorium as a tribute to Tharpe.[167] She is currently pulling 800,000+ monthly Spotify streams.

FOUNDATIONS OF BRITISH AMERICANA MUSIC

Back in 1950, Alan Lomax, a Texan musicologist and field recorder from a family of Southern Folk music collectors, was living in London. Lomax had come to London on a contract with Columbia Records to collect European Folk music recordings but had fallen foul of the House Committee on Un-American Activities (HUAC) the previous year. During his lifetime, Lomax strenuously denied that he moved to London to escape the anti-Communist 'witch hunts' of the McCarthy era. However, correspondence with his agent records his precipitous departure from the US once his name had been added to, what would become the notorious HUAC entertainment industry blacklist, in June 1950.[168]

Lomax used London as a base from which to record Folk musicians from all over Europe, notably Irish fellow song-collector and virtuoso piper Seamus Ennis. But in 1954, at a party hosted by Mancunian Folk singer Ewan MacColl, Lomax met a young singer from Sussex named Shirley Collins. Collins fell for Lomax and became his assistant, travelling widely in Europe with him to collect material for his Columbia project. Lomax, Collins, and MacColl formed a Skiffle group, 'Alan Lomax and the Ramblers', also featuring MacColl's wife-to-be, American Folk singer Peggy Seeger. The group helped to popularise transatlantic Folk music in the UK during the mid-1950s and can be regarded as an ancestor of British Americana.

After an ill-starred collecting trip to the US in 1959, Collins became disenchanted with Lomax for failing to acknowledge the extent of her contribution to his work,[169] but she continued her dedication to English Folk music, working in American Rock elements with the Albion Country Band featuring guitar virtuoso and latter-day Americana champion Richard Thompson. Although Collins' music remains to this day deeply British in aspect, her unadorned vocal style and penchant for gritty lyrical realism in her material is reflected in the same tradition running through contemporary Americana.

Fast forward to 1970. A young presenter named Bob Harris makes his debut on UK national broadcaster BBC's Pop channel Radio 1. Born in 1946, former Northamptonshire Police Cadet Harris recently celebrated his 50-year anniversary with the BBC. In the early 1970s, Bob became British TV's whispering voice of contemporary and progressive Rock music with his iconic show *The Old Grey Whistle Test*. The show's title refers to an anecdotal test applied by the music promoters of London's Tin Pan Alley, in which a cohort of 'old greys' drawn from the elderly uniformed doormen of nearby West End hotels were played a single. If the old greys were able to whistle the tune after a listen or two, the track was deemed to have passed the 'old grey whistle test', and thus likely to become a hit.

After a brief and traumatic hiatus during the 'Year Zero' period of UK Punk, when the marketing antics of managers like Malcolm McLaren (Sex Pistols) inspired violent physical and media vilification of anyone within the music scene suspected of harbouring 'hippie' tendencies,[170] Harris re-emerged on BBC adult contemporary station Radio 2 with a weekly Country music show that he has piloted surely and steadily through many schedule changes for over twenty years. His intimate 'whispering' delivery and encyclopaedic knowledge of recorded music continue to strike a chord with music aficionados. In 2011, Harris won the Americana Music Association's Americana Trailblazer Award for his achievements in popularising Roots music. Those achievements continue: since 2016 Harris has presented the Bob Harris Emerging Artist Award on behalf of the AMA UK. Harris even made it to the silver screen playing himself in the Scottish Americana 'Star is Born' movie *Wild Rose,* which was released in 2018.

It follows a young Glaswegian Rose-Lynn Harlan (played by Jessie Buckley) in her struggle to rehabilitate herself as a mother and to further her career as a Country singer, after a term in jail for smuggling heroin into a prison. During the process, Harlan pays a chaotic visit to London after receiving an unexpected invitation to meet Harris at BBC Broadcasting House, where he advises her to write songs and to stay true to herself. The meeting initiates a process of self-realisation and acceptance of adult responsibilities in the immature Harlan. Although painting a somewhat clichéd portrait of Glasgow's inhabitants, the movie does much to reveal the honest reverence in which Country music is held in that city. Its climax, a set-piece at Scotland's premier Roots festival Celtic Connections, features Harlan triumphing with a supposedly self-penned song to Glasgow 'No Place Like Home', written for the movie by Nashville team Caitlyn Smith, Mary Steenburgen, and Kate York. The song (and its title) mirror allegorical references to *The Wizard of Oz* in Nicole Taylor's screenplay, with Harlan's own yellow brick road leading eventually to happiness and redemption. Oh, and there are some nice location cameos in Nashville, too.

Kirsty MacColl, daughter of modern UK Folk icon Ewan, came to prominence as a singer-songwriter in the early 1980s. In 1985 MacColl's cover of fellow Folk/Punk artist Billy Bragg's song 'A New England' made the UK top ten. Her own song 'They Don't Know' reached the US Billboard top ten, covered by Tracey Ullman. In 1987 MacColl collaborated with Anglo-Irish band the Pogues on her most popular single 'Fairytale of New York'. If MacColl had not been literally cut down in her prime in a horrific boating accident in Mexico in 2000, she may have followed her compatriot Billy Bragg into the Americana arena. Bragg has parlayed his UK Folk/Punk Roots into recognition by the AMA.

In 2013, Bragg performed at Nashville's Ryman Auditorium as part of the Americana Honors and Awards ceremony. In an article in the UK *Guardian* newspaper, Bragg said of his appearance at the Opry's holiest of holies; "we Brits have as much right to be here as anyone else because – whisper it – we invented Americana."[171] Bragg cites the British enthusiasts including Ken Colyer, who travelled to the US to seek out obscure Roots musicians before they became widely popular in their own country. The tradition continued with bands like the Rolling Stones re-exporting the Chicago Blues into the US to find a new popularity with mainstream audiences.

I interviewed Welsh singer and session musician Jade Williams to get her take on the relationship between her background in Welsh Folk music and the Americana-tinged Roots music she is now mainly involved in.

> I remember listening to Billie Holiday in my grandmother's house. 'That Old Devil Called Love'…It's that mix of African and European culture that created American music. My family played Welsh traditional music together at the *Eisteddfod* [traditional bardic festival competitions]. Welsh music is about singing with the [chromatic] harp - it's more like a piano. When I play traditional American music, I use the autoharp, which is set up for American Folk, just certain chords [diatonic]. Americana artists are often writing looking back at us [European folk musicians], and we're looking back at them. I would love to work a session in Nashville. I would not write the way I do if it wasn't for Nashville. I need a vibe, and that comes from other people. It could be a bassline or just a drone that inspires a story. It does not belong to me. It's a genie that enters you.

THE UK'S AMERICANA ASSOCIATION

Stevie Smith is the CEO of the Americana Music Association UK. As an independent record shop owner, she got involved back in 2012 when the newly formed AMA-UK was establishing itself through a campaign of industry mailshots. Her first goal when she became CEO in 2014 was to establish the UK Americana Music Awards, which were inaugurated in 2016. When we interviewed her in 2017, she cited a big reason for the growing popularity of UK Americana in the previous decade as:

> The Celtic connection: Scotland is particularly strong in Roots music… It's becoming easier to fill larger venues… the Glasgow Opry… The Celtic Connections Festival, Southern Fried in Perth, and in England we now have AMA-UK stages at the Maverick Festival and SummerTyne in Gateshead… there's also the Bristol Americana Festival. We've been attracting audiences of two to three thousand. We're now looking towards audiences of ten to fifteen thousand.

Smith's predictions may take time to come true with the advent of Covid-19. Festival director Paul Spencer told me by email that the Maverick, one of the largest UK Americana festivals, has "seen a year-on-year increase since we began, and now [2019] typically has between two and three thousand attendees."

Like all festivals after February, the 2020 Maverick was cancelled. The good news is that the 2020 line-up has been rolled over into 2021. Let's hope that audiences to all music events are quickly restored beyond 2019 levels.

In contrast, Celtic Connections, a city-based festival which draws more liberally from the Celtic musical tradition, attracted a reported 130,000 attendees at venues all over Glasgow just before lockdown in 2020[172].

Smith's objectives for AMA-UK are closely allied to those of the AMA in the US, the organisation that inspired AMA-UK's co-founder, the late Bob Butler, back in 2012. She has assembled a board which has respected influence within the performing, recording, promotion, branding, retail, charts, events, and legal dimensions of the industry.[173] When we spoke to her, she singled out local and national radio as key drivers to acquiring a significant audience for Americana in the UK, noting BBC Radio 6 Music's move from Indie to Roots music, as typified by Tom Robinson's Saturday night show:

Americana is not a rural phenomenon in the UK... It is becoming the popular form of live music for older audiences at the same time being embraced by younger artists... it's not ageist... at live events you see as many bald heads as young heads... audiences are loyal, following artists across multiple venues, owning a song as an audience member.

Smith pointed out that the Americana journey has origins in the UK:

...alt-Country [a genre developed by young British bands in the 1990s] did not all come from the US. Music changes as it travels. Folk music from Europe fuelled US Roots music, which then came back to the UK and inspired a strand of modern Americana with a recognisable but indefinable 'Britishness'.

She cited 2017 AMA-UK festival stars Danni Nicholls and Lewis & Leigh as examples of this "indefinable Britishness".

Al Lewis from Wales and Alva Leigh from Mississippi scored two AMA-UK Awards for their 2016 album, *Ghost*. Leigh's Southern voice tells tales of love and memory, hard times, and family in the best traditions of Country, but set within lush Celtic-via-Nashville vocal harmony from Lewis and typically 'British' understated production. Lewis said:

> We've always felt that we could dabble in different types of production. I think the production often steers where you get categorised and we didn't want to pigeonhole ourselves with what instruments we used.[174]

We interviewed Lewis and Leigh in 2017. They played us the song 'Rubble' from *Ghost* to illustrate the UK-American connection between 21st century Depression towns in Mississippi and Wales. Leigh explained:

> Yeah, I think the resilience in 'Rubble' is important, and that is a common thread in Americana: looking at communities and their common problems. Even though that song is about South Mississippi and South Wales it's still two communities that dealt with something awful and tried to make it a better place. I think that's a very human reaction to any disaster… and I think that's an important thing. I wish it was in all genres of music, but I think it just seems to find its way into Americana.

The duo is currently taking a break but still attracting 12,000+ monthly listeners on Spotify.

UK radio presenter and singer-songwriter Mandolin Jack has this advice for young musicians heading to Music City, USA as a career move: "Going to Nashville will not make you a star, but it will focus you."

Danni Nicholls is a singer-songwriter from Bedford UK who travelled to Nashville in 2012 to record her first full album

A Little Redemption. Her focus on the album paid off when the song 'First Cuckoo of Spring' featured on the last season of popular US TV series *Sons of Anarchy* in 2014. On the team in Nashville was Alabama native Will Kimbrough, producer and 2004 AMA Instrumentalist of the Year (see chapter 'Americana Music in the US Today'). According to Stevie Smith, Nicholls applied seven times to play at Nashville's AmericanaFest, before being given a showcase at the AMA-UK's midday party stage there in 2017. At the AMA-UK Awards in January 2020, Nicholls opened the show with a magnificent gospel-tinged rendition of *Hear Your Voice,* from her 2019 album *Melted Morning*, featuring the Hannah Brine Singers.[175] Nicholls' vocal displays a hint of soft British vowels as a badge within her Nashville team of co-writers and producers.

Danni Nicholls, Americanafest 2017. Photo Brumby Media

GREAT COLLABORATIONS

The work of the AMA-UK has given rising artists like Nicholls the chance to perform on the same platform as their venerable compatriots who have embraced Americana, including Robert Plant, former front man of UK monsters of Rock, Led Zeppelin. Back in the early 1970s, Led Zeppelin was the hottest band in the world, and now ranks in the top ten best-selling musical artists of all time[176]. In 2005, Zeppelin's lead singer Robert Plant released his first original album of Americana. The title track, 'Mighty ReArranger', combines heavy Roots Blues twangage with Celtic-British Folk-Rock touches of flute lacing Plant's unmistakably British light-and-shade vocal. The year before *Mighty ReArranger*, Plant had met a singer from

Robert Plant, Palace Theatre, Manchester. Photo Phil King

Illinois called Alison Krauss, whose bell-clear vocal he had noted and admired on a UK radio show. Interviewed in 2011, Krauss was to recall: "I first met him at a Lead Belly Tribute gig in Cleveland in 2004 where we were both singing, and we hit it off over an old bluegrass artist called Ralph Stanley. "[177] By 2004, Plant had become an avid enthusiast for Roots music from all over the world.

Three years later in 2007, Krauss and Plant recorded together for the first time. *Raising Sand*, recorded and produced in Nashville by T Bone Burnett, won the AMA album of the year in 2008 and the mainstream Grammy Album of the Year in 2009, selling over a million units in the US alone. It's an album of classic tracks by a Who's Who of classic Americana including Dorothy LaBostrie (writer of hits for Little Richard), Gene Clark (The Byrds), Leslie Ann ('Sam') Phillips, Allen Toussaint, Townes Van Zandt, and 'Doc' & Rosa Lee Watson. Krauss noted of working with Plant that "he is always playing me new stuff and saying things like [speaking rapidly], 'You have to listen to this incredible Egyptian singer I've just discovered.'"

The production on *Raising Sand* is a supreme example of Burnett's signature brooding guitar-laden style backed by percussion so authentic you can imagine you are hearing every last creak, squeak and click coaxed from Jay Bellerose's kit. Krauss and Plant's harmonies on songs like 'Killing the Blues' pay homage to Emmylou Harris and Gram Parsons. Others borrow from right across the musical lexicon: Sam Phillips' 'Sister Rosetta Goes Before Us' raids a French chanson gypsy melody, embroidered through with careful muted banjo.

Meanwhile, in London, February 2009, music journalist for *The Independent* Tim Walker is in a small bar lined with torn band posters at the back of the 12-Bar Club in London's Denmark Street, chatting with singer-songwriter Emma-Lee Moss (aka 'Emmy the Great') and her friends after Moss' try-out gig before she departs on a UK tour to promote her new album *First Love*. Moss's songs on this album play superficially as sweet and innocent musings of young love, given a rhythmic backing of unusually clever Folk textures and tempo changes by her coalition of musicians. But listen to the lyrics: "People think we're harmless, unless they're really listening," said Moss during her tour, when asked about the aggrandisement signalled by the band's name.[178] Her songs deal, frankly, with lost virginity, potential pregnancy and termination anxiety, controlled drug (ab)use, fatal traffic collisions, and how an 'ex' ruined Leonard Cohen's masterpiece for her:

> You were stroking me like a pet / But you didn't own me yet/ And the tape in the cassette deck was choking / Spat out a broken Hallelujah.

For the past year or so, a small group of acts has been developing, in moderate-sized London venues like the Luminaire in Kentish Town, into something the press is learning to call the 'nu-Folk' – or even 'anti-Folk' – scene. A young friend of Moss's joins the conversation:

> Calling it a 'scene' sends shivers down my spine because that word has so much baggage. It suggests exclusivity and people trying to be really cool. But it's more of an open musical community.[179]

The speaker is 22-year-old Marcus Mumford, a middle-class lad from Wimbledon, South London, whose band Mumford and Sons had already gathered enough momentum with manager Adam Tudhope to achieve boutique status at the premier UK festival Glastonbury. A chance video fragment records a performance to some 200 enthusiasts squeezed into the festival's tiny Tango Café Tepee.[180] Back at the 12-Bar in 2009, the musicians gathered to chat with Walker recall the genesis of their 'anti-scene' in 2007 at the Bosun's Locker in Fulham, West London, and the 'Pick your Own' sessions in the Big Chill House in King's Cross. At the time, Laura Marling was singing for Indie-Folkers Noah and the Whale, sharing vocals with her then-partner, Noah's frontman Charlie Fink, with whom Moss previously shared a house; oh, and a band too, before Moss went solo. Singer Eugene McGuinness recalls:

> The same crowd turned up every week. It all feels very old-fashioned and unforced. It's not surprising to learn that people are good friends with each other. We have the same value-system of just songwriting and performance, without any hoo-hah.[181]

Marling's debut album *Alas I Cannot Swim*, produced by Fink, had gone gold in the UK a year before in 2008. That year she split with Fink and began dating Mumford. Interviewed in 2020 at the ripe age of 30, Marling, the daughter of an English baronet, considers the career she began at 16, and admits a strong element of character creation in her writing.

> My interest in my songwriting is in inhabiting the character of a kind of forsaken, hardworking woman. I ask myself why that should be? It's not my experience necessarily.[182]

Marling took Mumford as her drummer on her Australian tour in 2008, and again in January 2010. "I got a lot of confidence being on stage with Laura," says Mumford.[183]

Marling and Mumford's relationship lasted until 2010. By then it was as much about Mumford and Sons as Laura Marling. Mumford's band had gone gold worldwide, largely through their self-made album *Sigh No More* featuring the single 'Little Lion Man'. Mumford explained:

> We could have made [the album] earlier, or signed a deal earlier, but we wanted to be patient. The more we played live the better the songs got. We wanted to wait for more demand in the UK rather than force it on people.[184]

By making the album before being signed to a label, the Mumfords maximised their income from the record by creating a bidding war between the big players. Entrepreneur Paul Piticco was instrumental in turning the band into stars in Australia through a licencing deal with his label Dew Process. He recalled a call from Mumford's US label asking the secret

Mumford & Sons, Aviemore, Scotland. Photo Stefan Shafer, Lich

to the band's success downunder. He pointed them at 'Little Lion Man':

> I just said… 'That song will do the work for you. When people tell you that there's no room on their radio station for a banjo, you tell them they're wrong and you keep telling them 'till they play it.'[185]

True, there is something of that song that appeals especially to Australian audiences. Maybe it's the jaunty swagman pace the tune moves with. Great to mosh to. Maybe it's the F-word in the chorus. By February 2010, 18 months after that Glastonbury Tepee show, the song was #3 in Australia's ARIA charts. It peaked in the US at #45 in the US main *Billboard* chart and #24 in the UK charts, with estimated sales in those three countries topping 3.3 million by 2013 (2.3 million of that in the US). So, here is a bouncy but self-confessional song by some cute, slightly upper-crust English boys; a song that tips a wink, musically, to American Roots and English Folk, goes down great in Oz, and eventually gets to the US and sells a bunch. Here is a fully connected three-continent Americana trail if there ever was one. Just to complete the circles, Mumford was born in California, where his parents were active in the Vineyard Church.

Danny and the Champions of the World were the homegrown stars of the first UK Americana Awards, held in

2016. The band are the creation of Danny George Wilson, a talented singer-songwriter from London. With his brother Julian, Wilson formed the UK alt-Country band Grand Drive in 1998. Early Grand Drive albums are typical of the UK alt-Country scene around the millennium: lush Country Rock with mannered brushwork-anchored rhythm section. Speaking in 2018, Wilson recalled: "We were brought up on Doo-Wop and Bruce Springsteen records, and just made music that sounded like the music we liked."[186]

Actually, neither Grand Drive nor Wilson's more recent projects sound much like either of these American musical beacons. But you can hear the collective sounds of 1970s American FM radio in every note of their most recent album *Brilliant Light*. Danny doesn't think much of the Nashville songwriting process, nor does he believe that the band need to join the crowd of music-industry immigrants into Nashville, saying: "We like recording in London. There's nothing in the water in Nashville that we don't have in London."[187] Danny is something of a survivor. Out of the flowering of alt-Country in the UK in the 1990s and early 2000s, he has continued to make a successful career in music, whilst retaining a degree of credibility he sees appropriate with his community and fanbase:

> The best thing about Americana… is that it's built from the ground up. The people who watch it are as important, if not more important, than the musicians. It's a collaboration.[188]

Wilson's collaboration with Robin Bennett (The Dreaming Spires) and Tony Poole (Starry Eyed and Laughing), *Bennett Wilson Poole*, was nominated for AMA UK's 2019 album of the year.

Jade Bird is a young singer who grew up in the UK and Germany but has integrated into the Nashville Americana scene. A graduate of the British Recording Industry Trust (BRIT) school, she got her first break playing Austin loft venue Palm Door at South by Southwest in March 2017.[189] On that

Jade Bird, The Troubadour in Los Angeles,
California. Photo Justin Higuchi

same visit, Bird opened for tours with First Aid Kit, Son Little, and London Grammar.[190]

When writer/singer Brent Cobb (cousin of noted Nashville producer Dave Cobb) came to tour the UK a couple of months later, Bird had been chosen to open his shows. Cobb told us he remembers:

> It was my first trip to the UK. I had never left the country before. I get there, and I'm playing a show at the [London venue] Slaughtered Lamb, and Jade is opening that show.

Bird and Cobb did some co-writing on that tour which resulted in 'Feet Off the Ground', a duet released eventually in 2019.[191] In the summer of 2017, Bird signed to Indie label Glassnote, also home to Mumford and Sons and Childish Gambino.

Having come to the attention of the Americana community with her first album *Something American,* recorded in upstate New York, Bird released a hit single 'Uh Huh' in 2018, which went to #3 in the US Adult Alternative chart. 'Lottery', released the same year, did even better with a #1. On these records, Bird unleashes a voice that could stop traffic. "My voice has improved so much over the years... I've hammered it to try and get to places."[192] An early exemplar of that hammered voice is her cover of Son House's 'Grinnin' in your Face', a tune she was inspired to record by hearing Jack White's version.[193]

Like one of her icons Tori Amos, Bird is a passionate advocate for women: "I feel really strongly about women's rights and making young girls feel like they can do it. The more educated we can get as a gender, as women, the better."[194] Currently just surpassing Amos, with one million+ monthly listeners on Spotify, Bird is on a trajectory to match other icons of hers, Alanis Morissette and Patti Smith.

Emily Barker was born in Bridgetown, Western Australia, where she says, "We didn't have any television, so Mum used to play guitar and taught us how to sing harmonies and we'd play these old Folk songs and all sing together."[195] Barker credits the Bridgetown Blues Festival for launching her interest in American music at the age of 12.

Emily Barker, Nashville AmericanaFest. Photo Brumby Media

Every café and pub, the town hall…all became venues with Blues bass lines bouncing down the street... my high school music department suddenly upped its game and went from learning recorder… to having a drum kit, electric guitars, and vocal microphones.[196]

Barker played in a few school bands, working on her voice. She became focussed on American Roots music via the Coen Brothers' movie *O Brother Where Art Thou?* But unlike many of her compatriots, she chose London, rather than Nashville, for the next stage in her musical career. Emily tells us:

I moved to Cambridge, that was the first place that I sort of got a job in the UK. I was on a two-year working visa because one of my friends from Australia was there and I got a job in a record store and was doing lots of open mic nights around the town there, and ended up forming a band with some local musicians and we played at Cambridge Folk Festival.

Barker's two-year visa ran out after that gig, and she was backpacking in Canada, vaguely heading for home, when guitarist Rob Jackson, who had sent their demo to legendary UK radio presenter and discoverer of new music John Peel, emailed her:

… just saying, 'I think you'd better buy a return flight to the UK because John Peel's just played [our demo]…That was very 'John Peel': he just played whatever he liked and it didn't really matter how long the song was or what genre it was. He was so eclectic in his taste and allegedly listened to everything that he was sent. And from then on, things started happening for this band out in the UK. We were called The Low Country and just did everything DIY, that is, booking our shows, and one thing led to another, [and] another, and I ended up still being there sixteen years later.

By 2008 she had assembled the Red Clay Halo, an all-female multi-instrumental quartet. The band's second album *Despite the Snow* opens with 'Nostalgia', a song about being far from Bridgetown.

I was working as a waitress. This guy… I would make him a flat white every day. He invited me to play at a garden party in Tufnell Park. A few days later I got a call from Martin Phipps, whom I'd met at the party.

At the time, composer Martin Phipps was working on the score for BBC drama *Wallander* starring Kenneth Branagh. Barker recalls:

I went… 'OK?' I didn't know who Kenneth Branagh was. I didn't know anything about this Wallander character. But I certainly knew the BBC. Martin invited me to his studio to re-record 'Nostalgia'. We changed a few words to make it fit the setting. And it became the theme tune for the show. I'm so grateful to Martin for that.[197]

Phipps' score for *Wallander* was to win a BAFTA, and net Barker a Royal Television Society Award as writer of the theme. Barker went on to pen 'Pause', which was used as the theme tune to BBC2 noir thriller *The Shadow Line*, (and she collaborated with Phipps on the original score for US Civil War drama *The Keeping Room*). In 2015, she completed her first full feature film soundtrack, for Jake Gavin's debut feature *Hector*.

Success followed success. Early in 2012, Barker was on her way to a gig, when, she recalls, very clearly, she says:

I was in the Citroen Berlingo driving up the motorway in England with my band at the time called the Red Clay Halo. We took this call, and it's one of those calls where we all know that something big has just come in. And it was my friend Frank Turner, who's a great singer-songwriter, he's a British guy. And he had been asked to sing at the opening ceremony of the Olympic Games in London and he wanted us to perform the songs with him.

Barker was to make two more Red Clay Halo albums: *Almanac* (2011) and *Dear River* (2013). In 2014, she began a co-writing partnership with Nashville artists Amber Rubarth and Amy Speace. The resulting album *Applewood Road* was recorded live in Nashville on a single microphone to analogue tape, a homage to the pre-digital recording techniques of early

Americana. *Sunday Times* critic Clive Davis' praise was fulsome: "I think I've just found an early contender for the albums of the year list. Those close harmonies are so gorgeous, so relaxed."[198]

In 2015, Barker began releasing solo albums. 2017's *Sweet Kind of Blue* was recorded at Sam Phillips Recording Service in Memphis with Grammy-winning producer Matt Ross-Spang (Jason Isbell, Margo Price) and an all-star cast of Memphis session players. The album achieved worldwide success through Barker's hard-working tour schedule and landed Barker UK Artist of the Year at the 2018 UK Americana Awards.[199]

Her 2019 album, *A Window to Other Ways*, is a collaboration with Mary Waterson, of that renowned family of UK Folk artists. It features dark new Folk songs of modern life to stripped-bare swinging beats and jazz harmonies from the African American tradition. Barker's latest offerings are 'Shadow Box', "a collection of hard-to-find and previously unavailable recordings" named for the handmade box for mementos her grandfather gave her as a child,[200] and *A Dark Murmuration of Words*. This last album:

> ...shares stories on the backdrop of stellar and elevated Folk-Americana. Want protest songs to be loud and Punk...? This album isn't for you... Like your protest songs [as] calm melodies with inspiring stories? Then *A Dark Murmuration of Words* is your record.[201]

In contrast to that of Spotify sensation Jade Bird, Barker's musical career feels like it has greater strength in depth. Her film score work and range of collaborations may serve to give her a lasting reputation (and income) without the necessity to ride the charts as a performer. If she continues to produce work of such quality, one can imagine a future reputation up there with her teenage heroes Aretha Franklin and Emmylou Harris.

In 2015, Felix Bechtolsheimer (lead vocals and guitar) and Neil Findlay (drums) formed Curse of Lono, a leading UK Americana band named after a cult novel of Americana literature by Hunter S Thompson. Bechtolsheimer's gravel-and-treacle vocal soon attracted media attention, especially when their second studio album *As I Fell* made it to #10 in the UK Americana charts.[202]

The band helped promote the album with the short documentary *Somewhere in Their Heads* filmed as they made the record in London's Flesh and Bone Studios in Hackney, and in the Joshua Tree National Park in California, a sacred site for Gram Parsons enthusiasts.[203] At the start of 2019, the band were awarded the Bob Harris Emerging Artist Award by the UK Americana Music Association. The band share a record label (Submarine Cat Records) with The Alabama 3 (see below) and John Murry, with whom they toured in past (normal) years, and, in the sad year of 2020, collaborated on diverse online shows.[204] We snapped Bechtolsheimer with Lono bass player Charis Anderson onstage at The Water Rats in London, back in 2017.

A chapter on UK Americana collaborations would not be complete without mention of leading UK producer Ethan Johns. Johns is the son of Glyn Johns, who produced the Rolling Stones' greatest albums of the 60s and 70s. Johns Jr is the nearest

Curse of Lono, London. Photo Al Stuart

Ethan Johns. Photo GPS Management

the UK gets to the great American(a) producer T Bone Burnett: he is a guitarist and arranger of taste and dexterity who can capture effortlessly and repeatedly a fresh take on that brooding gospely-bluesy sound. Johns' recent collaboration with the great Welsh singer Tom Jones to recreate Todd Snider's 'Talking Reality TV Blues'[205] is a masterpiece: a valedictory swipe at the reality-TV star who became President. Johns has collaborated with Jones for over ten years on a series of Roots projects,[206] and has worked with the cream of contemporary artists including Americana subscribers Mary Chapin Carpenter, Ryan Adams, The Jayhawks, and Rufus Wainwright.[207]

Americana is alive and well and following its own trail in the UK. As in Australia, the lure of Nashville is strong, especially with younger artists, but UK musical culture is perhaps more equipped to offer its own internationally recognised rewards to signal talent than Australia thus far. This is not necessarily a situation that will continue in the future.

The exit of the UK from the European Union that came into effect from the beginning of 2021 will make access to what was previously the largest market for touring UK musicians harder. These changes affect entry requirements, professional qualifications, tax on money earned in the EU, insurance, and transport of equipment.

The UK Musicians' Union is lobbying for adoption of a 'Musician's Passport' to cover some of the new regulatory requirements affecting a market they estimate at £5.8 billion[208].

Music journalist Paul Sexton told me: "This is a problem coming down the line when musicians are allowed to tour again. The artists have been taking the lead [in campaigning on this issue] ... There's some benefit there, in that they are most likely to get the headlines."

Only time will tell us the real cost to the UK Music industry of leaving the EU trading bloc, under Brexit. A final strand to the UK Americana trail: Police Dog Hogan represents the apotheosis of a multitude of UK bands that spring from the desire of mature British musicians to explore their Folk roots clothed in the hobo chic of Americana. Founded by Devon native James Studholme, the band quickly gained influential fans including BBC Radio presenter Jo Good. By 2014, they were one of five UK bands selected to perform at the AMA Awards in Nashville, where they attracted the attention of Bob Harris, who provided a live recording session and a showcase radio show the following year. Pre-Covid, the band were regulars at major UK festivals including Glastonbury; they are aiming for a lockdown restart at the new UK Folk/Roots festival Black Deer in June 2021.

Photo courtesy Black Deer Festival

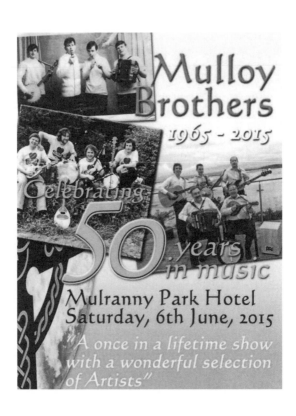

Mulloy Brothers 1965 - 2015

Celebrating 50 years in music

Mulranny Park Hotel
Saturday, 6th June, 2015

"A once in a lifetime show
with a wonderful selection
of Artists"

IRISH AMERICANA MUSIC

"You can't stay the same. If you're a musician and a singer, you have to change, that's the way it works."
– Van Morrison

Pat Mulloy is a veteran, last survivor of the Mulloy Brothers, an Irish traditional ensemble out of County Mayo. In their time, the Mulloys rivalled their Irish American mentors the Clancy Brothers. We meet online, kindly arranged by Mulloy's niece Elizabeth. "They went to New York to study acting," says Mulloy of the Clancys. "And they ended up in Greenwich Village teaching Woodie Guthrie and Bob Dylan traditional Irish tunes." Mulloy describes how Irish (and Scottish) workers began to emigrate to America "after the famine, 150 years ago. They bought the fiddle and the mandolin. That's two thirds of Bluegrass!"

In the middle of the 19th century, the Irish workers encountered African slaves, who played an instrument that was a reconstruction of similar native instruments. They called this instrument the *Banza* or *Banjul*, for 'bamboo [stick]', and also perhaps in memory of the place of departure, for many slaves, from Africa: the infamous Banjul [bamboo] Island at the mouth of the Gambia River. Musicologist Daniel Jatta believes the closest African instrument to the modern banjo is the *akonting*, the three-string folk stick-lute of the Jola people who live in what is now known as Senegal and The Gambia. Jatta cites two key pieces of evidence:

The *akonting* is most similar in construction to the banjo, with a pole passing through a wooden ring over which is stretched a goat-hide parchment; and the earliest recorded playing style for the American banjo is called frailing, which is uniquely the style used by the traditional players of the *akonting*.

Other less similar skin-lute instruments from West Africa (e.g. *jele n'goni*) have a different, very well maintained, historical playing style by virtue of their restricted use within the elite musical *griot* family tradition.[209] To support his thesis, Jatta concludes from historical data of the slave trade that the Gambian Jola folk formed a much larger proportion of the unfortunate souls removed from their homes by northern traders to be shipped across the Atlantic than the elite *griots* from further north.

Mulloy's nephew Enda Mulloy provides bass and vocals for London Irish Americana band, The Bible Code Sundays. He has his own colourful version of the evolution of the banjo, which is part of the mythological fabric of Irish Americana, based on the factual history of coerced labour in 19th century New Orleans:

> I was told some amazing stories over the years; some may be myth. One particular one inspired one of our songs, 'The Swamp Rats of Louisiana'. The Irish who were tricked (thought they were boarding a boat for New York but were rerouted to New Orleans to be slaved) and the black slaves built the Pontchartrain Canal. A reported 20,000 Irish died there. Apparently – and I love this story – the Irish had their fiddles with them on the journey. The Africans used to have an instrument that was made from goat skin and a wooden bowl when they were in Africa, and replicated the instrument using the empty biscuit tins and the goats they kept for milk – and the occasional stew no doubt. The instrument they made was the first banjo. The night-time music sessions allegedly created the original Cajun music. I hope that story is true!

One piece of music history that is beyond reasonable doubt is that the fusion of Irish/Scottish Folk tunes with the characteristic rhythmic licks of the African American banjo completed the holy trinity of Bluegrass. The original players were a mix of working folk of European and African heritage who powered the farms, plantations, and labouring gangs of the southern states. Pat Mulloy says:

> We started playing in about 1964–65. Originally in [our hometown] Mulrany, and then Dublin. As well as the Clancys, the Dubliners, and other traditional Irish musicians, we would listen to Bob Dylan and Pete Seeger from America. My late brother Martin played banjo in the band, mainly because the Dubliners had a banjo, but it wasn't a traditional Irish instrument.

By this time, the American banjo had evolved into four-string, and then five-string, variants with increased volume and power to suit the bar room and dance hall venues. Pat identifies the five-string banjo as the Irish variant: "Tommy Makem [of the Clancys] played the five-string banjo, the Irish banjo." Mulloy is somewhat correct in identifying this banjo variant as Irish, as its popularity is universally credited to one Joel Walker Sweeney of Appomattox, Virginia, whose family, like Mulloy's, are from County Mayo in the West of Ireland.[210]

"The Dubliners and the Clancys would have probably heard the Flanagan Brothers' records from the 1920s; they had banjo and accordion in their band," says Mulloy. The Flanagan Brothers emigrated from Wexford, Ireland, to New York in 1911. By the mid-1920s they were top of the bill in New York's dance halls, and made over 150 78rpm recordings in a wide range of musical styles from 1921 until the early 1930s.[211]

The Mulloys, like most of their Irish traditional music contemporaries, would include American songs in their sets: "We would play 'The Banks of the Ohio', 'Blowin' in the Wind', 'The Banks of Ponchatrain'." Like the Dubliners, and the Clancys, the Mulloy Brothers brought their music to America on tour. "We played The Irish Village and the Atlantic in Chicago, The Irish Centre in Cleveland, Ohio; we were on

Maureen O'Looney's radio show." O'Looney was a pillar of the Irish community in Chicago. Her radio show on WXRT in the 1970s was one of the most popular stations for Irish music in America. Interviewed shortly before her death in 2016 she recalled, "Every [Irish] musician that ever came to Chicago would come to my basement to record a session for my show."[212]

Later on, there was a great deal of musical traffic in the other direction. Mulloy recalls how Americana royalty Steve Earle spent time in Ireland in the late 1990s and early 2000s. "He recorded *The Galway Girl* with Sharon Shannon on accordion."

In 2012, 'The Galway Girl' was the eighth all-time best-selling song in Ireland, with *Riverdance* being the only other bigger selling Irish music.[213] The recording of the song by Shannon and fellow Irish musician Mundy (Eamon Enright) in 2008 was used to advertise Magners Cider, making the song a smash hit. Interviewed by Irish state broadcaster RTÉ in 2008, Shannon takes up the story:

> Steve wrote the song in Galway. Yes, we know the Galway Girl. She is real! It was his suggestion to record the original there with myself and some other local musicians.[214]

So here we have Earle, a US Americana artist of great repute working in Ireland with Irish musicians who then go on to make a hit in Ireland with one of his songs. There are many other examples of such complex cross-fertilisation between American and Irish music. This is no surprise for anyone who has experience of listening and playing music around the world. There are few other countries where ordinary people are more respectful and appreciative of popular music well played than Ireland and the US, in venues from the grassroots up to the great halls. Their intimately shared Roots musical culture marks out Ireland as a special place on the trail of Americana.

Two pairs of brothers make up Galway band We Banjo 3 (yes, we know). Such is the reputation of the band for their own particular fusion of Irish and American Roots music they have claimed for their own the tag "Celtgrass". The band's singer/guitarist David Howley attributes his appreciation of the "huge connection between Irish music and Bluegrass" to his father's mixtapes: "so we grew up with this myriad of schizophrenic music – sometimes one song recorded over half of another." The band, who are now based in Nashville, were planning to extend a sold-out fan-bus tour of Ireland starting in April 2020. Here's hoping that may be accomplished soon. A big source of inspiration (and out-of-comfort-zone terror) for Howley has been the American Legion in East Nashville: "…the most authentic Bluegrass you ever heard, around a single mic – nowhere to hide!" Howley singles out audiences in Ireland and the US as most typically receptive to uplifting live music: "there's a lot of pain in the [US] at the moment [2019], and they feel a need for connection."[215]

The band have worked hard to support US non-profit organisation Mental Health America with a merchandising partnership and a new song. Howley recounts:

> We were inspired to write 'Hold on to Your Soul' for a fan whose husband had suffered [a fatal] mental illness. The message is to hold onto life: it evolves; you will not recognise yourself in ten years' time.[216]

The therapeutic power of live music has been vastly under-estimated in past years. The pandemic throws this into stark highlight and gives us all an opportunity to recognise and reward musicians for their contribution. Howley notes:

> We see women of 70 or 80 [dancing] with twelve-year-olds, enjoying our music. Accessibility is one of the most important features of both [Irish Folk and Bluegrass]. The *bodhràn* - Irish for 'deaf man's drum' – is the common denominator for everyone.[217]

Elly O'Keeffe is an Irish singer/writer from Cork, who started in a family Folk band with her father, sister, and two brothers, the younger, Daniel, being "quite a young little

Elly O'Keeffe, Dublin. Youtube

famous singer," at the tender age of ten. "That's where I got my graft," she explains – and graft O'Keeffe certainly has. After the family band, she graduated into the Cork music scene when she was invited to join Karan Casey and Mick Flannery (the first Irish songwriter to have won Nashville's International Songwriting Competition),[218] to play a famous series of concerts 'The Junctions', organised by Armagh's premier music family the Vallelys. Elly recalls:

> In Cork there's a fantastic Bluegrass scene. Mick Daly is the king of that scene. I learned very quickly how important an inspiration he is to the younger folk like myself and [Americana singer-songwriter] John Bleck.

Two years ago, O'Keeffe teamed up with Willie Kelly, late of high-energy Irish Bluegrass combo Rackhouse Pilfer, to make her latest EP in Nashville. "Willie hooked me up with [Nashville musician] Jim Riley and before I knew it, we were in the studio making an EP," says O'Keeffe. The single 'Gold' was released in August 2020, but the EP release was delayed owing to contractual issues with the BBC reality show *The Voice*, where O'Keeffe progressed to the knockout rounds with mentor Welsh singing legend Tom Jones. One of O'Keeffe's fondest memories of *The Voice* is meeting Canadian Country star Shania Twain, who counselled her not to "hide where's comfortable" as a writer and performer.

> I like to compose intricate piano melodies and follow with my voice – the sort of thing where a producer might say, 'No, give it more space.' Shania Twain told me to push my voice, try five keys higher, and see what that brings… That advice is playing in my head when I'm writing – especially now in lockdown.

John Murry lives in Kilkenny. We had a long and far-ranging video call, much interrupted by the vicissitudes of the internet, but nevertheless, he is a fascinating man. "I would prefer to go back to not being so fascinating," he says, ruefully. I understand his meaning. Murry has endured loss and fame, all made chaotic by living with autism (a freely avowed constant) and addiction (thankfully a burden of the past). Murry was raised by Southern upper-class parents who adopted him at birth in Tupelo, Mississippi. They did not approve of his youthful ambition to be a Rock musician: "When I was growing up… I saw Tom Petty and I thought, 'I can do this!'"

Murry recounts a chance encounter with Petty in a music

John Murry in a Bristol studio.
Photo Rob Blackham/Blackham Images

149

shop in Tupelo back around 1994, when Petty came in to buy a white Vox Teardrop guitar. With some symmetry, Petty had become set upon the path of music by a fleeting encounter with Tupelo native Elvis Presley. But Murry's childhood was steeped in Country.

> My sixth-grade teacher played 'Negro League' baseball with Charley Pride; he was his best friend, and he'd come into our school. I just think [Pride] was one of the most massively underrated voices in Country music. He was a real redneck: like, he drove a big Bronco with a white deer-tail cover on the spare. And when he first appeared at the Grand Ole Opry the audience gasped to see him. They were not expecting a black man. But Charley says 'Guess I got a little sunburned at the weekend' [laughs]. And the guys at Stax and what have you, they were all listening to him at the Opry!

Murry headlined at Kilkenny Roots Festival back in 2013 after the untimely death of his mentor and producer Tim Mooney. But this was after he had become fascinating. The fascination originates from his writing on his debut solo album *The Graceless Age*, which deals candidly with his misadventures with abandonment, rejection by his adopted pedigree Southern family, and heroin addiction culminating in an ambulance ride off the pavement of 16th Street and Mission in San Francisco, documented in 'Little Colored Balloons', the song that inspired critics to dub him "Americana's coming man".[219]

Mooney's death combined with the stress of touring a universally acclaimed album left Murry lost and exiled, eventually settling as an Irish resident in 2016. Not until an encounter with Michael Timmins of Toronto Roots Rockers The Cowboy Junkies did Murry recover his artistic equilibrium with *A Short History of Decay*, "recorded in Toronto in five days". The album features the Pogues' Cait O'Riordan on vocals. Murry released four singles in 2020, in advance of an album he is recording at Mick Cronin's studio in rural County Longford.

The Kilkenny Roots Festival is a well-established (since 1998) hub for live Irish Americana. Founded by John Cleere around his venue Cleere's Bar and Theatre, the organisers proudly and justly describe their event thus:

> Audiences wind their way through the medieval streets sampling the huge range of music ...There's a mixture of old and new acts on the free pub gig trail and all styles are catered for, from Swing to Bluegrass, Rockabilly to Cajun, Folk, Blues and beyond.

Held in May, the festival has hosted some of the finest acts in the Americana/Roots canon, including Calexico, Giant Sand, Drive By Truckers, Jason Isbell, Alejandro Escovedo, Guy Clark, Chuck Prophet, Ray LaMontagne, Richmond Fontaine, Rodney Crowell, Phosphorescent, Sturgill Simpson, and Alabama Shakes.[220] Sadly, the 2021 festival, like the 2020 event, was cancelled due to the Covid-19 pandemic.

IRISH ARTISTS IN THE UK

Sir George Ivan Morrison OBE ('Van-the-Man' to his fans) was born in Hyndford Street, East Belfast, in 1945. Although on the relatively wealthy Protestant side of the much-divided city, Morrison's childhood friend Roy Kane described Hyndford Street as being "on the other side of the tracks".[221] His father, a shipyard electrician, had an outstanding collection of records from time he had spent in Detroit in the 1950s. Young Morrison grew up listening to the cream of American Soul music, and this is what one hears in his own voice. Morrison grew to prominence in the UK fronting Them, a 1960s beat combo. He had already acquired serious musical chops touring in Germany with Irish showband The Monarchs. Morrison's improvisational approach to performances was developed as Them performed regularly at Belfast's Maritime Hotel, an R&B club for sailors. Probably his most covered song, 'Gloria', was literally written onstage during this period. The band

Van Morrison, Northern Ireland. Photo Art Siegel

toured the US in 1966, but visa issues and a dispute with their management led to a split shortly thereafter.

Morrison signed with Bert Berns' newly formed Atlantic Records subsidiary BANG in 1967 and relocated to New York to record solo. Although he was unhappy with his contract, the sessions yielded what was to become Morrison's best-known hit 'Brown Eyed Girl'. On Berns' death, Morrison's contract was bought out, via a convoluted series of clandestine transactions, by Warner Bros. Records, during which time Morrison's income was contractually restricted. And so, at the tender age of 22, Morrison found himself hard-up in New York, about to record one of the best popular music albums of all time.

Astral Weeks was made by jazz producer Lewis Merenstein at Century Studios, NYC. Merenstein's choice of bassist,

Richard Davis, was key to the album's exceptional quality, as he explains:

> Richard was the soul of the album. Richard was the heart and beat of it, which I knew he would be…the other musicians would come in and see Richard, they knew they had to come up to top form.[222]

Davis and his fellow musicians, including Connie Kay of the Modern Jazz Quartet, turned *Astral Weeks* into a classic meditation upon Morrison's soul. Its slow-gathering critical reception and later worldwide appreciation has allowed Morrison the freedom to exploit the spirituality and Soul roots of his writing and the hypnotic voicing he gives to it across a staggering 41 studio albums to date. Along the way, his reinterpretation of American Roots music has garnered recognition from the Americana community, culminating in the 2017 AMA Lifetime Achievement Award for Songwriting.

Few contemporary Americana musicians fail to acknowledge Morrison's musical contribution, and many have claimed direct influence, including John Mellencamp, Joan Armatrading, and Nick Cave. In 2006, Morrison released his most overt Country album, *Pay the Devil*. "A project filled with steel guitars, fiddles and a variety of classic country songs," the album pipped Keith Urban in the *Billboard* Country top ten, the week that Morrison made his first visit to Nashville with a concert at the iconic Ryman Auditorium.[223]

Pay the Devil showed that Morrison could deliver Country classics with characteristic vocal grace, but despite its moderate commercial success (by Morrison's high standards) the self-produced album is musically unremarkable. In the same period, for example, Willie Nelson was stretching out, performing, and recording with Toots Hibbert, Ray Charles, and Wynton Marsalis.[224] Nelson's album *Songbird*, released that same year on the same label as Morrison's *Pay the Devil*, featured covers too, but ranging from Christine McVie's title track through the Grateful Dead's 'Stella Blue', to producer Ryan Adams'

'Blue Hotel'. Nelson, who has a good ten years on Morrison age-wise, was showing a degree of adaptability and class with younger colleagues, maybe not to the extent that Johnny Cash achieved in his valedictory *American IV*, but in contrast to Morrison's work at this time.

Throughout his career Morrison has acquired a reputation as a 'prickly' character, inviting comparison with Bob Dylan in that respect, as well as for the quality and prolificacy of his lyrics. In 2020, he attracted criticism for his advocacy of a return to capacity music events during the Covid-19 pandemic.[225] The *Belfast Telegraph*[226] reports US Americana star Jason Isbell criticising Morrison during an online performance which included a tribute to Morrison's classic song 'Into the Mystic'. Isbell was a close friend of another of Americana's elder statesmen, John Prine, who died from the virus on April 7th, 2020. Perhaps this will explain the bitterness in Isbell's words of introduction to the song, reported by *Rolling Stone*:

> There was a time… when our dear Van Morrison had… such beautiful songs… Now that time has passed… now he likes to say things like: 'The government asking you to not give everyone the Covid-19 virus is akin to slavery.'[227]

Back in spring 1955, jazz trumpeter Ross MacManus, of Irish heritage, got a big break with the Joe Loss Orchestra, then one of the UK's most popular acts. By the time his son Declan was 11, MacManus was a success, with a property in the leafy southwest London suburb of Twickenham. Ross MacManus' success meant more and more time on the road or out every night in town with the band, increasingly taking a front role, with own-name billing. Favouring white trousers, blue socks, and white Italian shoes, he would cause a flutter amongst the nuns when he came to pick up his son, young Declan, from school.[228]

But by 1969 his marriage was crumbling, and he soon fell in love with singer Sara Thompson who was to be his wife until their deaths within weeks of each other in 2011.

Declan and his mother Lilian moved back to her hometown of Liverpool. Meanwhile, Ross MacManus had a minor hit in Australia with a cover of the Beatles' 'Long and Winding Road' under the moniker Day Costello (his maternal grandmother's maiden name). As Ross MacManus moved into his forties, he started growing his hair and broadening his tastes in music.

When Ross's son Declan left school, he moved back from Liverpool to London, where he met Mary Burgoyne who was to become his first wife. Mary was also from an Irish family, steeped in the Irish showband tradition; she was also familiar with the works of American artists like Hank Williams and the later Country stars of the era. Declan, who had taught himself guitar during his schooldays, started playing in public, at first solo, and eventually with London Pub Rockers Flip City. In his 2004 biography of the man who would shortly become Elvis Costello, Graeme Thomson comments:

> Through his love of the Band, the Grateful Dead, and The Byrds, Declan had discovered what loosely could be called Americana, and was gradually tracing a rich seam of musical history back to its source.[229]

A live recording[230] of one of Flip City's last outings confirms Thomson's view of young Declan's musical influences in 1975. But it also gives an early taste of the nasally resonant, emotional tone that was to become Elvis Costello's plaintive yet sneering trademark vocal. Declan's long-haired laid-back Americana persona was to become abruptly suspended in 1976 when, after a year of severe frustration at his lack of recognition, he managed to get some solo demos of his new material (under the name DP Costello) to the ears first of influential Radio London DJ Charlie Gillett, and then, of one Andrew Jakeman (aka Jake Riviera), co-head of London's newest and coolest label Stiff.

Riviera was to give DP Costello his ironic first name during "a drunken meeting in a restaurant in the Fulham Road".[231] This was in March 1977. Nobody, least of all Riviera, had any idea how ill Elvis Presley really was. Riviera's partner at Stiff,

Dave Robinson, had arranged for the newly christened Elvis Costello to record his debut album *My Aim is True* with backing by experienced musicians from Huey Lewis's band, label-mates Clover who then happened to be residing in the UK. Clover were dealing out the laid-back Americana vibe with which compatriots Eggs Over Easy had started the UK Pub Rock trend in the first half of the 1970s, but in October 1976 Stiff had driven a stake through the heart of Pub Rock with the first UK Punk Rock single 'New Rose' by the Damned.

It's Monday August 29, 1977. I'm a callow youth of 19, working sound for a band up from the south coast trying to break into the London circuit. My diary says I worked a gig Saturday the 27th at Dingwalls Dancehall in Camden Town. I've taken a long weekend layover in the capital with a friend: guests of squatters in Maida Vale, if I recall correctly. Bank Holiday Monday can be a quiet night for music, but tonight is a bit special for those in the know. There's a crowd milling about outside Nashville Room in West Kensington. Somehow, I squeeze through and pass under the strangely curved glass arch of the main entrance. Hanging with the extra heavies on the door that night is Ieuan (not his real name), a tiny but combative Welsh drummer of my acquaintance. Ieuan waves me by, and I'm in! It's sweaty, smoky, and reeks of the slops of London Pride beer that donate that blackened patina to the carpet. I head into the back room and turn left to elbow my way through to the bar. On the other side of the room is the stage, backed by the most hideous synthetic lime-green curtains you ever saw. There's an unusually large contingent of smart folk up from Chelsea in tonight. Long-haired princesses in kinky boots trying to look like Marianne Faithfull did ten years before, accompanied by braying boyfriends in crisp Jermyn Street shirts open to the navel. And we're all excitedly gathered for the belated fourth gig of what has been a Sunday-night residency from our city's hottest young musical property. I'm just in time too: Elvis is already on stage, plugged into his dirty green Fender Jazzmaster and ripping through 'Blame it on Cain'. The band are a mighty engine. The crowd is heaving like a beast.

At the end of August 1977, *My Aim is True* had been out for a month, Elvis Presley – 'the King' – was dead, and the reverberations of the first, explosive, snarl of Punk were starting to die away amongst the musical trendsetters of the UK capital. The album is crisp, energetic, in-your-face, and waspish, without the brute aggression and bombast characteristic of vintage Punk. The Clover musicians contributed a level of maturity which Costello sought to replicate when selecting his touring band, The Attractions, when the album quickly launched him into the Rock 'n' Roll stratosphere. The 'king' of UK music journalists of the period, Nick Kent, asked Costello to comment on the songs on the album that expose a persona that is 'a complete loser':

> That's something totally new to the Rock idiom which, by its very nature, is immature and totally macho-orientated in its basic attitude. Only in Country music can you find a guy singing about that kind of deprivation honestly.[232]

Costello went swiftly on to fame and notoriety in the US and then all over the western world, but he didn't lose that respect of American Roots music. 'Elvis Costello' was marketed by Riviera as part of the shockwave created by the Punk attitude to authority and 'taste'; for Riviera, the timing of Presley's unexpected demise added to the shock value of the bitterness and frustration vented in Costello's material. Costello rode the wave diligently, while his contemporaries faded through illness (Ian Dury, Lee Brilleaux), or substance abuse. Riviera and Costello deliberately cultivated an unapproachable mystique about the young star, reinforced by Costello's diffidence with press, public, and fellow musicians.

By April 1984, Costello had been on a non-stop recording/ touring schedule for nearly seven years. His marriage to Mary was in trouble; his relationship with his band was on its last legs, touring the US with an album appropriately titled *Goodbye*

Elvis Costello, Riot Fest, Chicago

Cruel World. In support on the tour was one John Henry (aka T Bone) Burnett. Costello and Burnett bonded on that tour, hamming it up with a mock 'revival' harmony duo as Henry (Elvis) and Howard (T Bone) Coward. The 'Coward Brothers" set was songs that Elvis had loved in his youth: George Jones, the Beatles, and The Byrds. Another consolation for road-weary Costello was girlfriend Bebe Buell, with whom he would check in as 'Henry and Jane'. The romance and the clowning with Burnett affected Costello's onstage demeanour. He had become "warm, witty, and a little silly." Thomson quotes Buell: "Elvis is a very honest man. He was obviously participating in something he felt was wrong." Costello's marriage to Mary finally ended during the Japanese tour, after Mary had received a misdirected letter from Buell to Costello, informing him that she was pregnant. The vitriolic three-cornered international calls that followed also marked the end of his affair with Buell.[233]

Back in London, Costello asked his friend Philip Chevron to act as a guide to the new music that had sprung up there while he had been away. Phil ('Swill') Odgers, founder and singer-songwriter of the Anglo-Irish Punk Folk band The Men They Couldn't Hang (TMTCH), takes up the story. "We started in 1984 when my friend Paul Simmonds and I came to London and bumped into Stefan Cush."[iv] Cush was a roadie for The Pogues, formed after the Nipple Erectors' bassist Shanne Bradley had auditioned youthful vocalist Shane MacGowan. MacGowan's new Irish Punk Folk project hired another female bass player Cait O'Riordan, and by 1984 the *Pogue Mahone* ('kiss my arse' in Irish) had become a big noise. Bradley joined Odgers, his brother Jon, Simmonds, and Cush to form the first incarnation of TMTCH on the London busking scene. Odgers recalls the moment his band moved from buskers to big league:

> We were busking and people would come and chat with us. We were asked to play an alternative Country festival in Camden with The Pogues, Shillelagh Sisters, and the Boothill Foot Tappers. I think it was planned to coincide with the big Silk Cut Country Festival of the time. The Pogues were more of the Irish tradition, but a lot of their own songs have now become part of the American tradition! The Boothill Foot Tappers were Rockabilly and Country. Phil Chevron [later to join The Pogues] saw us. He had the ear of Elvis Costello. Costello saw us and put us on his show 'A Month of Sundays' at the Hammersmith Apollo.

Costello was much taken with TMTCH, but more so with The Pogues, particularly their 19-year-old bass player O'Riordan, whom he pursued relentlessly while he was producing The Pogues' second album *Rum, Sodomy, and the Lash*, much to the amusement of the rest of the band.[234] But the couple were totally serious about each other. Costello and O'Riordan were married in 1986.[v]

Odgers and I are discussing the oceanic currents that washed Irish music over to America, American popular music

i. iv   Sadly Stefan Cush passed away February 4, 2021
i. v   The 'marriage' was not actually a legal ceremony but was accepted by all parties while it lasted.

back to Europe, and his music back to the continent of North America, to which he says:

> I was born in Scotland, my mother was Irish, my father was English, in the navy. My grandparents would play 'cleaned up' traditional Scottish and Irish music like Kenneth McKellar, but at the same time I would hear my parents playing stuff like Hank Williams and Elvis Presley, both clearly drawing from Roots music. It sowed a seed that came back a long time later.

> I had my teenage musical awakening listening to Punk music in the 1970s. It was what really made me want to go onstage and play. But then I started to listen again to Irish music at the inception of The Men They Couldn't Hang. We did a lot of busking. We did songs that maybe came out of the struggles, the Troubles, in Northern Ireland. The great thing about it was it was simple to play and boil down… It propagated because it was easy to sing along to. And [Irish traditional music] had a humungous influence on American Roots!

For Odgers, UK Punk was the working class music of his time – "at least I thought it was". Like the American Country and Rock 'n' Roll musicians of his father's generation, he wanted to make music for working class people.

With further help from BBC's John Peel and The Pogues, TMTCH's debut single 'The Green Fields of France' was soon #1 in the UK Indie charts. Within a couple of weeks, the buskers were a band, touring the UK and then Europe.

> Miraculously, we found ourselves playing two nights at Milton Keynes opening for David Bowie on his Sound and Vision tour. I don't really know how that happened… I heard a story that his young son was a fan of ours and asked his dad if we could do it! But that was huge, as you can imagine.

In July 1985, Costello (reverting to the name DPA MacManus for the credits) began recording *The King of America* in Los Angeles with Burnett producing. The album marks a major redirection for Costello musically and the pinnacle in Costello's embrace of Americana. It was also the first he had made, since his debut, without his juggernaut band The

Attractions (except for one track, 'Suit of Lights'). The band for the sessions were, appropriately, Elvis Presley's former backing group, the 'TCB' ('taking care of business') band, augmented by musicians Burnett was able to call in from the cream of US talent, including Ray Brown (Ella Fitzgerald's long-time bass player) on 'Poisoned Rose'. Burnett creates a Rootsy feel for most of the album, and two tracks ('Glitter Gulch' and 'The Big Light') are downright Country.

Costello went in other directions musically after *King of America,* but Irish Punk-Folk bands he Pogues and TMTCH formed a major influence on later US bands. Odgers' band toured Canada extensively and played a few dates in the US in the 1990s. Odgers recalls:

> We never really caught on in the US. Perhaps because our music was maybe too American. I know that bands like the Dropkick Murphys were influenced by us, and by the Pogues, but we're seen there now as a sort of 'heritage' band.

Canadian alt-Country band The Tragically Hip makes a somewhat strange but, Odgers believes, respectfully intended, reference to TMTCH in their song 'Bobcaygeon'.

> It's always puzzled me… [vocalist Gord Downie] is sadly passed away now, but I heard the story goes he came to see us at a place called the Horseshoe Tavern in Toronto, at a rare time when there were riots going on in the city. The only thing I can think he means of that line, 'Their voices rang with that Aryan twang', apart from just looking for a rhyme, is a reference to our British accents!

Kaia Kater. Photo Al Stuart

CANADIAN AMERICANA MUSIC
COMES OF AGE

"Americana was formed from the rib of country music."[235]
– Kaia Kater

The Canadian banjo virtuoso Kaia Kater graduated from Davis & Elkins College in West Virginia on a scholarship won through her already remarkable banjo playing, which began when her mother fell in love with Bluegrass when Kater was eight.

> My mom was the Executive Director of the Ottowa Folk Festival and the Winnipeg Folk Festival. So, a lot of musicians crashed at our house and hung out, and I think it was a really interesting education for me.[236]

When Kater was contacted by Gerry Milnes, a well-respected folklorist at Davis & Elkins, she thought somebody was joking with her, but her dream college place really had come true. Kater graduated with experience of Appalachian dance techniques such as 'flatfooting', as well as consolidating her old-time music skills. By the time she had left college, her third album *Ninepin* had got the attention of *Rolling Stone* magazine, who tipped her as one of their 10 New Country Artists to Watch.

In October 2018, Kater released *Grenades*, an album which explores her Grenadian heritage from her father's family. Interviewed by *Rolling Stone,* Kater explains the inspiration of her father's experiences as a refugee from Grenada following

Ronald Reagan's invasion of 1983. Kater and her producer Erin Costelo looked to Joni Mitchell's 1975 album *Hissing of Summer Lawns* for inspiration – the fusion of Mitchell's impressionist jazz vibe with Kater's quest for her father's Grenadian roots makes music of great quality two or three generations removed from the mountain Folk of her previous recordings but still, discernibly, Americana. It marks Kater's attainment of a new level of musical maturity. Interviewed for her label Smithsonian Folkways, Kater says of the genesis of *Grenades*:

> Connecting the past with the present and the future is something at the forefront of my core beliefs, musically and otherwise… I wanted to give people a snippet of how I was feeling as a second-generation Canadian citizen.[237]

Kater discovered a 1957 Folkways recording of songs from Boca, Grenada, her father's home community, which she describes as "the missing puzzle piece for putting together that environment musically". One cold Canadian December day, Kater took her father down to the warm basement of his home and recorded his words as he took her for the first time through the whole story of his life and flight from Grenada. Some of those words appear in spoken interludes she describes as the "spine" of the album.[238]

Not all of the musical juxtapositions work totally well, as in the symphonic jumps of tempo, voicing, and signature early in 'Canyonland'. Others work brilliantly, like the use of Creole (or *Quebequois* perhaps?*)* in the Grenadian-tinted call and response acapella of 'La Misère'. The final track, 'Poets be Buried', is a father-daughter conversation summing up the life of an immigrant family haunted by "hatred hiding in the blue". Its French horns evoke Ontarian Neil Young's 'After the Goldrush', a song which references a different kind of refugee flight from a collapsing world. Erin Costelo describes her contribution as producer as "asking a lot of questions, sending [Kater] a lot of music:

'Do you like this? Do you hate it?' And through that, discovering the sound she wanted to have."[239] The two women go back a way: Costelo frequently takes keyboards in Kater's live set-ups, where, as on record, they are clearly a musical unit of some complexity and powerful understanding.

Kate McGarrigle was a singer-songwriter from Montreal, Quebec, Canada. With husband singer-songwriter Loudon Wainwright III she had two children, Rufus and Martha, both singers. The McGarrigle Sisters, Kate and Anna, made their

Kate and Anna McGarrigle. Photo Harold Barkley

first record, *Kate and Anna McGarrigle*, for Warner Bros. in 1976. A third sister, TV composer Jane, managed the sisters' musical career and co-wrote several of their songs. The album is unclassifiable and infectious in equal measure, bringing Canadian Folk music into the age of Rock 'n' Roll. It rolled through the industry awards system collecting accolades for Rock Album of the Year (*Melody Maker*, UK), Robert Christgau's Pazz and Jop (*The Village Voice*), and the Canadian heritage music Polaris Prize. Only Joni Mitchell comes close to the McGarrigle sisters as a North American female musical innovator of the period. Ironically, Rufus Wainwright admits that his mother was deeply jealous of Mitchell's relative commercial success and departure from what she valued as purist Folk tradition.[240] This despite the fact that the McGarrigles' albums were musically breaking through every wall of Folk tradition themselves.

With Rufus Wainwright, and friends including Emmylou Harris, the sisters are captured in some classic Americana performances, including a haunting rendition of the parlour[vi] classic, 'Hard Times Come Again No More'.[241]

Buffy Sainte-Marie is an Indigenous Canadian American musician, visual artist, educator, pacifist, and social activist. In all these areas, her work has focused on issues facing Indigenous peoples of the Americas. In 1983, Sainte-Marie stated that she believed herself to be the first indigenous American to win an Oscar.[242] Her song 'Up Where We Belong', co-written for the film *An Officer and a Gentleman*, won the Academy Award for Best Original Song at the 55th Academy Awards[243] and the Golden Globe for Best Original Song. Sainte-Marie, a member of the Cree Nation, writes songs which reflect the reality of American life. Her 1964 song 'Universal Soldier' is up there with Dylan in its message of protest against the nonsensicality of war.

Late in 2018, Canadian artist Belle Plaine quoted Sainte-Marie in a social post to express her gratitude for the increase in attention to the Saskatchewan music scene her album *Malice, Mercy Grief and Wrath* (*MMGW*) had generated. Her comments bring together older and new generations of musicians, for

---

i. vi   Parlour music is a form of popular music which was distributed as sheet music intended to be performed in the parlours of middle-class homes by amateur singers and pianists. Its popularity decreased in the 20th century as records and radio replaced sheet music as the most common method of mass-dissemination of music.

Buffy Sainte-Marie, NBC TV, 1970

she is acknowledging the coming-of-age of two Saskatchewan writers Blake Berglund and Colter Wall:

We wouldn't be where we are in this province if we weren't supporting one another, and that's something I've witnessed in spades between these two songwriters. I've learned a lot from them about building community. As Buffy Sainte-Marie would say, 'Build up in spite of, and beyond.'[244]

Plaine's magnificently titled 2018 album was produced by Jason Plumb, who has also produced for fellow Saskatchewan Americana artists The Dead South. Critics described *MMGW* as:

The kind of album you'd imagine playing on the jukebox in the background of a small-town bar on a drizzly Friday night… Her voice makes the record tender, but its content really makes you stop and think.[245]

Plumb plays a big part in the Canadian scene based around the tiny city of Regina, Saskatchewan. He started as lead singer for Folk Rockers The Waltons and went on to work with Ontario Rockers the Barenaked Ladies.

We caught up with Plaine in Nashville after her AmericanaFest showcase in September 2017, before a US tour for the release of *MMGW*. She shared the following:

> For me, the umbrella of Americana gave a lot of focus into what we were doing. And it did give us a bit of a home in terms of what we were looking for and what community to connect with, whether that's in Canada or Australia or the UK or in America. That community is seamless in a lot of ways, and Americana embraces Soul, and it embraces Blues and Country and Bluegrass. I think it's this vehicle that so many artists can use when a commercial radio isn't going to be interested in what you're doing, but Americana has such a strong connection with other people that you can find your place.

Belle Plaine, Americanafest, 2017. Photo Brumby Media

Plaine's writing has a wit and vigour derived from prairie self-sufficiency. There is a little gem of a song on *MMGW* which narrates the duel between Laila Sady Johnson, a "matriarch of seven" in her "silver half-ton Ford" and a transcontinental train, when she crosses the tracks to "check on her potato patch".

Notwithstanding the pandemic, 2020 was an especially bad year for The Dead South. The Regina, Saskatchewan band formed around the idea of "a rockin' stompin' bluegrass band" in 2012,[246] and rose to prominence in popular culture with their song 'In Hell I'd be in Good Company',[247] which has to date notched up more than 42 million streams on Spotify. But in July of this inauspicious year, allegations of historical sexual misconduct emerged against founder member Danny Kenyon, which led him to "step down" from the band.[248] Lyrically, the band have always played upon the dark side of American Roots culture, evidenced by criticism of their 2014 song 'Banjo Odyssey', a tale of incest and misogynistic violence.[249] Until this year, one could have accepted this content as deriving from the murder ballad tradition, brought up to date with elements from Rap culture. But the allegations against Kenyon have cast a personal shadow which may leave a lasting scar on the band's professional career. Time will tell.

Lindi Ortega likes to wear black. Like her "all-time hero"' Johnny Cash. Back in 2013, the UK newspaper *The Guardian* quotes a nameless critic's description: "a country-fried Amy Winehouse in widow's robes."[250] Ortega was living in Nashville then, having left her native Toronto in 2011 to make her fourth album, *Cigarettes and Truckstops*, off the back of her third, *Little Red Boots*, that had made it into the US charts.[251] Ortega traces her ancestry as Mexican-Irish, a heritage which noticeably colours her take on Americana music. She told us:

> My dad was a bass player in a Latin band, so I grew up listening to a lot of Latin music, like... Los Lobos and Linda Ronstadt... But my mom was into Country music, so she loves

Hank Williams and Johnny Cash. And she had a big crush on Kris Kristofferson. And I remember watching the Dolly Parton variety show on TV and that's how I fell in love with music. So, my music, it's a mix of everything. I listened to Country, and I listened to Blues and I listened to Soul, and there's little pieces of that in everything that I do.

By 2015 Ortega had collected a couple of Canadian Country Music Awards. That year she made *Faded Gloryville*, her last Nashville-based record and her most popular album to date. Ortega's voice is more ripped silk than grit to the ears. Songs from this album reference Dolly Parton's vocal ('Ashes') and the New Orleans groove of The Meters ('To Love Somebody'). It's impossible to avoid reading into the title track a sense of disillusion with Ortega's adopted home:

> I won't get back all the dues I've paid / Here in Faded Gloryville.

In 2017 Ortega left Nashville and moved back to her native country. She explained:

> It got to the point I couldn't pay the rent… I left my former label, management…. I wasn't commercial…. But over a bottle of wine I sat at the piano and decided I'd write one more song.[252]

Lindi Ortega, Nashville. Photo Brumby Media

That 'one more song' turned into an EP, *Til the Goin' Gets Gone*, recorded in an old mansion, with Saskatchewan co-producer Jay Tooke at the controls. Ortega admits it took a while to find a suitable room in which to record her vocal, but they found the desired acoustics in that mainstay of home recording, the bathroom.[253] Ortega lives quietly now in Canada but her social media reports encouragement from her fans and a promise of more songs to come.[254]

Matthew Swann met legendary Canadian experimental musician Dan Mangen in 2008, while Swann was playing bass for Hot Little Rockets, a Calgary, Alberta, indie band. Mangan's career exploded – he has won two Juno Awards and a Polaris Prize – but he remained an admirer of Swann's music. Mangan signed Swann's indie/Canadian project Astral Swans to his label Madic in 2014.[255] Astral Swans' debut album was the oblique Outlaw homage *All My Favorite Singers Are Willie Nelson*. 2018's *Strange Prison* opens with 'Blow Away', a dark dream fantasy with explicit and disturbing lyrics of sexual revenge and paranoia:

Of Swann's latest single 'Bird Songs' (2020), *Americana UK* asks the reader to imagine, if you will, that:

> You're walking through Vondelpark in Amsterdam…Love has abandoned you, …all the birds are mocking you …letting you know that you never deserved love anyway. Pretty heavy, and if you imagine it then there's a good chance that you are Matthew Swann….[256]

Canada has its share of festivals for Americana music. The aforementioned Ottawa (now known as CityFolk) and Winnipeg Folk Festivals lead the field in showcasing new and established Canadian Roots artists. Tamara Kater has served as Executive Director of both festivals. Kater has acted to instil green initiatives[257] and sustain the cultural traditions of these long running events by limiting audience growth.[258] Whilst entertaining a diverse sprinkling of international artists, these Canadian festivals focus on native talent and national musical tradition, and have embraced, whilst avoiding being overwhelmed by, the inevitable influences from south of the border. CityFolk's virtual line-up for November 2020 featured only two US acts (Jason Isbell and Steve Earle) amongst more than a dozen home-grown headliners, including Hannah Georgas, Hawksley Workman, and the achingly beautiful music of the Great Lake Swimmers, whose latest album *The Waves, The Wake* comes in original and acoustic editions.

As well as receiving supportive recognition in their own country, Canadian Americana artists are being helped to gain recognition in Americana's capital city. In September 2020, the Canadian Independent Music Association (CIMA) presented *Thriving Roots 2020,* a virtual showcase of twelve Canadian, British, and Australian "emerging Americana" artists at Nashville's AMA Music Festival and Conference. The event was supported by the AMA Foundation[259].

Astral Swans at Broken City, Calgary, Canada. Photo Etherbug

First Aid Kit, Coachella, California. Photo Raph PH

EUROPEAN AND OTHER OFFSHOOTS

"It's not 'me too,' it's 'we too,' us as a collective. Now we have each other's backs. If everyone speaks out, things will change, and a change is coming."

– First Aid Kit

SCANDINAVIA

First Aid Kit are a well-connected and popular band with Columbia Records, fronted by Swedish sisters Klara and Johanna Söderberg. Their song 'Emmylou' was chosen by *Rolling Stone* magazine as the number ten Single of the Year in 2012. They describe the song as "about the joy and the magic of singing together with someone you love". At the Polar Music Awards in 2015, the duo performed the song with Emmylou Harris in the audience, who was moved to tears. The sisters blend their voices in an enchanting incantation dedicated to the great vocal partnerships of Americana, namechecking Emmylou Harris and Gram Parsons, June and Johnny Cash.[260]

They represent perfectly the current generation of high-profile Americana acts, in the truly international spirit of the genre. Like many Millennial stars, the sisters began their career with posts on *MySpace* from back in 2007. Their juvenilia has, unsurprisingly, been sanitized from cyberspace, but a London busking performance of their song 'In the Morning' perhaps gives a flavour of the sound that made the industry sit up and take notice.[261]

By 2015, in their early twenties, the sisters had already reached the burnout that is the frequent fate of those sucked into the industrial fame cycle.[262] After a break from touring, they recorded *Ruins*, an album of mature and harder-edged material, illustrating their female strength acquired from the psychological and physical assaults of the road. Having made a debut in the modest Mojave Tent in 2012, in 2018 amid a blaze of mainstream publicity (including an article in the hyper-corporate *Forbes* magazine), First Aid Kit made a postgraduate appearance at the influential Millennial festival Coachella.[263] In 2019, *Ruins* was nominated by UK's Brit Awards and the UK-AMA Awards as Best International Album. The album peaked at #3 in the UK and #47 in the US mainstream charts.

Of their next record, they said, "It's not going to sound like anything else we've done. The core – our vocal harmonies, our songwriting – will still be there, but everything else could change."[264] Then came the pandemic. The band streamed from home lockdown and released a single of Willie Nelson's 'On the Road Again' as a benefit for Crew Nation, in support of workers stranded by the loss of live music employment. In June 2020, Johanna gave birth to a daughter. Let us hope that next record gets made, so we can hear where the trail takes them.

Saving Country Music blog points out that Americana receives a better per capita commercial reception in Europe than in the US:

> Europe is a better support center for independent country and roots music… with venues and festivals in the UK, France, Germany, Italy, and beyond full of thankful and appreciative fans… willing to go the extra mile to support authentic music.[265]

The Country Side of Harmonica Sam pay respectful homage from Sweden to the Stetson wearing, suited honky-tonk bands of 50s Nashville. Their albums to date, *Open Letter to the Blues* (2015), *A Drink After Midnight* (2017), and *Broken Bottle, Broken Heart* (2019), are carefully packaged in the graphics of the period, and contain original dance tunes, 2/4 hops and four-to-the-floor shuffles, authentically rendered in classic retro style. Tours of Sweden and Europe have led to appreciation the other side of the Atlantic, with a nomination for 2020 Honky-Tonk Group of the Year at the Memphis Ameripolitan Awards.

Originating from Stockholm, Bluegrass band The Spinning Jennies "fuse Swedish poetry and North American Mountain music".[266] Their 2015 album, *Istallet for Visor*, is a collection of original songs ranging across American forms: Blues, Cajun, Rhumba, Polka, and, of course, Bluegrass. Their steadfast adherence to their native language for lyrics has so far confined the band's popularity to Scandinavia, but the quality of their musicianship is notable.

Johan Örjansson is a songwriter from Falkenberg, Sweden, who in 2013 took all his money and his dream to Texas to record (as 'Basko Believes'), *Idiot's Hill*,[267] an album that gracefully straddles Folk, Country, and Soul with a vocal delivery that inevitably references Van Morrison, without entering the latter's meandering streams of consciousness. Basko chose to debut his new performing moniker with an Australian tour.[268]

BMG artist Ellen Sundberg from Bjärme, central Sweden describes her music as "Grunge Americana".[269] Her earlier work borrows musically from Bruce Springsteen, but her latest album, *Levi's Blue Eyes* (2020), stretches in more and different directions, combining Rootsy instrumentation and techniques with a very 21st century attitude. Sundberg's vocal on this album throws faint shades of classic Icelandic singer-songwriter Björk, without appropriating any of her more extreme mannerisms.

A popular Swedish Country act, and most faithful in their reproduction of home-grown modern Country music, is the Willy Clay Band. The band have been a little quiet in terms of recent recorded output, but their social media promises new songs in the pipeline.[270]

Benjamin Folke Thomas "was born in the coldest winter recorded in modern day history in Gothenburg; perhaps his obsession for sad, lamenting country songs was inevitable"[271]. He was raised on a secluded Swedish island populated by evangelical Christians. Rather than finding religion, Thomas discovered grunge music. By the time he was 11, he was playing drums in a Punk band before turning to Folk and Americana music after seeing Kurt Cobain's performance of 'In the Pines' on TV. Thomas steeped himself in Americana – Lead Belly, Bob Dylan, and Leonard Cohen. By 2013, he had mastered the finger-picking guitar style and was a mature songwriter, performing his material mainly in London, UK.[272] That year he returned to Gothenburg to record the first of two well-received studio albums. In 2015, his second album, *Rogue State of Mind*, triggered an invitation from UK's premier Americana radio personality Bob Harris to a BBC showcase in Nashville. By 2017, Thomas was fronting major festival appearances including UK's Cropredy, and had released his third studio album *Copenhagen*. We caught him on camera that year with fellow guitarist Dave Burn and tour manager Peter Christopherson at Camden's Green Note club.

Thomas has a distinctive baritone dripping with the whiskey and smoke of the poolhall, a habitat the Swedish nine-ball aficionado is not unfamiliar with.[273] His press pack describes him as "the missing link between Johnny Cash and Ingmar Bergman". As with Bergman, dreams weigh heavy in Thomas's work. 'Stuff of Dreams' is a wry homage to the ghost of Paul Newman. An early live recording features 'Dreams of High Quality Truth', an epic of infidelity that could easily have been penned by Leonard Cohen himself.

September 2018 found Thomas touring with dark Americana aristocrat John Murry out of Tupelo, Mississippi. More of the Dark Earl elsewhere (see chapter: Irish Americana

MUSIC). 2019 saw a move in a more European folk direction, with Thomas working with UK Folk artist Jay McAllister (aka 'Beans on Toast') and Kathryn Williams, among others. On August 6, 2019, Thomas announced his last UK gig "for a year or two (maybe ever!)",[274] prior to a move back to Sweden, where he now lives and works with his wife and young family.

FRANCE, GERMANY, NETHERLANDS, ITALY

In France, La Maison Tellier fly the American flag in a land which at one and the same time manages to be resistant to anglophone culture whilst valuing artistic endeavour across the globe. Their eponymous 2010 debut ranges boldly across the American musical landscape with a convincing degree of twang. A highlight is the restrained cover of Rage Against the Machine's 'Killing in the Name', but by far their most-played offering on Spotify is *Sur un Volcan:* picked guitars, claps, and claves back a lyrical dance of doom around the crater,

Benjamin Folke Thomas, Green Note Club, London. Photo Al Stuart

waiting for the hungry tiger. The band are from Normandy, the location of the fictional brothel in Guy de Maupassant's short story, from which they take their name.[275]

Dietmar Leibecke is "an insatiable supporter of Americana music" and curator of what he claims is Germany's "one and only"[276] festival of that ilk, Static Roots. The venue is a former zinc factory in the industrial town of Oberhausen on the Ruhr, converted into a lofty and inspiring performance space. Interviewed in 2018, the festival's third year, Leibecke said:

> [Americana] is definitely on the rise [here] ...a few more radio stations put on Americana shows, [but] I would still consider it a niche genre in Germany. ... half of the tickets have been sold to fans from other countries than Germany.[277]

Leibecke is planning a "postponed 2020 festival" for 2021 which he hopes will feature California Southern Rockers Robert Jon & the Wreck in addition to a selection of acts from UK and Canada, including UK band Curse of Lono.[278]

Out of Amsterdam comes VanWyck, a songwriter whose dusky voice has, she says, been compared with "Leonard Cohen, Natalie Merchant, and Laura Marling"[279]. VanWyck is attracting very nearly 100,000 monthly listeners on Spotify, a most respectable following. 'Carolina's Anatomy' from her 2019 album *Molten Rock* is a lilting and gently erotic hymn to a lover. Her lockdown album *God is in the Detour* is an intimate conversation with the deity (female, of course). VanWyck's songwriting reflects her much-travelled past: "a fragmented upbringing, moving all over the world and playing different roles in different bands." [280]

Nero Kane (aka Marco Mezzadri) is an Italian Americana artist whose music is about as gothic as you can get, paradoxically for a follower of the Italian Renaissance. Kane eschews the temptation to apply a fake Southern accent to his vocal, instead adopting the tone of a young Cardinal intoning a delicately sung Roman Mass in English as a second language. Kane is a polymath, admitting:

> I have become quite obsessed by the aesthetic dimension of the Christian religion, as it was evidenced in my solo photo and installation exhibition *God Loves You* featured in an Italian art gallery in 2017.[281]

Kane's music has the flavour of originality and careful craft required to become a future force in Americana. It will be interesting to see how he fares in the lottery that is the world of professional music.

Many of the larger festivals in Continental Europe have started to include Americana in their line-ups. Totaalfestival, held since 1978 in Bladel, Netherlands featured on their 2019 bill a selection of homegrown acts who tribute American Roots music with covers and faithful reproductions from the Opry c1950, along with some more original artists, notably Maurice Van Hoek, who makes thoughtful Americana for the 21st century without feeling the need to push the envelope too far. 'Last Light', from his 2016 album *Live Forevermore* has some

Nero Kane, *Love in A Dying World*. Photo Samantha Stella

skilful little twists in its chord structure (VII - I - VII - IV - I at the start of the refrain works very well with the hopeful melody and lyric). Wikipedia lists over 50 small Bluegrass festivals in more than half a dozen countries in Continental Europe.[282] Each of these represents hundreds of enthusiasts who are willing to travel to participate in a weekend of finger-lickin' pickin' and general good times. The post-pandemic survivors from these events will form the green shoots of recovery in the grassroots scene.

ISRAEL

Mark Smulian is an English-born musician, educator, and producer. He identifies as a "nice Jewish boy from a middle-class North-London family." He moved with his mother to Israel at the age of 11, after his parents divorced.

> I was teaching myself the guitar, really working at it, and my parents noticed that. The agreement was that I was to attend an English-speaking school in Israel, and the only one at the time was the American International School in Tel Aviv. It was totally a piece of America… all the music, all the culture… I went to Israel and fell in love with America.

This was 1969. Smulian fondly recalls the weekly school 'hop', where he became immersed in roots Rock 'n' Roll, still without any formal teaching. "I was absorbing Americana without even knowing it," he says.

Smulian returned to England in 1971 to continue his English education in a progressive boarding school near Bristol. There he was encouraged to learn bass guitar to a high level of proficiency, stimulated by the "dominant" UK Rock scene: "More American than Americana… the 'British invasion'." In hindsight, Smulian feels fortunate not to have stayed in Israel at this critical point in his musical development, when American music was being innovatively evolved in the UK by bands like Led Zeppelin, The Jimi Hendrix Experience, and The Who, because as he says, "In Israel they were still copycatting". At the age of 16, Smulian

Mark Smulian in the studio, Lucerne, Switzerland

chose to return to Israel – the place he considers home – to begin his journey as a musician. He remembers: "I was this kid with long curly hair and the girls loved me. I was 'authentic', I was 'British'!"

Smulian quickly found work entertaining troops stationed in desert outposts in the aftermath of the Yom Kippur War. In a parallel with the Nashville Country music purist culture of the 1950s and 1960s, which insisted on 'doing it the way Hank [Williams] did'. He recalls:

> Israeli musicians I worked with would frequently say, 'You're not playing that right.' And I'd be, like, 'We're playing a Bowie cover and you're telling the kid from Britain how to play?' They didn't get it – the spirit of the music – to improvise and develop.

The Israeli elite, Smulian notes, were less than encouraging of immigration from Jewish cultures in the Middle East and North Africa, which had their own highly developed musical traditions. So, it was Northern European classical and Western popular music that ordinary Israelis appreciated. "Israeli Pop [in the 1970s] was sticking Hebrew lyrics onto over-faithful copies of American and British four-chord tunes." It was only twenty or thirty years later, around the Western millennium, that there was "this influx of 'Eastern' music into Israel, to create this new fusion with Americana, and this is the reason that now, Israeli musicians are some of the best on the 'world music' scene".

After studying in New York, and an interlude playing free jazz in a Tel Aviv transgender club, Smulian spent time cutting his Americana teeth in Austin, Texas in the late 1980s and early 1990s. A story from this experience is quoted in the chapter Outlaw Country. Raising a family in Israel curtailed his touring in the 1990s, but it allowed him to concentrate on recording and production work.

Smulian's production on Mosh Ben-Ari's 2004 second album, *Derekh* ('A Way'), helped win it an Israeli Gold certification, combining American structures and rhythms with Middle Eastern melodies and instrumentation. Ben-Ari's music developed further after he relocated to India to study. By 2016, Ben-Ari could even be heard incorporating tantalising elements of Irish Folk into his music.[283] *The Times of Israel* was more restrained, in deference perhaps to Ben-Ari's upcoming US tour, describing the single 'Flower' as "a sound that is rock 'n' roll at its core but with touches of Eastern elements.[284]

Smulian's later work has been influenced by two other American Roots forms, Jazz and Afro-American Hip Hop. His *WhiteFlag* project involves Palestinian musicians exploring Hop and Dub rhythms behind traditional local themes and vocal melodies.[285]

Tel Aviv trio Jane Bordeaux "is kicking up the local music scene with some incredibly original Hebrew-language Americana folk music."[286] The band surmounted the language barrier to achieve international attention via a brilliantly original video by Uri Lotan and Yoav Shtibelman for the band's 2016 single 'Ma'agalim' ('Cycles'): "In a forgotten old penny arcade, a wooden doll is stuck in place and time."[287] Tel Aviv is also the origin of punk-Americana collective On the Shoulders of Giants (OSOG). Their song 'Wanted' combines Tango, slide guitar, and Klezmer style *Rhaita* (Arabic oboe) work in an engaging story of long-anticipated revenge.[288]

A 2017 article in the *Jewish Telegraphic Agency,* a long-established organ of international Jewish culture, opined that "Americana could be having its biggest moment in the Jewish community right now. The trend follows a train of greater experimentation throughout the Jewish music world."[289] The corresponding rise in popularity of Jewish folk music in Europe and the US may also be contributing to this crossover trend. Groups such as the London Klezmer Quartet have regularly featured at international Folk/Roots festivals in recent years.[290]

Seattle singer-songwriter Ben Fisher, a self-described "liberal, left-wing Jewish-American"[291], uses the medium of Americana music to tell song-stories of Israel's chequered history. The opening song 'Shell Lottery', from his 2018 album *Does the Land Remember Me?* tells the story of the founding of Tel Aviv from the sand dunes. But the album includes a cover of Anaïs Mitchell's 21ˢᵗ century anti-war classic 'Why We Build the Wall', a song that was also covered in 2017 by popular UK punk-Folk/Americana artist Billy Bragg. Fisher says "It's like good journalism; You tell both sides of the story. If I make everybody mad, then I'm doing the right thing. But I want them to also find things they like about it."[292]

Kasey Chambers, Australian BBQ Showcase, Nashville 2017.
Photo Brumby Media

WOMEN CALL THE SHOTS

"If you're not pissed off with the world, you're just
not paying attention."
–Kasey Chambers

Back in 2018 we spoke with Michael Chugg, head of Chugg
Music and one of Australia's most successful music executives
about how he sees the issue of gender equality in the music
industry:

> Well 70% of my staff are women so I'm doing my bit. There
> are more and more female road crew than there have ever
> been, it's a growing area, the last two American tours and
> UK tours [brother/sisters-led indie band] Sheppard has had
> female tour managers. It's just a growing thing and I think …
> if a female wants to be anything in our industry they can in
> these days. I've always employed women and I think women
> are a really major part of our industry. To the point now where
> the head of our international label, Decca, is a woman. More
> and more, [the] people we're dealing with are women, there's
> a girl that looks after Chugg Music acts in South America ….
> Sheppard's American agent is a female, so there's more and
> more women in our industry.

Chugg was anxious to demonstrate that he was ahead of
the curve. The UK music rights management organisation PRS
recently revealed that: "the proportion of women working in
the music industry rose from 45.3% in 2016 to 49.1% in 2018,
while the percentage of young women (aged 16 to 24) in the
industry was up from 54.6% in 2016 to 65.3% in 2018."[293]

However, the figures showed a lower representation for women over 35. In senior and technical roles, the music business is still male-dominated, with *Rolling Stone* noting:

> There are 13 frontline major record label groups operating in the United States…. One [Sony's Epic Records] is run by a woman – Sylvia Rhone. One [Warner's Atlantic Records] is co-run by a woman – Julie Greenwald. All of the rest, *literally all of the rest*, are run by men.[294]

Reporting UK pay-gap data, *Rolling Stone* pointed out that, predictably, the biggest average pay differences came at the top levels of the business "Amongst the highest-paid quartile at Universal, 73% of employees were male; at Warner, 70% were male; at Sony, 60% were male." This is significantly above the average for all UK major businesses (58% male)[295]

In technical roles the gender imbalance remains stunning. Leading production software vendor ProTools quotes 5-7% women engineers and producers across the industry based on membership of professional bodies, a figure that has not changed significantly in the last decade[296].

*

The path to lucre in the popular music business was for most of the 20th century via record sales through a small number of major labels. Modern musicians, male and female, have a genuine but harsh choice in the way they market their products. Whilst streams are now the current sales currency, there is little return on investment for all but the most popular bands. When a band is signed to a major label, the company will typically recoup their large marketing investment from sales and licensing. Musicians achieving more niche positions in the market (and this covers a large proportion of current Americana acts) will frequently choose greater control and access to their revenues by using independent labels or doing their own marketing and distribution with the aid of many available online platforms such as Bandcamp and Distrokid (other platforms are available). Most up-and-coming acts earn more from performance and merchandise sales (including physical recordings) than from streaming, so more direct control of these revenues is a desirable objective. Right now, all the bets are off. The pandemic has pretty much frozen out live music altogether, and who knows whether the relatively small (in commercial terms) niche that is Americana will survive, but we have to assume in our crystal ball that the industry somehow eventually picks up where it left off in March 2020.

Where many artists now need to make the largest investment is in management and promotion. Image is the key here, and it is here that female artists have always had to make bigger choices than male artists. Sex appeal has been a key marketing tool since the advent of mass production,[297] and traditionally it was the female form that was most exploited in this manner. By the mid-20th century, popular music began to exploit masculine beauty (particularly the androgynous male image), and this use has accelerated into the 21st century and widened into the context of LGBTQ sexual imagery. But the major labels, who still control the marketing of the most popular musical product, are still largely focussing on the sexual aspect in marketing young female artists because this they find still shifts the most units in the popular market. Back in the mid-90s Australian star Kasey Chambers was persuaded to pose nude for a Country Music magazine.[298] More recently, under the big umbrella of Americana, many musicians are attempting to buck that trend. Alva Leigh, from Gulfport, Mississippi, who is half of duo Lewis & Leigh, has this to tell us about how female artists within Americana are marketed:

> I think for me it's one of the strange things about Americana, that in many ways has got all this traditionalism behind it, and yet it's one of the music genres where women can be more equal... I think that the female singers are not pressurised to appear in the same way. The rest of the music industry

expects you to think of somebody like Miley Cyrus… the lengths they go to get themselves on YouTube.

We asked Australian singer-songwriter Catherine Britt why it seems there is less pressure on female Americana artists to comply with the standard music industry demands to market their music than in some other genres, to which she responded:

> Maybe it's because of what the music is about and where it comes from originally; that it's not so much about sex and selling a person and a body as much as it is about selling a story, or a song, or a lyric. I think in Country music especially, we're very lucky, coming from, that early Appalachian [tradition]. It's really about family and singing songs about your history, and love, and all those things that are important to us as people. [In other genres] it is about how you look and you're selling an artist rather than the music that they're making. And all of a sudden, the artist becomes more famous than their music. And you never want to do that as an artist. You always want the music to be more famous than you.

Slim Dusty's daughter Anne Kirkpatrick has this to tell us about the positive presentation of women in Americana:

> The fact that there were two women in [the Carter Family] sets the scene… yet they were natural-looking women too… Women became very stylised in Country Music in the 60s and 70s in America. Still the case, slightly, but it's turned round with the Americana movement …it's come back for a more natural look. Maybelle and Sarah Carter are really important because [they've] enabled a sort of authenticity…Whereas in the rest of the music industry women are still dressing off: scantily clad and trying to look like sex symbols.

Watching the Highwomen perform at the 2019 Newport Festival was the grown-up Americana equivalent of watching the Spice Girls burst girl power onto the world on BBC's Top of the Pops in 1996. The raw oestrogen with which Brandi Carlile (refugee mother), then Amanda Shires (healer), then Yola (freedom rider), then Natalie Hemby (preacher), then Maren Morris and Sheryl Crow join their voices:

"Singing stories still untold / We carry the sons you can only hold".

They verily take that song to church; and it is a wonder to harken unto. Meanwhile, the boys in the band (including Shires' husband, Jason Isbell) wisely take a backseat. *Rolling Stone* magazine commented, "Yola became the single most sought-after voice at this year's festival."[299]

Americana is a more gender-neutral part of the popular music industry than most, as far as the musicians go. This is a legacy from Folk and early Country music. There is still a big gender gap in terms of promoters, producers, and technical crew. Interviewed at the Brit Awards in 2019, First Aid Kit commented on the role of women in their industry.

> There's a long way to go… It's a patriarchy; men decide who gets to play, and behind the stage it's almost all male, unless bands make a deliberate choice to employ women, as we do.[300]

Sara Silver is Head of European Operations for Nashville-based entertainment company Thirty Tigers. The company provides management, label, and promotion services for a diverse and high-quality roster of Americana artists including Emily Barker, Amanda Shires, Brent Cobb, Jason Isbell, and Lucinda Williams.[301] Silver has built a career in music promotion from early days in Pop promotion at Stiff Records and Polydor. When I spoke with journalist and presenter Paul Sexton recently, he singled out Silver as someone who has "grown into a role as spokeswoman-defender of a huge number of 'real artists'…There aren't many women [in the industry] with her wealth of experience based on enthusiasm for the music."

Helen Thomas was appointed Head of BBC Radio 2 in June 2020. She has recently been named in *Music Week*'s Women in Music Roll of Honour[302]. Thomas is justly proud of her radio station, which attracts an unprecedented 14 million weekly listeners: "I think it's the greatest radio station in the world, bar none. We have an incredible line-up of presenters who play the broadest mix of music you will hear anywhere across both our mainstream and specialist output."[303] To the relief of Roots music fans, Thomas has retained respected music presenters Bob Harris and Mark Radcliffe in that line-up.

Women like Silver and Thomas recognise, along with many of their male peers, that sustainability is a key factor in maintaining sales and audiences for music outside of the teen Pop market. Maintaining diverse rosters and playlists, constantly discovering and promoting new music, making decisions founded on an appreciation and enthusiasm for originality and quality, are strategies that are appreciated and rewarded by true lovers of music, who form a high proportion of the Americana audience.

WITHOUT LABELS

The dominance of IP streaming, and the poor revenues available to grassroots musicians therefrom, makes live music events a key source of revenue. Live music is also a deeply powerful social experience, something we all missed in the plague year of 2020. Whether live streaming events and virtual festivals will retain much popularity after the pandemic remains to be seen, but there have certainly been some significant Americana offerings this year[304]. Whatever happens post-pandemic, how to market their music in order to achieve fair return on investment for time and hard work spent developing their art remains the biggest dilemma for Americana musicians, particularly female ones.

Lula Wiles and Wildwood Kin are two all-female trios named from Carter Family classics ('Lula Walls' and 'Wildwood Flower'). But they have very different approaches to marketing their music. Lula Wiles are Northerners (Maine), who, like some of their illustrious predecessors (Neil Young to name one) display a somewhat cynical attitude to (white, Southern) American culture ('Good Old American Values'). The band market their records with Smithsonian Folkways, not a major player in the commercial music business.

Wildwood Kin, who hail from Exeter, UK, marry distinctly twangy vocal harmonies with contemporary British commercial arrangements. Lyrically, their songs are less confrontational and more commercial than Lula Wiles' (dealing more with the emotional interior than political issues); and, judging by their latest work, their label seems intent on morphing them into a sort of latter-day Fleetwood Mac. When we interviewed the band a year or two back, they were still fresh from their first major break, courtesy of their radio plugger:

> ...who is an amazing lady, one of the best. So, we got involved with BBC Radio two when our radio plugger took our tracks in. And it was quite a surprise for us. The first song that she took to radio, we weren't really known at that point, so yeah, we were all thinking, 'Oh, this isn't gonna make the playlist.' And then, I think it got pushed back a few weeks, but then it eventually got C list, which was such a surprise for us. We didn't think we would ever get that at that stage. But since then, we've had two singles from the album also on the playlist... massive support!

Wildwood Kin, Nashville, AmericanaFest. Photo Brumby Media

But these two bands co-exist comfortably under the great umbrella that is Americana. To support this statement, I offer today's almighty arbiter, the Spotify algorithm. Both bands exist in the same niche (but appreciable ballpark) of the order of 100,000 when it comes to monthly listeners, although Wildwood Kin have the edge because of their major label backing. But what of comparable musicians who dispense with labels altogether?

Rising Appalachia are two sisters, Chloe and Leah Smith, out of Atlanta, Georgia, who are popular (560,000+ monthly on Spotify) without the aid of a major record label. Founded in 2005 when they decided to make a record in a friend's basement, they make a kind of new-age Appalachian folksy sound using musicians from all over the world, notably Burkina-Fasso *griot* Arouna Diarra on *kora*. Their sisterly vocal harmonies have modern rock school cadences with ancient mountain genes.

From the start, the duo proved supremely adept at managing their online image and marketing to the extent of having one of the most comprehensive and well-maintained YouTube footprints I can testify to have witnessed. Says Chloe of the band's first outing:

> In celebration of the musical connections between Appalachia and Ireland, I remember specifically being both utterly nervous to sing… in front of 700 people. While simultaneously thinking, 'We should put out a mailing list on the table outside by our CDs.'[305]

In 2011, they raised over $11,000 to finance the making of their album, promoting the project as "FULL band. Crunk-folk style: sister harmonies, heavy rhythm, live drum, bass, banjo, and infectious groove."[306]

Their enthusiasm and sincerity are somewhat infectious, even through the filter of YouTube. Their protest anthem 'Resilient', from 2019's *Leylines*, concludes with yelping, howling vocal coyote music bringing to mind the songs of the Apache nations of the American Southwest. Now based in

New Orleans, the band employs a small management team and are stand-out representatives of a positive future manifestation of Americana.

Jenny and the Mexicats are fronted by Jenny Ball (UK, vocals, trumpet), with her band from Mexico, Spain, and occasionally Scotland and other nations. Their connection to American Roots comes mainly via the Mexicat brothers Ichio (bull fiddle) and Pantera (guitar), but Ball plays a mean mariachi trumpet, as well as singing in a style that swaps adeptly between Lily Allen and Carmen Miranda in a single number. She is equally compelling in English or Spanish. Keen to avoid omitting anything that might be of inspiration, the band themselves identify their output as "Roots music from Mexico, Cumbia, Rockabilly, Reggae, Flamenco, Jazz, and Country."[307]

The band were 'discovered' by NPR's Felix Contreras at SXSW a few years before their dazzling yet intimate performance on *Tiny Desk* in 2018. With 700,000+ monthly listeners on Spotify, the band have had considerable success in marketing their own musical product without benefit of a record label.

Irish singer Elly O'Keeffe is disillusioned with the way social media works as a marketing tool for emerging musicians: "People who actually have the talent are not using social media [effectively]. We live in a society that expects to be spoon-fed." Working musicians, she says, do not have the time or energy to maintain the kind of social feeds that major label artists backed by pluggers achieve.

> I was the grafter. I'd go out and do 250 gigs per year. But that doesn't work anymore because you are competing with such a mass of stuff online. If I'd been working that way 20–25 years ago I'd have had a lot more industry success.

O'Keeffe has recently enlisted US management to help her operate the media launch of her forthcoming EP *Gold*. She compares the situation around financial backing for emerging performers in Ireland and in the UK where she now lives.

I receive no support in the UK. Both here and in Ireland, the funding scene is really cliquey. The best thing about starting as a musician in Ireland was that it was easier to get the dole! I was better off in Ireland, I would be better off in America, but there's a great scene in Germany too.

Liv Austen is a singer-songwriter from Norway who came to the UK to study drama but stayed for the music, and now lives in Belgium.[308] Her debut album *A Moment of Your Time* (2018) has a poppy Country feel with catchy hooks. "I grew up listening to all sorts of Scandinavian Folk music and the melodies are just so beautiful. When I get ideas for hooks and stuff that's what comes in," she explains.[309] Austen co-produced with multi-instrumentalist partner Jon Wright and assistance from experimental Manchester-based producer Loft on some tracks.[310] Austen worked hard on launching and promoting the album without management or label backing. During lockdown, Austen and Wright have been live streaming to support the release of new material. Here's hoping all that hard work will pay off in 2021. Austen believes:

Whenever people manage to be themselves that's the most powerful thing that you can do... I've managed to do something that just sounds like me. It's all subjective, whether people like it or not. At least then I know I'm unique.[311]

Americana, with its focus on Roots and tradition, is not a musical genre that one expects to see presented with expensive sets and lighting. It lends itself especially to simple, intimate presentation, close to the audience, in small venues. An archetypal grass-roots Americana venue is Nashville's Bluebird Café, founded by Amy Kurland in 1982. Kurland ran the venue until 2008, when she donated the ownership and management to the Nashville Songwriters Association International. Kurland grew the venue from a restaurant with live music to an iconic performance space featured both in fictional drama (*Nashville*, 2012) and in real-life documentary (*Bluebird*, 2019). Kurland was an innovator of the oft-imitated 'writers' nights', where auditioned performers would entertain in the round, surrounded and supported by customers who appreciated the craft of songwriting. She sums up the role of the Bluebird: "[it] gives musicians a pathway, from open mic, to auditions, to writers' nights, to showcase performances. We can't guarantee you success, but we can show you what you need to do."[312]

In the UK, Camden's Green Note, owned and run by childhood friends Immy Doman and Risa Tabatznik, is an Americana venue of less fame than the Bluebird, but held in similar respect by musicians who have had the pleasure of playing there. Green Note opened in 2005. Doman and Tabatznik are proud to say "we have established a reputation as one of London's best spots for roots, world and acoustic music, and we're constantly astonished by the wealth of incredible musicians who grace our stage."[313] That wealth includes Emily Barker, Ed Sheeran, Amy Winehouse, Emmy the Great, Danni Nicholls, Pokey LaFarge, Will Kimbrough, and Lewis & Leigh. In normal times Doman and Tabatznik travel widely to see new artists, and run their club with unquenchable enthusiasm:

Green Note Club, Camden, London. Photo Risa Tabatznik

We both agree that the gigs we have most enjoyed have been ones at Green Note! There is nothing like seeing music in such a cosy, intimate environment. It really feels like being in someone's living room and sharing something very special.[314]

From grassroots to major labels, women have played a key role in the development of Americana music since Sara and Maybelle Carter first stepped up to the microphone in 1927. Women like the Carters, Dolly Parton, Emmylou Harris, Rosanne Cash, and Lucinda Williams continue to offer strong role models to today's female members of the industry, blazing a trail that sings of women's lives, loves, trials and tribulations, with love, but devoid of sugar coating. Jed Hilly was proud to announce that all of 2019's AMA Award nominees for Best Artist were female. [315]

Hannah Aldridge. Photo Al Stuart

WHERE TO NEXT?

Rolling Stone heads up their top Ten New Country and Americana Artists for Winter 2019 with Carsie Blanton out of New Orleans,[316] whose hilarious obscenely titled cover of Sheeran, Blanco, and Bieber's *Love Yourself* features the kazoo, an instrument hitherto vastly overlooked in the canon of the tools of Americana. The title track of her 2019 album *Buck Up* features a talking hound who delivers the immortal lines:

Buck up baby, come on sick 'em/

Make 'em laugh if you can't lick 'em.

Good advice for struggling musicians of every stripe. Musically, Blanton uses conventional Country rock settings featuring vintage electric piano, Gibson 320, and bull fiddle. Lyrically, she is anything but conventional: a juxtaposition that defines Americana. Blanton has not had major label marketing for her seven studio albums to date, using, like many modern artists, her own online store via the Bandcamp platform.[317]

Another Americana act with a distinct sense of humour is Pokey LaFarge, brainchild of Midwesterner Andrew Heissler. LaFarge plays and dresses in the style of 1940s swing jazz, with a hokey sound gathered from busking the West Coast and his love of Bill Monroe and Jimmie Rodgers.[318]

The retro revival direction followed by Blanton and LaFarge is mirrored (usually more reverentially) in the direction Americana seems to be following in parts of Europe, but in Australia and the US the trail is fanning out in other directions.

After Kasey Chambers released her *Campfire* album, we caught up with aboriginal musician Alan Pigram, who contributes music and words in his mother tongue to the album. Pigram is talking about giving Australian native peoples a voice in today's world:

> I've thought about it obviously with [Kasey], asking me to do the spoken word stuff. So, it's taken us to another level, not only just indigenous people seeing it within their [own] language. It's taken us to where it's going to get heard in a totally different space. And then [people] probably question exactly what you're saying, and can be taught … just those little things… I've taken out of Broome and from my circle of music.

Pigram's voice is certainly being heard in the home of Americana. One US reviewer wrote of *Campfire*:

> American listeners, if you're still sleeping on Kasey Chambers, wake up. She's as good or better than any of our best singer-songwriters stateside, and she's making the best music of her career lately.[319]

Lilly Hiatt's recent work with Lincoln Parish on *Walking Proof* is a perfect fusion of Americana songwriting themes in an Indie Rock setting. Parish's antecedents are as a founder member (at the tender age of 14) of Cage the Elephant, a band steeped in classic rock from Bowling Green KY, which relocated to London when Parish was 16. By 2013, the band had moved through Punk Blues to psychedelic Indie; Parish left to pursue solo projects as a writer, performer and producer. Reviewer Stephen Thomas Erlewine describes the band Hiatt and Parish assembled for the album as a "lean and lithe combo, as capable at delivering nuance as noise, they follow their leader whenever she raves, wails, or sighs".[320]

Walking Proof, features restrained and sophisticated Indie rocker 'Some Kind of Drug'. The song emerged after Hiatt accompanied her sister Rae on a mission to help Nashville's homeless.[321] Lyrically, the song is a lament to the gentrification of the city of Nashville, a process Hiatt observes with trepidation like many other Nashville natives.

Nashville's gentrification is not just about the regeneration of poorer areas. The city is growing as, apart from Music Production and Tourism, it is a good central location for industries such as Technology, Logistics, Insurance and Health Care which have expanded recently. Nevertheless, it continues to be a magnet for musicians of all stripes, not just Country music as in former days. There is a parallel between the gentrification of parts of the city such as East Nashville and the assimilation of every type of American music under the Americana umbrella. The city is a living, standing, embodiment of the process.

The international allure of Nashville is not confined to Australian artists. Ontario singer-songwriter Cat Clyde told us she thought it was "an awesome place to be". Like most musicians who visit, Clyde enjoys Nashville's small-town, community vibe, with big-city benefits. Clyde's brand of Americana is modern but gothic, her beautifully poised angular and insistent voice bringing life to dark pools of song such as 'All the Black' from 2019's *Hunters Trance.*

Indie/psychedelic influences in new Americana music are not confined to Nashville. LA musicians Conor Oberst and Phoebe Bridgers' project LP *Better Oblivion Community Centre* is a fine example. It is described as:

> [This] gorgeous and golden record... allows both artists to contribute and coordinate with a touching and engaging vulnerability. Offering an indie spin on Americana folk the pair come together in one triumphant sound.[322]

The project is currently generating a buzz on Spotify, nudging 400,000 monthly streams. It is definitely one to watch.

Early in 2018, Australian promoter Michael Chugg told us: "It's taken Keith Urban nearly twenty years to get on mainstream pop radio. But because 'Country' is becoming 'Country Pop/Country Rock', it's becoming more accessible to radio." Urban's 2020 album *The Speed of Now Part 1* is about as accessible as they come, because he is now working with artists including Nile Rodgers, Pink, and rapper BRELAND. So would Urban fit under the umbrella of Americana today? Rather than his commercial success, it's the lack of true grit in his lyrics which probably rules him out. Commonly referred to as a Country Music artist, some critics argue[323] that Urban has always been a Pop artist and his recent work certainly seems to defy genres. But it's too easy to equate high sales with low artistic value. Even if you find Urban's music is not to your taste, it is indisputably of very high quality. And audibly made with a sense of joy and sincerity, as well as benefiting from considerable commercial backing in its marketing. And when Urban explores elements of modern American forms such as rap and funk, he is drawing on other strands of American Roots music.

Keith Urban, Washington DC. Photo Shawn Miller/ Library of Congress

Rolling Stone put it this way: "With every album since 2013's *Fuse*, Keith Urban has had less and less creative fucks to give. Sticking to the confines of the country music genre hasn't interested him in years."[324] Like most musicians, Urban pays less regard to genre than to quality. As he says: "I just make music and find where it lives."[325]

Gangstagrass, out of New York City, are a Bluegrass trio mashed up with two urban Rap artists. Surprisingly, the musical surgery necessary has been somewhat successful, with their song 'Long Hard Times to Come' selected as the theme for popular TV series *Justified* and nominated for an Emmy Award for Outstanding Original Main Title Theme Music (2010).[326] The man behind this radical departure for Americana is Brooklyn producer and DJ Rench (aka Oscar Owens), who explains:

> I grew up in Southern California with my dad playing Willie Nelson, George Jones, and Gram Parsons records at home, but liked Run-DMC as a kid. I became a trip-hop producer, but I rediscovered a love for the old honky-tonk sounds.[327]

Rench references particularly the recordings of Ralph Stanley and the Clinch Mountain Boys from the 1970s when Keith Whitley and Ricky Skaggs were in the band.

UK's coolest Americana label Submarine Cat artists Alabama 3 are known chiefly for their song 'Woke Up This Morning', which made the sync deal from heaven when it was used for the opening credits of hit TV show *The Sopranos*. The band was formed in 1995 after the late Jake Black met Rob Spragg at a rave in Peckham and decided that a fusion of Country with acid house was a musical possibility.[328] The band's ludicrous stage names and comedic live delivery led them to be dismissed initially as a novelty act, but their continued success as sync artists has built up critical respect.[329] As Electropop sensation Halsey puts it, so succinctly, "We are the new Americana, high on legal marijuana."[330]

The 'back-to-basics' drive to a resurgence of interest in American Roots music in the 1990s, culminating in the enormous sales of the soundtrack album *O Brother Where Art Thou?* has been sustained, but the purist element has happily given way to respectful re-assimilation into 21st century musical forms by musicians and promoters who love and respect the traditions of their craft but continue to look forward in artistic and commercial development.

After long periods of confinement during the pandemic and the cancellation of music festivals across the world, musicians are longing to perform in front of live audiences once more. As John Hiatt commented in a recent interview for *Blues Matters* magazine[331]:

> People are hungry to go see some live music and it's looking like in some form it may need limited-size audiences but we're gonna start this tour in as safe a manner as we can. Hopefully, not too long after that, we can get back over to Europe. That would just be great.

Perhaps the term Gram Parsons gave to the genre he helped to create was prophetic: perhaps we can find a new way forward, through our enjoyment of music, to heal the grief and loss so many have experienced and begin to repair the social divisions that have plagued us too. Then Americana music truly will be "Cosmic American Music".

Alabama 3, Tramshed, Cardiff. Photo Nvg

ENDNOTES

1   Batts, Daniel "Review: The Nashville Sound by Jason Isbell and The 400 Unit", *Medium*.com, August 31, 2017 https://medium.com/@dbatts11/review-the-nashville-sound-by-jason-isbell-and-the-400-unit-c739bd78c506

2   "A Different Kind of Twang: Q&A With Jed Hilly", Relix Live Music Conference, May 28, 2019 https://www.youtube.com/watch?v=2oZBMEEXch0

3   Schlansky, Evan. "'Americana' Now In Webster's Dictionary", *American Songwriter*, August 25, 2011 https://americansongwriter.com/americana-now-in-websters-dictionary

4   Coroneos, Kyle. "Green River Ordinance Excluded from Billboard Country Charts While Other Acts Go Unquestioned", *Saving Country Music*, February 2, 2016 https://www.savingcountrymusic.com/green-river-ordinance-excluded-from-billboard-country-charts-while-other-acts-go-unquestioned

5   "Americana/Folk Albums", *Billboard*, February 13, 2016 https://www.billboard.com/charts/americana-folk-albums/2016-02-13

6   Rau, Nate. "Billboard adds Americana music to charts", *The Tennessean*, May 15, 2016 https://eu.usatoday.com/story/life/music/2016/05/15/billboard-adds-americana-music-charts/84419420/

7   Smith, Harry (compiled by). *Anthology of American Folk Music*, 1952, Folkways Records, catalogue FP 251, FP 252, FP 253

8   Fahey, John. *How Bluegrass Music Destroyed My Life: Stories* (Chicago: Drag City, 2000)

9   Cantwell, David. Merle Haggard: The Running Kind. (Austin: University of Texas Press, 2013), p 151

10   La Chapelle, Peter. *Proud to be an Okie: Cultural Politics, Country Music, and Migration to Southern California* (Oakland: University of California Press, 2007), 192

11   "The Conservative Evolution of Country Music", *All Things Considered* on *NPR*, February 18, 2007, radio transcript *https://www.npr.org/templates/story/story.php?storyId=7484160&t=1594298983728*

12   Feder, J Lester. "When Country went Right", *The American Prospect*, February 16, 2007 https://prospect.org/article/country-went-right/

13   Malone, Bill. "Country Music & Politics", *Talk of the Nation* on *NPR*, October 25, 2004 https://www.npr.org/templates/story/story.php?storyId=4125687

14   "The Conservative Evolution of Country Music", *All Things Considered* on *NPR*, February 18, 2007, radio transcript *https://www.npr.org/templates/story/story.php?storyId=7484160&t=1594298983728*

15   Malone, Bill C, and David Stricklin. *Southern Music/American Music* (Lexington: University Press of Kentucky, 2014), 130

16   Ibid.

17   *The Unfortunate Rake*, Album No. FA 3805 (New York: Folkways Records and Service Corp., 1960)

18   Pruett, Barbara J. *Marty Robbins: Fast Cars and Country Music* (The Scarecrow Press, 2007)

19   Smorodinskaya, Anastassia. 'Hipsters' in "Country, Honky Tonk and Americana: The New Sounds of the Indie Scene?", *Guff*, 2014 https://guff.com/country-honky-tonk-and-americana-the-new-sounds-of-the-indie-scene

20   Zhang, Joseph. "A Systematic Breakdown of The Atlantic Magazine", *Medium*.com, August 30, 2019 https://medium.com/@josephhhz/a-systematic-breakdown-of-the-atlantic-magazine-aed8ce0725b6

21   Russonello, Giovanni. "Why Is a Music Genre Called 'Americana' So Overwhelmingly White and Male?", *The Atlantic*, August 1, 2013 https://www.theatlantic.com/entertainment/archive/2013/08/why-is-a-music-genre-called-americana-so-overwhelmingly-white-and-male/278267/

22   Petrusich, Amanda. *It Still Moves: Lost Songs, Lost Highways, and the Search for the Next American Music* (London: Faber & Faber, 2008)

23   Neumann, Fredreich. "Hip Hop: Origins, Characteristics and Creative Processes", *The World of Music*, 42 (1): 51–63 (2000), JSTOR 41699313

24   Woolaver, Alex. "Top 10 Hip Hop Festivals in the USA 2021", *Festicket*, November 6, 2020 https://www.festicket.com/magazine/discover/top-10-Hip Hop-festivals-usa

25   Hughes, Charles L. *Country Soul: Making Music and Making Race in the American South* (Chapel Hill: University of North Carolina Press, 2015)

26   Drive by Truckers, *Decoration* Day, 2003 *https://www.youtube.com/watch?v=O3k7TLDR7O4&t=338s*

27   Wilco, Nick Lowe and Mavis Staples rehearse *The Weight* https://www.youtube.com/watch?v=2WmlUXsjSv8&feature=youtu.be&fbclid=IwAR01moe2Tt8Vh78aLCFOGffH-Hzbi0CqFrn68Lhaty3Ry3r03bhlITa6F5k

28   Gross, Terry. "Remembering Guitarist Link Wray", *Fresh Air* on *NPR*, November 23, 2005 https://www.npr.org/templates/story/story.php?storyId=5024749

29   Ibid.

30   Ibid

31   "Link Wray", *Mojo*, October 1995 http://colin-harper.com/journalism/link-wray/

32   Berry, Chuck. *Chuck Berry: The Autobiography* (London: Faber 1988)

33   Wegman, Jesse. "The Story Of Chuck Berry's 'Maybellene'", *NPR*, July 2, 2000 https://www.npr.org/2000/07/02/1076141/maybellene

34   Briggs, Kara. "Exploring Native American Influence on the Blues, American Indian News Service", *TankaBar*, 2009 http://www.tankabar.com/cgi-bin/nanf/public/viewStoryLeftRightImages.cvw?storyid=101330&sectionname=Blog:%20In%20Our%20View&commentbox=Y

35   "HOUSE of LUX Presents – John Murry plus guests at Tŷ Pawb, WXM", *Evensi*, September 15, 2018 https://www.evensi.uk/house-lux-presents-john-murry-guests-ty-pawb-wxm-market-street-ll13-8bb-wrexham/265367433

36   Roy, William. "'Race Records' and 'Hillbilly Music': Institutional Origins of Racial Categories in The American Commercial Recording Industry", *Poetics*, Volume 32, Issues 3–4, 265–279 (2004)

37   Porcaro, Lorenzo. "20 Years of Playlists: A Statistical Analysis on Popularity and Diversity", 20th Conference of the International Society for Music Information Retrieval, Delft, the Netherlands, July 2019 https://www.researchgate.net/publication/334230728_20_Years_of_Playlists_A_Statistical_Analysis_on_Popularity_and_Diversity

38   Cush, Andy. "How Musicians Are Fighting for Streaming Pay During the Pandemic", *Pitchfolk*, June 29, 2020 https://pitchfork.com/features/article/how-musicians-are-fighting-for-streaming-pay-during-the-pandemic/

39   "Deezer wants artists to be paid fairly: By adopting a User-Centric Payment System (UCPS)", *Deezer* https://www.deezer.com/ucps

40   Ingham, Tim. "Should Spotify Change the Way It Pays Artists?", *Rolling Stone*, December 7, 2018 https://www.rollingstone.com/music/music-features/should-spotify-change-the-way-it-pays-artists-763986/

41   Coldrick, Annabella. ""The Great Big Spotify Scam", *Medium.com*, February 22, 2018 https://medium.com/@AnnabellaCF/the-great-big-spotify-scam-exposed-in-music-business-worldwide-this-week-highlights-one-of-the-9eadd5fc4c42

42   https://committees.parliament.uk/work/646/economics-of-music-streaming/publications/

43   See below. Extended quotes by kind permission of Diana Stone

44   Ukmusiccity. "Barry Everett on House of Mercy Radio", *YouTube*, August 20, 2012 https://www.youtube.com/watch?v=JBYqavOrJek&t=1372s

45   "Ken Burns' Country Music episode 2: 'Hard Times'" (1933 –1945)", *PBS*, transcript, 2019 https://transcripts.fandom.com/wiki/Ken_Burns%27_Country_Music_episode_2:_%22Hard_Times%22_(1933_–1945)

46   Simmonds, Sylvie. "The Carter Family: Into the Valley", *TeachRock*, 2002 https://teachrock.org/article/the-carter-family-into-the-valley/

47   Sounes, Howard. *Down the Highway: The Life of Bob Dylan* (New York: Grove Press, 2001), 194

48   Nelson, Willie. *My Life: It's a Long Story* (London: Sphere, 2015)

49   Jennings, Waylon, with Kaye, Lenny. *Waylon: An Autobiography* (New York: Warner Books 1996) 221–226, quote as abridged in the audiobook version https://www.amazon.com/Waylon-Waylon-Jennings-Lenny-Kaye-audiobook/dp/B01CWHJN06

50   Christgau, Robert. "Consumer Guide Album: The Flying Burrito Brothers: Burrito Deluxe [A&M, 1970]", *Robert Christgau: Dean of American Rock Critics* https://www.robertchristgau.com/get_album.php?id=3617

51   Simmonds, Jeremy. *The Encyclopedia of Dead Rock Stars: Heroin, Handguns, and Ham Sandwiches*, second edition (Chicago: Chicago Review Press, 2012), 66

52   Cain, Michael Scott. *The Americana Revolution* (Lanham: Rowman & Littlefield, 2017)

53   Edgers, Geoff "It was The Byrds album everyone hated in 1968. Now, "Sweetheart of the Rodeo" is a classic", *The Washington Post*, August 17, 2018 https://www.washingtonpost.com/entertainment/music/it-was-the-byrds-album-everyone-hated-in-1968-now-sweetheart-of-the-rodeo-is-a-classic/2018/08/16/a2534a88-9a8f-11e8-b60b-1c897f17e185_story.html

54   https://www.rollingstone.com/interactive/lists-100-greatest-songwriters/#lucinda-williams

55   Ibid

56   Hudak, Joseph "Lucinda Williams Previews New Album With Scathing 'Man Without a Soul'" *Rolling Stone* February 4, 2020 *https://www.rollingstone.com/music/music-country/lucinda-williams-new-album-trump-song-947347/*

57   Petrusich, Amanda, Ibid., 127

58   Ibid., 133

59   Hodge, Will "O Brother, Where Aren't Thou?: The Two-Decade Cultural Impact of 'O Brother, Where Art Thou?'" *No Depression* December 14, 2020 https://www.nodepression.com/o-brother-where-arent-thou-the-two-decade-cultural-impact-of-o-brother-where-art-thou/

60   Ibid.

61   "The Duet Known as Gillian Welch" *Today* September 3rd, 2003 https://www.today.com/popculture/duet-known-gillian-welch-wb-na3075863

62   Wilkinson, Alec "The Ghostly Ones: How Gillian Welch and David Rawlings Rediscovered Country Music" *The New Yorker* September 20, 2004 https://www.newyorker.com/magazine/2004/09/20/the-ghostly-ones

63   Ibid.

64   Friskics-Warren, Bill "Gillian Welch: Orphan Girl of the Hollywood hills finds a high lonesome musical home in the heart of the Appalachians" *No Depression* Summer 1996 https://web.archive.org/web/20090719021207/http://archives.nodepression.com/1996/07/orphan-girl-of-the-hollywood-hills-finds-a-high-lonesome-musical-home-in-the-heart-of-the-appalachians/

65   Christgau, Robert *Consumer Guide* January 28, 1997 https://www.robertchristgau.com/xg/cg/cgv297-97.php

66   Bowers, William "Soul Journey: Gillian Welch" *Pitchfork* October 7, 2003 https://pitchfork.com/reviews/albums/8623-soul-journey/

67   https://en.wikipedia.org/wiki/The_Harrow_%26_The_Harvest

68   https://www.gillianwelchanddavidrawlings.com/GandD/music/33/covering-the-grateful-dead

69   Lesh, Phil *Searching for the Sound*. Little, Brown & Co., New York, NY., 2005. Chapter 11. ISBN 978-0-316-00998-0.

70   Bernstein, Jonathan. "Inside the Americana Genre's Identity Crisis", *Rolling Stone*, September 13, 2017 https://www.rollingstone.com/music/music-country/inside-the-americana-genres-identity-crisis-202818/

71   Ibid

72   Denton, Andrew. "Paul Kelly: Transcripts". Enough Rope with Andrew Denton. Australian Broadcasting Corporation(ABC), 5 July 2004

73   Ritz, David "The Fighting Side of Sturgill Simpson" *Rolling Stome* October 6, 2016 https://www.rollingstone.com/music/music-country/the-fighting-side-of-sturgill-simpson-123657/

74   "Sturgill Simpson" *The Charlie Rose Show* 13 October 2016 https://charlierose.com/videos/29307

75   Ibid.

76   Simmonds, Jeremy. *The Encyclopedia of Dead Rock Stars: Heroin, Handguns, and Ham Sandwiches*, second edition (Chicago: Chicago Review Press, 2012), 66

77   "Emmylou Harris – Album By Album", *Uncut*, January 25, 2013 https://www.uncut.co.uk/features/emmylou-harris-album-by-album-26653/

78   Abramovich, Alex. "'Satan Is Real,' the Story of the Louvin Brothers", *The New York Times*, February 17, 2012 https://www.nytimes.com/2012/02/19/books/review/satan-is-real-the-story-of-the-louvin-brothers.html

79   Pinnock, Tom. "This month in Uncut!", *Uncut*, January 3, 2013 https://www.uncut.co.uk/features/gram-parsons-torn-and-frayed-27459/

80   Christgau, Robert. "Consumer Guide Album: Gram Parsons: Grievous Angel [Reprise, 1974]", *Robert Christgau: Dean of American Rock Critics* https://www.robertchristgau.com/get_album.php?id=1431

81   Deming, Mark "John McEuan Biography" https://www.allmusic.com/artist/john-mceuen-mn0000222298/biography

82   Larkin, Colin (ed.) (1997). The Virgin Encyclopedia of Popular Music (Concise ed.). Virgin Books. pp. 905/6. ISBN 1-85227-745-9.

83   https://www.riaa.com/gold-platinum/?tab_active=default-award&ar=Nitty+Gritty+Band&ti=Will+the+Circle+Be+Unbroken#search_section

84   McEuan, John *The Life I've Picked: A Banjo Player's Nitty Gritty Journey* Chicago Review Press 2015 ISBN 9781613738955

85   Huffman, Eddie. *John Prine: In Spite of Himself* (Austin: University of Texas Press, 2015)

86   "John Prine Setlist at The Bitter End, New York, NY, USA, November 4, 1971", *Setlist.fm* https://www.setlist.fm/setlist/john-prine/1971/the-bitter-end-new-york-ny-43d7a783.html

87   https://web.archive.org/web/20110708082742/http://www.bonnieraitt.com/press_detail.php?id=37

88   Tunis, Walter. "Stephen Colbert to Roger Waters: Tributes to John Prine poured in after singer's death", *Lexington Herald Leader*, April 15, 2020 https://www.kentucky.com/entertainment/music-news-reviews/article241970636.html

89   "Bob Boilen: Host, *All Songs Considered*", *NPR*, last accessed December 10, 2020 https://www.npr.org/people/2100252/bob-boilen

90   Crockett, Zachary. "Tiny Desk: how NPR's intimate concert series earned a cult following", *Vox*, November 21, 2016 https://web.archive.org/web/20200307173554/https://www.vox.com/culture/2016/11/21/13550754/npr-tiny-desk-concert

91   Boilen, Bob, Stephen Thompson, and Robin Hilton. "2019 SXSW Wrap-Up: Our Favorite Discoveries And Memorable Moments", *All Things Considered* on *NPR*, March 19, 2019 https://www.npr.org/sections/allsongs/2019/03/19/704593812/2019-sxsw-wrap-up-our-favorite-discoveries-and-memorable-moments

92   Statt, Nick, and Jay Peters. "SXSW 2020 canceled due to coronavirus", *The Verge*, March 6, 2020 https://www.theverge.com/2020/3/6/21162247/sxsw-2020-cancelled-coronavirus-austin-texas-virus-fears-public-health-event

93   Boilen, Bob. "Hear From SXSW Artists Who Entered The 2020 Tiny Desk Contest", *All Things Considered* on *NPR*, March 19, 2020 https://www.npr.org/sections/allsongs/2020/03/19/817705793/hear-from-sxsw-artists-who-entered-the-2020-tiny-desk-contest

94   Shapiro, Ari, and Noah Caldwell. "Meet Linda Diaz, The Winner Of The 2020 Tiny Desk Contest", *All Things Considered* on *NPR*, August 4, 2020 https://www.npr.org/sections/allsongs/2020/08/04/898907981/meet-linda-diaz-the-winner-of-the-2020-tiny-desk-contest

95   NPR Music. "Isbell, Jason 2020 Tiny Desk (home) concert", *YouTube*, September 30, 2020 https://www.youtube.com/watch?v=dJm_RW8Rm10

96   Booth, Jared "Jason Isbell talks writing, war, and family life". *Charleston City Paper*. May 11, 2011 https://www.charlestoncitypaper.com/story/jason-isbell-rests-his-case?oid=3345499

97   Sculley, Alan "Jason Isbell: Estranged Trucker" *Shepherd Express* August. 13, 2009 https://shepherdexpress.com/music/music-feature/jason-isbell-estranged-trucker/

98   Garner, Dwight "Jason Isbell, Unloaded". *The New York Times*. May, 31 2013 https://www.nytimes.com/2013/06/02/magazine/jason-isbell-unloaded.html?pagewanted=all&_r=0

99   Moss, Marissa R. "15 Things You Learn Hanging Out With Brandi Carlile", *Rolling Stone*, March 9, 2019 https://www.rollingstone.com/music/music-country/brandi-carlile-things-you-learn-hanging-out-805570/

100   Kayce, Aaron. "Reviews: Brandi Carlile", *HARP* magazine, June 2007 https://web.archive.org/web/20081201195951/http://harpmagazine.com/reviews/cd_reviews/detail.cfm?article_id=5741

101   Leftridge, Steve. "Brandi Carlile: Give Up the Ghost", *popMatters*, October 14, 2009 https://www.popmatters.com/112366-brandi-carlile-give-up-the-ghost-2496091542.html

102   'Sweeney, Sabrina. "Brandi Carlile Finds Her Rock And Roll Voice", *BBC News*, February 10, 2015 https://www.bbc.co.uk/news/entertainment-arts-31310552

103   "Brandi Carlile discography", *Wikipedia*, last accessed December 10, 2020 https://en.wikipedia.org/wiki/Brandi_Carlile_discography

104   Basilan, Rebelander. "Brandi Carlile's Relationship with Her Wife of 8 Years Catherine Shepherd — Inside Their Love Story", *AmoMama*, June 22, 2020 https://news.amomama.com/214172-brandi-carliles-relation-ship-her-wife-8.html#:~:text=Brandi%20Carlile%20has%20enjoyed%20eight,reported%20by%20Wide%20Open%20Country.

105   The Late Show with Stephen Colbert. 'Brandi Carlile Pays Tribute To John Prine: "Hello In There"', *YouTube*, April 9, 2020 https://www.youtube.com/watch?v=CFLqYKjOVOk

106   Alex, Sam. "Travis Tritt on His Friendship With Marty Stuart and Loving Chris Stapleton", *Taste of Country*, November 28, 2016 https://tasteof-country.com/travis-tritt-loves-chris-stapleton/

107   Scissortwins. "Adele - If It Hadn't Been For Love lyrics", *YouTube*, September 14, 2011 https://www.youtube.com/watch?v=cpN11Df6fSg

108   "The Steeldrivers - Angel of the Night (Live)", Bluegrass Underground on *Youtube*, July 17, 2009 https://www.youtube.com/watch?v=kIGXlHOk23I

109   "Chris and Morgane Stapleton – Interview", *Paste Magazine*, August 1, 2015 https://www.pastemagazine.com/music/chris-and-morgane-staple-ton/chris-and-morgane-stapleton-interview

110   Justin Timberlake Brasil. "Tennessee Whiskey/Drink You Away - Justin Timberlake & Chris Stapleton (CMA 2015)", *YouTube*, April 22, 2020 https://www.youtube.com/watch?v=jZG82iqP06A

111   Coroneos, Kyle. "Chris Stapleton Announces New Album & Song 'Starting Over'", *Saving Country Music*, August 29, 2020 https://www.sav-ingcountrymusic.com/chris-stapleton-announces-new-album-song-starting-over/

112   Harrington, Richard "Robert Randolph, Man of Sacred Steel", *The Washington Post*, December 13, 2002 https://www.washingtonpost.com/ar-chive/lifestyle/2002/12/13/robert-randolph-man-of-sacred-steel/6221e370-ebb5-4490-8623-87de2f25c3e0/

113   Robert Randolph and The Family Band. "Robert Randolph And The Family Band - We Walk This Road", *YouTube*, June 20, 2011 https://www.youtube.com/watch?v=8J2rdht8LpE

114   "Hannah Aldridge", *Facebook*, last accessed December 10, 2020 https://www.facebook.com/HannahAldridgeOfficial

115   "Hannah Aldridge – Razor Wire", *American Roots UK*, 2014 https://www.americanrootsuk.com/hannah-aldridge---razor-wire.html

116   "Bio", *Hannah Aldridge*, last accessed December 10, 2020 https://hannah-aldridge.myshopify.com/pages/bio-1

117   Stormymonday56. "Brigitte DeMeyer & Will Kimbrough @ Gibson Studios 2017", *flickr*, March 30, 2017 https://www.flickr.com/photos/beaconrun/33777068745/in/photolist-TsLiLe-SdUFnV-bt1B2V/

118   Hill, Corbie. "Former Brooklyn Rocker Kamara Thomas Pursues a Singer-Songwriter Future in Durham" Indy Week Jun. 19, 2013 https://indyweek.com/music/features/former-brooklyn-rocker-kamara-thomas-pursues-singer-songwriter-future-durham/

119   Country Soul Songbook "Amplifying Indigenous Voices in Country & Americana: a special re-broadcast from CSSB's 2020 Summit", Nov 28, 2020 https://www.youtube.com/watch?v=QqmzkQDue88

120   https://www.billboard.com/charts/americana-folk-albums

121   Roth, Arlen. *Arlen Roth's Complete Acoustic Guitar* (New York: Schirmer Books, 1985), 47

122   Traverse Area Community Media. "Family Strings: Billy Strings and His Dad Terry Barber - 2/28/2020", *YouTube*, March 10, 2020 https://www.youtube.com/watch?v=_6U6NCvOfl8

123   Teton Film Works HSMF- 2017. "Billy Strings Shady Grove: The Music of Doc Watson", *YouTube*, November 13, 2018 https://www.youtube.com/watch?v=Nk4SWmDbMNI

124   Stormymonday56. "Billy Stings", *flickr*, February 16, 2020 https://www.flickr.com/photos/beaconrun/49564601397/in/photolist-2ivRyo7-2ivRxc4/

125   Billy Strings. "Voodoo Chile - Billy Strings with Umphrey's McGee", *YouTube*, June 11, 2020 https://www.youtube.com/watch?v=y9JUjxUcJv4

126   "Official Launch Of The Americana Music Association Of Australia", *Dirty TV*, last accessed December 10, 2020 https://dittytv.com/official-launch-americana-music-association-australia/

127   "How Tamworth became Country Music Capital", *History of Country Music in Australia*, last accessed December 10, 2020 https://www.historyofcountrymusic.com.au/htbcmc.html

128   "History", *Country Music Association of Australia*, last accessed December 10, 2020 https://www.country.com.au/about/history

129   O'Neill, Peggy. "The Arts Factory: where did it all begin?", *Nomads*, last accessed December 10, 2020 https://nomadsworld.com/arts-factory-lodge-history/

130   "Out On The Weekend", *Facebook*, last accessed December 10, 2020 https://www.facebook.com/outontheweekend/

131   LeFevre, Jules. Ed Droste quoted in "'Literally Losing Money': Why It's So Hard For Bands To Tour Australia", *Junkee*, March 20, 2018 https://junkee.com/tour-australia-difficulties/134768

132   "True Blue bust up: Williamson walks: Golden Guitars 'too American'", *The North Daily Leader*, December 10, 2013 https://www.northerndailyleader.com.au/story/1961962/true-blue-bust-up-williamson-walks-golden-guitars-too-american/

133   Galvin, Nick. "Troy Cassar-Daley, Adam Harvey out of Golden Guitar Awards over John Williamson row", *The Sydney Morning Herald*, December 13, 2013 https://www.smh.com.au/entertainment/music/troy-cassardaley-adam-harvey-out-of-golden-guitar-awards-over-john-williamson-row-20131213-2zba7.html

134   Cashmere, Paul. "CMAA President Dobe Newton Addresses Cassar-Daley, Harvey CMAA Withdrawal", Noise111, December 13, 2013 http://www.noise11.com/news/cmaa-president-dobe-newton-addresses-cassar-daley-harvey-cmaa-withdrawal-20131213

135   Cashmere, Paul. "ARIA Recount Places Kanye West At Number One", *Noise111*, June 24, 2013 http://www.noise11.com/news/aria-recount-places-kanye-west-at-number-one-20130624

136   "Awards Information" *CMAA* https://www.country.com.au/awards/awards-info

137   "Past Golden Guitar Award Winners", *CMAA*, last accessed December 10, 2020 https://www.country.com.au/awards/past-award-winners

138   http://www.markmoffatt.com/landmarks/

139   "Nashville Songwriters' Residency", Australia Council for the Arts, last accessed December 10, 2020 https://www.australiacouncil.gov.au/international/nashville-songwriters-residency/

140   Lucid Hats feat Larissa Tandy. "Don't Steal My Bounce", *Larissa Tandy*, May 25, 2020 https://larissatandy.bandcamp.com/track/dont-steal-my-bounce

141   Jones, Helen. "Josh Rennie-Hynes "Patterns" (Soundly Music, 2019)", *American UK*, August 21, 2019 https://americana-uk.com/josh-rennie-hynes-patterns-soundly-music-2019

142   Gibson TV. "Sinead Burgess at Summer NAMM 2019", *YouTube*, July 20, 2019 https://www.youtube.com/watch?v=pPrH-_52zbA

143   Kasten, Roy. "SXSW 2017 Highlights From the First Three Days: Lemon Twigs, Spoon, New Pornographers, Kasey Chambers, Valerie June, She Drew the Gun and More", *Riverfront Times*, May 17, 2017 https://www.

riverfronttimes.com/musicblog/2017/03/17/sxsw-2017-highlights-from-the-first-three-days-lemon-twigs-spoon-new-pornographers-kasey-chambers-valerie-june-she-drew-the-gun-and-more

144   Kaseychamberstv. "Sinead Burgess Live at Summer NAMM 2019", *YouTube*, July 20, 2019   https://www.youtube.com/watch?v=tua2SBHsrsU

145   Gordon, Bob "Ruby Boots Wasn't Ready To Sink When She Moved To Nashville" *SceneStr* July 31, 20§7https://scenestr.com.au/music/ruby-boots-wasn-t-ready-to-sink-when-she-moved-to-nashville

146   https://www.dailymail.co.uk/news/article-3917906/Keith-Urban-Nicole-Kidman-lead-Australian-celebrities-voting-election-Naomi-Watts-Caitlin-Stasey-Pia-Miller-reveal-backing-Clinton-Trump.html

147   https://www.usa.gov/who-can-vote

148   https://www.nzherald.co.nz/entertainment/lifes-a-sweet-thing/Q6JFJXY543L7RXTFEOR5336KLE/

149   https://www.nfsa.gov.au/collection/curated/took-children-away-archie-roach

150   https://eu.usatoday.com/story/life/nation-now/2017/04/26/keith-urban-just-call-him-mr-platinum/100959150/

151   Alden, Grant, and Peter Blackstock. *The Best of No Depression: Writing about American Music* (Austin: University of Texas Press, 2005), 151

152   Ibid., 157

153   "Weddings Parties Anything", *Howlspace*, last accessed December 10, 2020 https://web.archive.org/web/20120206165942/http://www.whiteroom.com.au/howlspace/en2/weddingspartiesanything/weddingspartiesanything.htm

154   Mushroomvideos. "Mick Thomas - *Most of the Time* feat. Ruby Boots (Official Video)", *YouTube*, February 19, 2017 https://www.youtube.com/watch?v=uhdZphLr7rA

155   "Mick's Story", *Mick Thomas*, last accessed December 10, 2020 https://www.mickthomas.com/category/micks-story

156   Bloodlines. "Mick Thomas - *Anything You Recognise* (Mick Thomas' Roving Commission)", *YouTube*, October 10, 2019 https://www.youtube.com/watch?v=8Jf4fQ6kWLM

157   Bracknell, Clint. *Identity, language and collaboration in Indigenous music* (Edith Cowan University Research Online, 2019) https://ro.ecu.edu.au/cgi/viewcontent.cgi?article=7648&context=ecuworkspost2013

158   "Next Big Thing – Presented by Aim: Julia Jacklin" in "Here are All the Winners in the 2016 FBi SMAC Awards", *FBi Radio*, January 17, 2017 https://fbiradio.com/here-are-all-the-winners-in-the-2016-fbi-smac-awards

159   Martoccio, Angie. "Julia Jacklin Is Living in the Moment", *Rolling Stones*, May 14, 2019 https://www.rollingstone.com/music/music-features/julia-jacklin-crushing-interview-831512

160   Mackay, Emily. "Julia Jacklin: Crushing review – ghostly, rollicking second album", *The Guardian*, February 24, 2019 https://www.theguardian.com/music/2019/feb/24/julia-jacklin-crushing-review

161   Horn, Olivia. "Julia Jacklin: Crushing", *Pitchfolk*, February 27, 2019 https://pitchfork.com/reviews/albums/julia-jacklin-crushing/

162   "Little Georgia", *Music Collective*, last accessed December 10, 2020 https://musiccollective.com.au/listing/little-georgia/

163   Little Georgia. "Little Georgia (Full Show) Live at Hay Mate 2019", *YouTube*, April 2, 2020 https://www.youtube.com/watch?v=acv3SUDc5wI

164   Ross, Ricky. "Another Country with Ricky Ross: Yola Interview" *Another Country* on *BBC Sounds*, 2019 https://www.bbc.co.uk/sounds/play/p07c8pck

165   Ibid.

166   Kroll, Justin. "Yola to Play Sister Rosetta Tharpe in Baz Luhrmann's 'Elvis' (Exclusive)", Variety, February 21, 2000 https://variety.com/2020/film/news/yola-elvis-presley-movie-sister-rosetta-tharpe-1203510668/

167   "Yola", *Facebook*, last accessed December 10, 2020 https://www.facebook.com/iamyolaofficial/videos/444861939827290

168   Szwed, John. *Alan Lomax: The Man Who Recorded the World* (New York: Viking, 2010)

169   Collins, Shirley. *America Over the Water* (London: SAF Publishing, 2004)

170   GriefTourist. "Bob Harris talks about being attacked by Sid Vicious", *YouTube*, October 15, 2008 https://www.youtube.com/watch?v=5mUO8LmzdeI

171   Bragg, Billy "whisper it … but the British invented Americana" *The Guardian* September 20th, 2013 https://www.theguardian.com/music/musicblog/2013/sep/20/billy-bragg-americana-british-teenagers

172   Jobson, Johnny "130,000 in Attendance at Celtic Connections 2020 Events" *The National* February 6, 2020 https://www.thenational.scot/news/18213698.130-000-attendance-celtic-connections-2020-events/

173   "Welcome to the Americana Music Association UK", *The Americana Music Association UK*, last accessed December 10, 2020 https://theamauk.org/

174   Haskell, Duncan. "Interview: Lewis & Leigh", *Songwriting*, August 19, 2016 https://www.songwritingmagazine.co.uk/interviews/interview-lewis-leigh

175   Americana Music Association UK. "UK Americana Awards 2020 Full Show", *YouTube*, April 29, 2020 https://www.youtube.com/watch?v=i6nSoYEyDOA

176   Digital Music News (updated for 2020) https://www.digitalmusic-news.com/2017/10/17/riaa-best-selling-artists-of-all-time/

177	Hernu, Piers. "'Robert Plant asked me if there was anything wrong with him. His kids tell him he's not a normal dad': The world according to Alison Krauss", *Daily Mail*, April 23, 2011 https://www.dailymail.co.uk/home/moslive/article-1378857/Alison-Krauss-Robert-Plant-asked-wrong-him.html

178	Sullivan, Caroline. "Emmy the Great: First Love", *The Guardian*, February 6, 2009 https://www.theguardian.com/culture/2009/feb/05/emmy-the-great

179	Walker, Tim. "Folk music in the city", *The Independent*, February 6, 2009 https://web.archive.org/web/20100115083502/http://www.independent.co.uk/arts-entertainment/music/features/folk-music-in-the-city-1547431.html

180	Simon Vine. "Mumford & Sons, Glastonbury 2008, Little Lion Man in Tango Cafe tepee, Greenpeace field", YouTube, July 1, 2013 https://www.youtube.com/watch?v=6GjmbRJ-0fc

181	Walker, Tim. "Folk music in the city", *The Independent*, February 6, 2009 https://web.archive.org/web/20100115083502/http://www.independent.co.uk/arts-entertainment/music/features/folk-music-in-the-city-1547431.html

182	Watters, Gemma. "Laura Marling On Maya Angelou And Arming A Younger Generation Of Women", *All Things Considered* on *NPR*, April 11, 2020 https://www.npr.org/2020/04/11/832052963/laura-marling-on-maya-angelou-and-arming-a-younger-generation-of-women

183	"Lion Kings" *Melborne Herald-Sun* March 25, 2010 https://www.pressreader.com/australia/herald-sun/20100325/285890204008436

184	Ibid._

185	Collins, Simon. "Dew recognition", *The West Australian*, December 21, 2012 https://thewest.com.au/entertainment/music/dew-recognition-ng-ya-341897

186	uDiscover Music. "Danny Wilson Interview Long Road Festival 2018", *YouTube*, September 14, 2018 https://www.youtube.com/watch?v=1TBKMiPsUYM&list=PL2VivD1Kh51tWPZFEoQLjDHfiwll7LYKJ

187	Ibid.

188	Ibid.

189	"Jade Brid", *SXSW* Schedule, 2017 https://schedule.sxsw.com/2017/artists/10225

190	Vain, Madison. "See U.K. country music breakout Jade Bird cover 'Grinnin' In Your Face'", *Entertainment Weekly*, October 4, 2017 https://ew.com/music/2017/10/04/jade-bird-grinnin-your-face-cover/

191	"#NewMusicEveryday: Brent Cobb and Jade Bird", *The Boots*, last accessed December 10, 2020 https://theboot.com/brent-cobb-jade-bird-feet-off-the-ground/

192	Swift, Jacqui "AMERICANA DREAM Welsh singer Jade Bird tells how she's already surpassed her wildest dreams by touring and releasing her debut album". *The Sun* April 18, 2019 https://www.thesun.co.uk/tvand-showbiz/8895339/jade-bird-americana-debut-album/

193   Vain, Madison. "See U.K. country music breakout Jade Bird cover 'Grinnin' In Your Face'", *Entertainment Weekly*, October 4, 2017 https://ew.com/music/2017/10/04/jade-bird-grinnin-your-face-cover/

194   Swift, Jacqui. "Americana Dream: Welsh singer Jade Bird tells how she's already surpassed her wildest dreams by touring and releasing her debut album", *The Sun*, April 18, 2019 https://www.thesun.co.uk/tvand-showbiz/8895339/jade-bird-americana-debut-album/

195   Newton, Allen. "Bridgetown-born musician Barker returns home for double celebration", *WAtoday*, January 18, 2020 https://www.watoday.com.au/national/western-australia/bridgetown-born-musician-barker-returns-home-for-double-celebration-20200112-p53qu5.html

196   Bourke, Kevin. "Sweet Kind of Blue: acclaimed musician Emily Barker talks to Northern Soul", *Northern Soul*, December 9, 2017 https://www.northernsoul.me.uk/emily-barker-sweet-kind-of-blue

197   David Barrs. "Nostalgia Performed by Emily Barker and Lukas Drinkwater", *YouTube*, November 27, 2016 https://www.youtube.com/watch?v=GTmeRiGPIxE quoted by permission (TBC)

198   *Clive Davis*, last accessed December 10, 2020 https://clivedavis.net/tag/folk

199   Barker, Emily. "Sweet Kind of Blue", *Linn*, last accessed December 10, 2020 https://www.linnrecords.com/recording-sweet-kind-blue

200   Barker, Emily. "Shadow Box", *Emily Barker*, last accessed December 10, 2020 https://www.emilybarker.com/shadow-box/

201   "Album Review: Emily Barker – A Dark Murmuration Of Words", *High Fives & Stage Dives*, September 3, 2020 https://highfivesnstagedives.com/2020/09/03/album-review-emily-barker-a-dark-murmuration-of-words

202   "Curse of Lono, *As I Fell*, Official Americana Albums Chart Top 40 24 August 2018 – 30 August 2018", *Official Charts*, last accessed December 10, 2020 https://www.officialcharts.com/charts/americana-albums-chart/20180824/americana

203   Curse of Lono. "Curse of Lono *Somewhere Inside Their Heads* (Documentary)", *YouTube*, May 10, 2018 https://www.youtube.com/watch?v=LyJWwl1qmk4

204   "Submarine Cat Music", *Facebook*, last accessed December 10, 2020 https://www.facebook.com/subcatmusic

205   Tom Jones - Talking Reality Television Blues (Official Video) https://www.youtube.com/watch?v=khgdwZmWkXc

206   Tom Jones in the studio with Ethan Johns https://www.youtube.com/watch?v=KWoqnuRBzgA

207   "Ethan Johns: Credits" *AllMusic* https://www.allmusic.com/artist/ethan-johns-mn0000171535/credits

208   https://musiciansunion.org.uk/campaigns/musicians-working-in-the-eu

209   Allen, Greg. "The Banjo's Roots, Reconsidered", *All Things Considered* on *NPR*, August 23, 2011 https://www.npr.org/2011/08/23/139880625/the-banjos-roots-reconsidered

210   "Joel Sweeney & The Musical Sweeneys of Appomattox", *The Official Sweeney Clan*, last accessed December 10, 2020 http://www.cgim.org/sweeneyclan/misc/musical.html

211   "Flanagan Brothers", *Wikipedia*, last accessed December 10, 2020 https://en.wikipedia.org/wiki/Flanagan_Brothers

212   Ward Irish Music Archives. "Interview with Maureen O'Looney", *YouTube*, June 28, 2016 https://www.youtube.com/watch?v=cXj8VAXTXug

213   Reilly, Gavan. "Top 20: The best-selling singles in Irish history", *The Daily Edge*, May 20, 2012 https://www.dailyedge.ie/top-20-the-best-selling-singles-in-irish-history-455737-May2012/

214   "Sharon Shannon", *The Will Leahy Show* on RTÉ Ireland, 2008 http://www.rte.ie/podcasts/2008/pc/pod-v-070408-6m45s-willleahy.mp3

215   Stockbridge, Katie "Interview: An In Depth Conversation With We Banjo 3 About Their New Album 'Roots To Rise'" *NYS Music* July 23, 2019 https://nysmusic.com/2019/07/23/interview-an-in-depth-conversation-with-we-banjo-3-about-their-new-album-roots-to-rise/

216   Ibid.

217   Ibid.

218   "Cork man wins top songwriting prize in Nashville", *RTÉ*, April 30, 2016 https://www.rte.ie/entertainment/2016/0429/785211-irish-man-wins-top-prize-in-nashville/

219   "John Murry Official", *Facebook*, last accessed December 2020 https://www.facebook.com/johnmurryofficial/photos/a.375633621909/10151409742886910

220   Kilkenny Roots Festival https://kilkennyroots.com

221   "Daily Visual 31.08.15: Van Morrison Down On Cyprus Avenue", *culturedarm*, August 31, 2015 https://culturedarm.com/daily-visual-31-08-15-van-morrison-down-on-cyprus-avenue/

222   Shteamer, Hank. "In Full: Lewis Merenstein, producer of Astral Weeks", *Punches*, March 1, 2009, updated September 9, 2016 http://darkforcesswing.blogspot.com/2009/03/in-full-lewis-merenstein-producer-of.html

223   Gilbert, Calvin. "Van Morrison, Norah Jones Visit the Country Top 10", *CMT*, March 18, 2006 https://web.archive.org/web/20081015062750/http://www.cmt.com/artists/news/1526478/20060317/lost_trailers.jhtml

224   Nelson, Willie, and David Ritz. *It's A Long Story: My Life*. (Boston: Little, Brown and Company, 2015)

225   "Van Morrison: 'Fight the Covid-19 pseudoscience and speak up'", *The Irish Times*, August 25, 2020 https://www.irishtimes.com/culture/music/van-morrison-fight-the-covid-19-pseudoscience-and-speak-up-1.4338343

226   Little, Ivan. "US country star Jason Isbell rails at Van Morrison's Covid songs", *Belfast Telegraph*, September 26, 2020 https://www.belfast-telegraph.co.uk/news/world-news/us-country-star-jason-isbell-rails-at-van-morrisons-covid-songs-39563019.html

227   Martoccio, Angie "Jason Isbell Blasts Van Morrison, Covers 'Into the Mystic'" *Rolling* Stone September 21, 2020 https://www.rollingstone.com/music/music-country/van-morrison-jason-ibell-amanda-shires-1064133/

228   Thomson, Graeme. *Complicated Shadows: the life and music of Elvis Costello* (Edinburgh: Canongate, 2004)

229   Ibid., 40

230   Anthony John. "Flip City", *YouTube*, March 6, 2015 https://www.youtube.com/watch?v=NotOtWbwwaE

231   Thomson, Graeme. *Complicated Shadows: the life and music of Elvis Costello* (Edinburgh: Canongate, 2004), 29

232   Kent, Nick. "D. P. Costello of Whitton, Middlesex, it is your turn to be The Future of Rock & Roll" *New Musical Express*, 1977 http://www.elvis-costello.info/wiki/index.php/New_Musical_Express,_August_27,_1977

233   Thomson, Graeme. *Complicated Shadows: the life and music of Elvis Costello* (Edinburgh: Canongate, 2004), 209–211

234   Thomson, Graeme. *Complicated Shadows: the life and music of Elvis Costello* (Edinburgh: Canongate, 2004), 218

235   Kater, Kaia. "Inside the Americana Genre's Identity Crisis", *Rolling Stone*, September 13, 2017 https://www.rollingstone.com/music/music-country/inside-the-americana-genres-identity-crisis-202818/

236   Deutsch, Joni. "Kaia Kater: A Portrait of a Young Quebecalachian", *WV Public Broadcasting*, June 3, 2016 https://www.wvpublic.org/post/kaia-kater-portrait-young-quebecalachian#stream/0

237   Smithsonian Folkways. "Kaia Kater Discusses Inspiration Behind 'Grenades' [Interview Video]", YouTube, October 23, 2018 https://www.youtube.com/watch?v=0_7lA6bvXnE

238   Thorne, Tara. "Kaia Kater's folk bomb", *The Coast*, November 22, 2018 https://www.thecoast.ca/halifax/kaia-katers-folk-bomb/Content?oid=19376116

239   Ibid.

240   Reynolds, Daniel. "How Rufus Wainwright Finally Became a Joni Mitchell Fan", *Joni Mitchell*, August 21, 2017 https://jonimitchell.com/library/view.cfm?id=3661

241   Xavier Héraud. "Kate & Anna McGarrigle - *Hard times come again no* more", YouTube, November 19, 2006 https://www.youtube.com/watch?v=4YrfLnlrquo&list=RDEMtHk_9vIxErwJuXxwxTxwMQ&start_radio=1

242   Simon, Scott, and Ian Stewart. "Buffy Sainte-Marie's Authorized Biography Serves As A 'Map Of Hope'", *Weekend Edition* Saturday on *NPR*, September 29, 2018 https://www.npr.org/2018/09/29/652791230/buffy-sainte-maries-authorized-biography-serves-as-a-map-of-hope

243   "An Officer and a Gentleman", Oscars, last accessed December 10, 2020 https://www.oscars.org/events/officer-and-gentleman-ny

244   "Plaine Belle", *Facebook*, November 30, 2018 https://www.face-book.com/belleplainemusic/posts/its-not-often-that-i-get-to-be-at-the-show-with-these-folks-but-i-had-the-chance/10155668305126603

245   Pynn, Morgan. "Album Review: Belle Plaine – Malice, Mercy, Grief & Wrath", *Lula*, November 29, 2018 http://lula1892.com/album-review-belle-plaine-malice-mercy-grief-wrath

246   "The Dead South", *Sputnick Music*, last accessed December 10, 2020 https://www.sputnikmusic.com/bands/The-Dead-South/81194

247   Dwilson, Stephanie Dube. "'Umbrella Academy' Season 2 Soundtrack: See Videos of the Best Songs", *Heavy.*, July 31, 2020 https://heavy.com/entertainment/2020/07/umbrella-academy-season-2-soundtrack-songs

248   "Code of Conduct", *The Dead South*, last accessed December 10, 2020 https://www.thedeadsouth.com/code-of-conduct

249   Soloducha, Alex. "Women detail sexual misconduct allegations against former The Dead South band member", *CBC News*, August 30, 2020 https://www.cbc.ca/news/canada/saskatchewan/women-detail-sexual-misconduct-allegations-against-former-the-dead-south-band-member-1.5699608

250   Simpson, Dave. "Country musician Lindi Ortega: 'I'm a kickass thing'", *The Guardian*, January 27, 2014 https://www.theguardian.com/music/2014/jan/27/country-musician-lindi-ortega

251   "Chart History: Lindi Ortega – Heatseekers Albums", *Billboard*, last accessed December 10, 2020

252   Schultz, Chuck. "Lindi Ortega Leaves Nashville Behind, But Not Country Ahead of New EP", Saving Country Music, March 1, 2017 https://www.savingcountrymusic.com/lindi-ortega-leaves-nashville-behind-but-not-country-ahead-of-new-ep

253   Ibid.

254   "Lindi Ortega", *Facebook*, last accessed December 10, 2020 https://www.facebook.com/lindiortegamusic

255   Lucas, John "Calgary musician Matthew Swann goes it alone as Astral Swans" *The Straight* March 19, 2014 https://www.straight.com/music/609411/calgary-musician-matthew-swann-goes-it-alone-astral-swans

256   Aird, Jonathan "Astral Swans 'Bird Songs' – Listen" August 20, 2020 https://americana-uk.com/astral-swans-bird-songs-listen

257   McPhee, Joyce "A History of the Ottawa Folk Festival" http://wordpress-mea.s3.amazonaws.com/wp-content/uploads/sites/8/2011/05/Folk-Festival-History-1994-2012-August-28-2014.pdf

258   MacDonald, Michael B "Back to the Garden: Territory and Exchange in Western Canadian Folk Music Festivals" PhD Thesis, Uni. of Alberta 2010

259   "Thriving Roots 2020" https://cimamusic.ca/events/canadian-blast-events/display,details/14990/thriving-roots-2020

260   Tinkham, Chris. "First Aid Kit: Healing From Sweden", Under the Radar, October 18, 2010 http://www.undertheradarmag.com/interviews/first_aid_kit

261   Bandstand Busking. "First Aid Kit – In the Morning", YouTube, October 20, 2009 https://www.youtube.com/watch?v=39jJyB6FLPY

262   Kot, Greg. "First Aid Kit 'divorce' leads to renewed music", Chicago Tribune, January 25, 2018 https://www.chicagotribune.com/entertainment/music/ct-ott-first-aid-kit-interview-0126-story.html

263   Baltin, Steve. "First Aid Kit: A Coachella Can't-Miss Act", Forbes, April 3, 2018 https://www.forbes.com/sites/stevebaltin/2018/04/03/first-aid-kit-are-a-coachella-cant-miss-act

264   NME. "First Aid Kit at the Brits 2019: 'We live in a patriarchy, we need more women in the music industry'", YouTube, February 21, 2019 https://www.youtube.com/watch?v=beq3izedcdg

265   Coroneos, Kyle. "How Sweden Became A Surprising Enclave for Country and Roots Music", Saving Country Music, May 3, 2018 https://www.savingcountrymusic.com/how-sweden-became-a-surprising-enclave-for-country-and-roots-music

266   "Press", Spinning Jennies, last accessed December 10, 2020 http://spinningjennies.com/press.html

267   Basko Believes. "Idiot's Hill", April 2, 2014 https://baskobelieves.bandcamp.com

268   Tonkin, Corey. "Basko Believes", Tone Deaf, August 7, 2013 https://tonedeaf.thebrag.com/basko-believes

269   "Ellen Sundberg", BMG, last accessed December 10, 2020 https://www.bmg.com/sc/artist/ellen-sundberg

270   "Willy Clay Band", Facebook, last accessed December 10, 2020 https://www.facebook.com/Willy-Clay-Band-125142937167

271   "Benjamin Folke Thomas – Album Launch", Green Note, last accessed December 10, 2020 https://www.greennote.co.uk/production/benjamin-folke-thomas

272   ibid.

273   "Benjamin Folke Thomas – Stuff of Dreams", Facebook, October 25, 2018 https://www.facebook.com/benjaminfolke.thomas/videos/2546149245456126

274   "Benjamin Folke Thomas", *Facebook*, last accessed December 10, 2020 https://www.facebook.com/benjaminfolke.thomas

275   Celeste. "Now THIS Is How You Do Americana", *French Music Blog*, September 15, 2014, updated June 2, 2016 https://www.frenchmusicblog.com/la-maison-tellier

276   https://staticrootsfestival.com/

277   Day, Del "Interview: Dietmar Leibecke" *Americana UK* June 22, 2018 https://americana-uk.com/interview-dietmar-leibecke

278   https://staticrootsfestival.com/

279   VanWyck, https://www.vanwyck.nl/about

280   Ibid.

281   Johnson, Martin "Interview: Nero Kane discusses mixing Johnny Cash and Ry Cooder with Italian gothic" December 18, 2020 https://americana-uk.com/interview-nero-kane-discusses-mixing-johnny-cash-and-ry-cooder-with-italian-gothic

282   https://en.wikipedia.org/wiki/List_of_bluegrass_music_festivals#Europe

283   "חרפ | ירא נב שומ‎ (Mosh Ben-Ari *Flower*)", *YouTube*, February 15, 2016 https://youtu.be/-y5TBry2tF4

284   Steinberg, Jessica. "Elements of the east in Mosh Ben-Ari's latest", *The Times of Israel*, February 16, 2016 https://www.timesofisrael.com/elements-of-the-east-in-mosh-ben-aris-latest

285   Smulian, Mark. "Whitefang – Talk", *SoundCloud*, last accessed December 10, 2020 https://soundcloud.com/marksmulian/sets/whiteflag-talk

286   Press, Viva Sarah "12 of the Hippest Emerging Israeli Bands" *Israel21c* March 26, 2017 https://www.israel21c.org/12-of-the-hippest-emerging-israeli-bands/

287   "Jane Bordeaux: Ma'agalim (2016)" *IMDb* https://www.imdb.com/title/tt6106302/

288   OSOG "Wanted" 2016 https://www.youtube.com/watch?v=MqddzCNAYYU

289   Friedman, Gabe "'Jewish Americana' Music Gets Its Moment In The Spotlight" *Jewish Telegraphic Agency* January 12, 2017 https://www.jta.org/2017/01/12/united-states/jewish-americana-music-gets-its-moment-in-the-spotlight

290   "About the London Klezmer Quartet" https://www.londonklezmerquartet.com/about.html

291   Graff, Gary "Ben Fisher Looks at 'Human Aspects' of Israel-Palestine on 'Does the Land Remember Me?' Album" *Billboard* August 16, 2018 https://www.billboard.com/articles/columns/rock/8470537/ben-fisher-does-the-land-remember-me-premiere/

292   Ibid.

293   Ducker, Faye "UK Music's head of diversity discusses gender equality" March 6, 2020 https://www.prsformusic.com/m-magazine/news/uk-music-head-of-diversity-on-gender-equality/

294   Ingham, Tim "The Major Record Companies Have a Big Gender Problem – But There are Positive Signs for the Future" *Rolling Stone* April 15, 2019 https://www.rollingstone.com/music/music-features/the-major-record-companies-have-a-big-gender-problem-but-there-are-positive-signs-for-the-future-821037/

295   https://www.gov.uk/government/publications/home-office-gender-pay-gap-report-and-data-2019/home-offices-gender-pay-gap-report-2019

296   Martinovich, Audrey "We Need Women To Break Through The Glass Ceiling In Music Production To EQ The Gender Imbalance" December 2nd, 2019 https://www.pro-tools-expert.com/production-expert-1/2019/2/12/we-need-women-to-break-through-the-glass-ceiling-in-music-production-to-eq-the-gender-divide

297   Tedlow, R. *New and Improved: The Story of Mass Marketing in America* (New York: Basic Books, 1990)

298   Deming Mark "Artist Biography: Kasey Chambers" *Allmusic* https://www.allmusic.com/artist/kasey-chambers-mn0000359658/biography?cmpredirect

299   Bernstein, Jonathan, and Suzy Exposito. "Yola Becomes the Voice of 2019 Newport", *Rolling Stone*, July 29, 2019 https://www.rollingstone.com/music/music-live-reviews/newport-folk-fest-2019-recap-864579

300   NME. "First Aid Kit at the Brits 2019: 'We live in a patriarchy, we need more women in the music industry'", *YouTube*, February 21, 2019 https://www.youtube.com/watch?v=beq3izedcdg

301   https://www.thirtytigers.com/

302   Meet the 2020 Music Week Women In Music Roll Of Honour Music Week October 19, 2020 https://www.musicweek.com/media/read/meet-the-2020-music-week-women-in-music-roll-of-honour/081573

303   Paine, Andre "Radio 2's New Boss Helen Thomas On Her Vision For The Station" *Music Week* June 5, 2020 https://www.musicweek.com/media/read/radio-2-s-new-boss-helen-thomas-on-her-vision-for-the-station/079980

304   https://americana-uk.com/uk-americana-festivals-go-virtual-for-the-end-of-summer https://americana-uk.com/will-oldham-ron-sexsmith-and-more-to-play-livestreamed-cat-stevens-festival

305   "The Making of Rising Appalachia", *Bandsintown for Artists*, last accessed December 10, 2020 https://manager.bandsintown.com/support/blog/the-making-of-rising-appalachia

306   Rising Appalachia. "Rising Appalachia. NEW ALBUM!!!!", *Kickstarter*, December 29, 2011 https://www.kickstarter.com/projects/1288238485/rising-appalachia-new-album

307   "Bio", *Jenny and the Mexicats*, last accessed December 10, 2020
https://www.jennyandmexicats.com/en

308   "About", *Liv Austen*, last accessed December 10, 2020 https://livausten1.webs.com/about

309   Costa, Monica. "Exclusive! Contemporary country singer Liv Austen Talks her debut album 'A Moment Of Your Time'", *London Mums*, November 27, 2018 https://londonmumsmagazine.com/activities/attractions-for-families-in-london/exclusive-contemporary-country-singer-liv-austen-talks-her-debut-album-a-moment-of-your-time

310   Klonowski, Laura. "Exclusive: Liv Austen Talks Debut Album 'A Moment Of Your Time', CelebMix, 2018
https://celebmix.com/exclusive-liv-austen-talks-debut-album-a-moment-of-your-time

311   Costa, Monica. "Exclusive! Contemporary country singer Liv Austen Talks her debut album 'A Moment Of Your Time'", *London Mums*, November 27, 2018 https://londonmumsmagazine.com/activities/attractions-for-families-in-london/exclusive-contemporary-country-singer-liv-austen-talks-her-debut-album-a-moment-of-your-time

312   "Nashville, Part One: Amy Kurland and the Bluebird Café" *American Songwriter* October 2020 https://americansongwriter.com/amy-kurland-episode-of-prine-time/

313   Doman, Immy & Tabatznik, Resa http://www.greennote.co.uk/about-us/

314   "Immy Doman & Risa Tabatznik – Founders and Owners, The Green Note, London" *INDIE50* 2017 https://indie50.wordpress.com/portfolio/immy-doman-risa-tabatznik-managers-the-green-note-london/

315   A Different Kind of Twang: Q&A With Jed Hilly", Relix Live Music Conference, May 28, 2019 https://www.youtube.com/watch?v=2oZBMEEXch0

316   Bernstein, Jonathan, Robert Crawford, Jon Freeman, Joseph Hudak, and Marissa R Moss. "10 New Country and Americana Artists You Need to Know: Winter 2019", *Rolling Stone*, February 13, 2019 https://www.rollingstone.com/music/music-country-lists/10-new-country-and-americana-artists-you-need-to-know-winter-2019-793958

317   "Cassie Blanton", *Bandcamp*, last accessed December 10, 2020
https://store.carsieblanton.com/music

318   Steinhoff, Jessica. "Pokey LaFarge is a musical time traveler", *Isthmus*, December 8, 2011 https://isthmus.com/music/pokey-lafarge-is-a-musical-time-traveler

319   Coyne, Kevin John. "Year-End Album Review: Kasey Chambers & The Fireside Disciples, *Campfire*", *Country Universe*, November 28, 2018
http://www.countryuniverse.net/2018/11/28/year-end-album-review-kasey-chambers-the-fireside-disciples-campfire

320   Erlewine, Stephen Thomas. "Lilly Hiatt: *Walking Proof*", *Pitchfolk*, March 31, 2020 https://pitchfork.com/reviews/albums/lilly-hiatt-walking-proof

321   Erlewine, Stephen Thomas. "Lilly Hiatt: Walking Proof", *Pitchfolk*, March 31, 2020 https://pitchfork.com/reviews/albums/lilly-hiatt-walking-proof/

322   Far Out Staff. "Stream: Conor Oberst and Phoebe Bridgers' new project Better Oblivion Community Center drops surprise LP", *Far Out*, January 24, 2019 https://faroutmagazine.co.uk/stream-conor-oberst-and-phoebe-bridgers-new-project-better-oblivion-community-center-drops-surprise-lp

323   https://www.savingcountrymusic.com/keith-urban-says-the-country-definition-is-totally-meaningless/

324   https://www.rollingstone.com/music/music-country/keith-urban-speed-of-now-pandemic-concerts-1066553/

325   https://tasteofcountry.com/keith-urban-new-songs-album-interview/

326   https://skopemag.com/2010/07/08/emmy-nomination-for-gangstagrass

327   "Emmy Nomination for Gangstagrass", *Skope*, July 8, 2010 https://skopemag.com/2010/07/19/stoli-congrats-gangstagrass-for-their-2010-emmy-nom

328   "Alabama 3 - Interview: Contact music spoke to Jake Black", *Contactmusic*, October 22, 2002 http://www.contactmusic.com/interview/alabama3x22x10x02

329   Virtue, Graeme. "Alabama 3 review – raucous ravers soak up mashup outlaws' sin and soul", *The Guardian*, December 15, 2019 https://www.theguardian.com/music/2019/dec/15/alabama-3-review-club-country-barrowland-glasgow-jake-black-sopranos

330   Halsey. "Halsey - New Americana (Official Music Video)", *YouTube*, September 25, 2015 https://www.youtube.com/watch?v=b-eYbUVZedY

331   Riding with the King. Interview with John Hiatt by Iain Patience in *Blues Matters* Magazine June 2021 https://bluesmatters.com/

INDEX

A

Abramovich, Alex, 68
ACDC, 13
Acuff, Roy, 71
Adams, Ansell, 15
Adams, Ryan, 140, 153
Adele, 83
Ain't no Little Girl, 111
akonting instrument, 143–144
The Alabama 3, 139, 203
Alas I Cannot Swim, 131
Aldridge, Hannah, 86–87, 198
Aldridge, Walt, 86
All Along the Watchtower, 50
All My Favorite Singers Are
    Willie Nelson, 171
All the Good Times, 62
All the While, 115
All Things Considered, 75
AmericanaFest programme, 15,
    17–18
Americana music, 8
    and AMA, 12–19
    Australia. See Australian
    Americana
    Britain. See British Americana
    Canadian Americana, 163–174
    vs. Country Music, 19–24
    European. See European
    Americana
    France, 179–180
    Germany, 180–181
    history of, 11–42
    Irish. See Irish Americana
    Israel, 182–185
    Italy, 180–181
    Netherlands, 181
    Scandinavia, 175–179
    Streets of Laredo, 25–27
    Umbrella, 24–25

US. See US Americana
Americana Music Association
    (AMA), 9, 12–19
    AMA-UK, 124–127
    of Australia, 94
    Australia Advisory Group, 99
    Spotify charts, 79
The Americana Revolution (book),
    56
American Beauty, 63
"American Roots music", 9
Amos, Tori, 135
Anderson, Charis, 139
Angel from Montgomery, 72
Angel of the Night, 83
Anka, Paul, 71
Apple, Fiona, 114
Applewood Road, 137
Armatrading, Joan, 153
Armstrong, Kyshona, 29
As I Fell, 139
Astral Swans, 171, 173
Astral Weeks, 152–153
Atkins, Chet, 13, 23, 49, 51, 101
The Atlantic magazine, 27–28
ATO Records, 82
audio reproduction technology, 34
Auerbach, Dan, 118–119
Austen, Liv, 196
Australia Advisory Group (AMA),
    99
Australia, Country Music in, 9
Australian Americana, 93–116
    Australiana, 97–99
    Do You Have to Go to Nashville,
    100–109
    Today's Australian Americana
    Scene, 109–116
Australian Recording Industry
    Association (ARIA), 98
Autry, Orvon Grover (Gene), 47

B

Bakersfield sound, 47
Ball, Jenny, 195
Bandcamp, 189
banjo, 145
Banjo Odyssey, 169
Banza (Banjul) instrument, 143
Barber, Terry, 90
Barenaked Ladies, 168
Barker, Emily, 135–138, 191, 197
Barricades and Brickbats, 104
Basko Believes, 177
Bayes, Coy, 44
Beam, Sam, 90
Beans on Toast, 179
The Beatles, 31, 155, 158
Be-Bop-a-Lula, 30
Bechtolsheimer, Felix, 138–139
Belfast Telegraph, 154
Bellerose, Jay, 129
Ben-Ari, Mosh, 184
Bennett, Robin, 133
Berglund, Blake, 166
Bergman, Ingmar, 178
Berns, Bert, 152
Berry, Chuck, 32
Best Folk Album Grammy Award, 62
Better Oblivion Community Centre, 201
Bevan, Fiona, 38
The Bible Code Sundays, 144
Billboard magazine, 15–16, 54
Bird, Jade, 133–134, 138
Bird Songs, 171
Bitter Suite (Pajero), 90
Björk, 177
Black, Cilla, 119
Black Deer Festival, 141
Black, Jake, 203
Black Keys, 118
Black Panther Party, 20
Black Sabbath, 13

Blame it on Cain, 156–157
Blanton, Carsie, 199
Bleck, John, 148
Bleetstein, Rob, 56
Bleyer, Archie, 31
Blonde on Blonde, 49
Bluebird, 196–197
The Bluebird Cafe, 6
Bluegrass, 90
Bluesfest, 95–96, 115–116
Boggs, Dock, 18
Boilen, Bob, 38, 75
Boots, 105
Boots No 1: The Official Revival Bootleg, 62
Boots, Ruby, 105, 114
Borderline club, in London, 40
Bowie, David, 160
Bradley, Owen, 13
Bradley, Shanne, 159
Bragg, Billy, 123
Branagh, Kenneth, 137
Breadline Blues, 22
BRELAND, 202
Bridgers, Phoebe, 201
Brighter Days, 86
Brilleaux, Lee, 157
Brilliant Light, 133
Brinkley, John R., 43–44
Bristol Sessions, 46
British Americana, 117–142
    foundations of, 120–124
    great collaborations, 128–141
    UK's AMA, 124–127
British invasions, of popular music, 9
Britt, Catherine, 65, 105, 190
Brooks, Garth, 17
Brown Eyed Girl, 152
Brown, James, 23
Brown, Ray, 161
Brumby Media Group, 8
Buck Up, 199
Buddy Holly, 24

Buell, Bebe, 158
Burgess, Sinead, 101–102
Burgoyne, Mary, 155
Burn, Dave, 178
Burnett, Chester (Howlin' Wolf), 64
Burnett, Richard, 59
Burnett, T Bone, 59–62, 82, 85, 129, 139, 158
Burns, Joey, 89
Burris, Roy Edward, 20
Bushwackers, 99
Butler, Bob, 125
The Byrds, 55, 158
Byrne, David, 58
Byron Bay, Australia, 95–96, 115–116
By the Way, I Forgive You, 82

C
Calexico, 89–90
California, 55
Campbell, Glen, 49
Campbell, Mike, 84
Campfire, 34, 104, 200
Canadian Americana, 163–174
Canadian Independent Music Association (CIMA), 172
Can't Help You Now, 110
Cantwell, David, 20
Capital Country Music Association (CCMA), 95
The Captain, 104
Carlile, Brandi, 12, 72, 73, 81–83, 190
Carolina's Anatomy, 180
Caroline, 82
Carpenter, Mary Chapin, 57, 140
Carter, Alvin Pleasant (AP) Delaney, 44
Carter, James, 60–61
Carter, Justin, 115
Carter, Maybelle, 44, 71, 190, 198
CarterRollins, 115

Carter, Sara, 43, 190, 198
Car Wheels on a Gravel Road, 58
Case, Neko, 57, 75
Casey, Karan, 148
Cash, Johnny, 21, 50, 154, 169, 178
Cash, Rosanne, 17, 19, 64, 198
Cassar-Daley, Troy, 97–98, 99, 105–106
cassette tapes, 35
Cavanagh, Robbie, 87
Cave, Nick, 94, 153
Celtic Connections, 124–125
"Celtic" music, 9
Celtic Rock, 33
Chambers, Bill, 112
Chambers, Diane, 112
Chambers, Kasey, 34, 67, 96, 102, 104, 110–112, 186–187, 189, 200
Chambers, Nash, 37, 102–104, 110, 112
Chambers, Veronica, 102
Charcoal Lane, 108
Charles, Ray, 153
Chess, Leonard, 32
Chevron, Philip, 159
Chicks, Dixie, 23
Chilcott, Bex (Boots), 105
Childish Gambino, 134
Christgau, Robert, 56, 70, 165
Christopherson, Peter, 178
Chugg, Michael, 96, 187, 201
Cigarettes and Truckstops, 169
City Fathers, 49
Clancy Brothers, 143
Clark, Gene, 129
Cleere, John, 150–151
Clinch Mountain Boys, 203
Clooney, George, 60
Clyde, Cat, 201
Cobain, Kurt, 67, 178
Cobb, Brent, 12, 134, 191
Cobb, Dave, 12, 66–67, 80, 84, 86, 134
Coen, Ethan, 59

Coen, Joel, 59
Cohen, Leonard, 130, 178
Colbert, Stephen, 73
Coldrick, Annabella, 37
Collins, Shirley, 121
Colyer, Ken, 123
Colter, Jessi, 54
Connors, Graeme, 98
Convertino, John, 89
Copenhagen, 178
Coroneos, Trigger, 108–109
Cosmic American Music, 55
Costello, Elvis, 155, 157–161
Costelo, Erin, 163, 164
Country Music, 9
    vs. Americana music, 19–24
Country Music Association (CMA),
    16, 18, 21–22, 23-4, 48, 84
Country Music Association of Aus-
    tralia (CMAA), 95, 97
Country Music Radio (CMR), 39
The Country Side of Harmonica
    Sam, 176
Covid-19 pandemic, 10, 36
Coward Brothers, 158
The Cowboy Junkies, 150
Cronin, Mick, 150
Crow, Sheryl, 191
Crushing, 114, 115
Cush, Stefan, 159
Cuttin' Grass (1 & 2), 67
Cyrus, Miley, 190

D

Daly, Mick, 148
Damaged Goods, 102
Danny and the Champions of the
    World, 41, 42, 132–133
Davis, Clive, 137
Davis, Richard, 152–153
Davis, Tex, 30
Dead Ringers, 104, 112
The Dead South, 29, 167–168

Deezer, 37
DeMeyer, Brigitte, 87–88
Denver, John, 72
Derekh (A Way), 184
Despite the Snow, 136
The Diamonds, 30
Diaz, Linda, 76
Dickinson, Jim, 113
DiDia, Nick, 115
Didn't Leave Nobody but the Baby,
    60
digital rights management (DRM)
    technology, 35–36
disruptive technologies, 35
Distrokid, 189
DJ Rench (Oscar Owens), 203
Doeppel, Dan, 95–96
Does the Land Remember Me?, 185
Doman, Immy, 197
Donovan, Jason, 94
Don't Steal My Bounce, 101
Dragonfly, 104, 111
Dreams of High Quality Truth, 178
Drive By Truckers, 29, 57, 80
Dr John, 15
Droste, Ed, 97
DuMont network, 48
Dury, Ian, 157
Dust Bowl migration, 46–47
Dusty, Slim, 95, 106, 112
Dylan, Bob, 49–50, 114, 143, 145,
    154

E

Earle, Steve, 58, 75, 146, 171
Easy Eye, 118–119
Edge of the Sun, 90
The Ed Sullivan Show, 48
Eisenhower, Dwight, 21
Elephant, 81
Ellis, Max, 94, 95
Ely, Joe, 17
Emmylou, 175

Emmy the Great, 197
Ennis, Seamus, 121
Enright, Eamon, 146
Erlewine, Stephen Thomas, 200
European Americana, 175–186
Everitt, Barry, 40–41
Everly Brothers, 31, 69

F
Faded Gloryville, 170
Fahey, John, 18
Fairytale of New York, 123
Faraway Look, 119
Father's Day, 113
Faulkner, William, 33
Feder, J. Lester, 21–22
Feet Off the Ground, 134
Ferguson, Bob, 13
Fifteen, 16
Findlay, Neil, 138–139
Fink, Charlie, 130–131
The Firewatcher's Daughter, 82
First Aid Kit, 174–176, 191
First Love, 130
Fisher, Ben, 185
Fitzgerald, Ella, 161
Flanagan Brothers, 145
Flannery, Mick, 148
Flying Burrito Brothers, 56
400 Unit, 80
France
    Americana music, 179–180
Franklin, Aretha, 138
Fuji Rock Festival, 115

G
The Galway Girl, 146
Gambian Jola folk, 144
Gangstagrass, 203
Gavin, Jake, 137
gender bias, 79
Georgas, Hannah, 172
Georgia, Little, 115, 116

Germany
    Americana music, 180–181
Ghost, 126
Gibson, Laura, 76
Gilded Palace of Sin, 56
Gillett, Charlie, 155
Gilmore, Colin, 24–25
Gilmore, James, 24
Ginty, John, 85
Girl from the North Country, 50
Give Up the Ghost, 82
Glaser, Tompall, 54
Glastonbury Festival 130, 132, 141
God is in the Detour, 180
Golden Guitar Awards, 95, 99
Good, Jo, 141
Goodbye Cruel World, 157–158
Goodman, Steve, 72
Good Souls Better Angels, 58
The Graceless Age, 150
Graffiti U, 108
Grammy Awards
    Americana Album in, 14, 27
Grand Drive, 133
The Grand Ole Opry, 48
Grant, Milt, 30–31
Grateful Dead, 153
The Great Country Songbook,
    97–98
Great Depression, 46
Great Lake Swimmers, 172
The Green Fields of France, 160
Green Note Club, 178, 197–8
Green River Ordinance, 16
Green Tea Ice Cream, 76
Grenades, 163–164
Grievous Angel, 68–73
Grizzly Bear, 97
Grossman, Albert, 50
Guthrie, Woody, 47, 143
Guy, Buddy, 15

H

Haggard, Merle, 19–21, 47
Halsey, 203
Hannah Brine Singers, 127
Hanna, Jeff, 71
Hanseroth, Phil, 82
Hanseroth, Tim, 82
Hard Time Killing Floor Blues, 60
Harlan, Rose-Lynn, 122
Harpo, Slim, 39, 59
Harris, Bob, 38, 39, 121, 141, 178, 192–193
Harris, Emmylou, 11, 17, 34, 56, 58, 60, 68–69, 70–72, 104, 113, 129, 138, 139, 166, 175, 198
The Harrow and the Harvest, 62
Harvey, Adam, 98
Heartbreakers, 84
Heavy Rock, 29–30
Heissler, Andrew, 199
Hell Among the Yearlings, 62
Helm, Levon, 27
Hemby, Natalie, 190
Henderson, Mike, 83
Hendrix, Jimi, 30, 50, 90, 182
Hiatt, John, 204
Hiatt, Lilly, 7, 200
Hibbert, Toots, 153
Higgins, Missy, 94, 96
High Top Mountain, 84
The Highwomen, 12, 83, 190
Hill Country Blues, 33
Hillman, Chris, 56
Hilly, Jed, 14–17, 60, 67–68, 99, 103, 198
Hip Hop, 28, 29, 32
Home on the Range, 47
home taping, 35
Hood, David, 80
Hood, Patterson, 80
Hookey, Harry, 37, 92, 93
House Committee on Un-American Activities (HUAC), 120–121

House of Mercy Radio (Radio Borderline), 40
Howley, David, 147
How to Make Gravy, 108
Hughes, Charles, 29
Hunters Trance, 201
Hurt, John (Mississippi), 18

I

Idiot's Hill, 177
If It Hadn't Been For Love, 83
I'm So Lonesome I Could Cry, 49
I'm Stranded, 100
I'm Thinking Tonight of my Blue Eyes, 44
In Bloom, 67
In Hell I'll be in Good Company, 29, 166
Internet radio, 38–39
In the Morning, 175
IP streaming, 35, 192
Irish Americana, 143–162
    Irish artists in UK, 151–162
Iron and Wine, 90
Isbell, Jason, 12, 13, 29, 79–80, 87, 103, 138, 151, 154, 172, 191
Israel
    Americana music, 182–185
    Americana music in, 182–185
Istallet for Visor, 177
Italy
    Americana music, 180–181

J

Jacklin, Julia, 114–115
Jack, Mandolin, 39–41, 126
Jackson, Rob, 136
James, Skip, 18
Jane Bordeaux, 184
Jatta, Daniel, 143–144
The Jayhawks, 140
Jennings, Shooter, 12, 13
Jennings, Waylon, 54–55

Jenny and the Mexicats, 195
John, Elton, 82
Johns, Ethan, 139, 140
Johns, Glyn, 139–140
Johnson, Laila Sady, 168
Johnson, Lyndon, 20
Johnson, Robert, 64
Johnston, Bob, 49
John Wesley Harding, 50
Jones, Booker T., 15
Jones, George, 158
Jones, Paul, 85, 86
Jones, Tom, 140, 148

K

Kane, Nero, 180–181
Kane, Roy, 151
Kater, Kaia, 162–164
Kater, Tamara, 171
Kay, Connie, 153
Keep Music Alive, 36
Keep on the Sunny Side, 44
Kelly, Paul, 38, 64, 93, 94, 104, 109, 112–113
Kelly, Willie, 148
Kennedy, John F., 20
Kent, Nick, 157
Kenyon, Danny, 169
Kidman, Nicole, 108
Kilkenny Roots Festival, 150
Killing in the Name, 179
Kimbrough, Will, 87–88, 127, 197
King, Chris Thomas, 60
King, Marcus, 79
The King of America, 160
Kirkpatrick, Anne, 106–108, 190
Kooper, Al, 49
Krauss, Alison, 60, 129
Kravitz, Lenny, 86
Kristofferson, Kris, 55, 71
Kurland, Amy, 196

L

LaBostrie, Dorothy, 129
La Chapelle, Peter, 20
LaFarge, Pokey, 197, 199
Leibecke, Dietmar, 180
Leigh, Alva, 126, 189
Levi's Blue Eyes, 177
Lewis & Leigh, 126, 197
Lewis, Al, 126
Lewis, Huey, 156
Lewis, Jerry Lee, 49
Lickety Split, 86
Life is Fine, 112
Lightning Slim, 39
Lincoln, Abraham, 21
Little Lion Man, 132
Little Red Boots, 169
A Little Redemption, 127
Live Forevermore, 181–182
Live in Black and White, 87
Live music, 192
Living in the Circle, 112
Lockhart, Jim, 33
LOFT, 196
Lomax, Alan, 120–121
London Grammar, 101, 134
London Klezmer Quartet, 185
The Lone Bellow, 79
Long Hard Times to Come, 203
Look at Miss Ohio, 62
Lord, Dennis, 56
Lotan, Uri, 184
Louvin Brothers, 68, 69
Louvin, Charlie, 68
Louvin, Ira, 68
Lowe, Nick, 29
Lucinda Williams, 57–58, 67, 191, 198
Luhrmann, Baz, 120
Lula Wiles, 192–193
Lynn, Loretta, 22
Lynyrd Skynyrd, 29
Lyu, Oliver, 7

M

Ma'agalim, 184
MacColl, Ewan, 121, 123
MacColl, Kirsty, 123
MacGowan, Shane, 159
Mackay, Emily, 115
MacManus, Declan, 154–155
MacManus, Ross, 154
The Maddox Brothers and Rose, 47
Maddox, Rose, 47–48
Maghett, Sam (Magic Sam), 30
Makem, Tommy, 145
Malice, Mercy Grief and Wrath (MMGW), 166
Malone, Bill, 22–24
Mamma Raised a Ramblin' Man, 102
Mandrell, Barbara, 13
Mangan, Dan, 171
Mannix, Ashleigh, 104, 115
Man Without a Soul, 58
Marinelli, Matt, 88
Marling, Laura, 130–131
Marsalis, Wynton, 153
Martin, George, 119
Maverick festival, 125
Maybellene, 32
McAllister, Jay, 179
McDonald, Bill, 112
McEuen, John, 71
McGarrigle, Anna, 165
McGarrigle, Kate, 165
McGarrigle Sisters, 165
McGuinness, Eugene, 131
McKean, Joy, 95
McLaren, Malcolm, 122
McLaughlin, Pat, 119
McVie, Christine, 153
Mean Mary, 40
Melba, Nellie, 94
Mellencamp, John, 153
Melted Morning, 127
The Men They Couldn't Hang (TMTCH), 99, 159–161

Merenstein, Lewis, 152
Metamodern Sounds in Country Music, 66
The Meters, 170
Mezzadri, Marco, 180-181
Might be Losing my Mind, 105
Mighty ReArranger, 128
Miller, Bill, 33
Miller, Jimmy, 40
Milnes, Gerry, 163
Minogue, Kylie, 94
Mitchell, Anaïs, 185
Mitchell, Joni, 163–164, 165–166
Mockingbird Soul, 88
Moffatt, Mark, 99, 100
Molten Rock, 180
A Moment of Your Time, 196
Monroe, Bill, 68, 199
Mooney, Tim, 150
More Gunfighter Ballads and Trail Songs, 26
Morgan, Danyel, 85
Morissette, Alanis, 135
Morris, Maren, 72, 191
Morrison, George Ivan, 143, 151–154, 177
Moss, Emma-Lee (Emmy the Great), 129–131
Moss, Jerry, 61
Muddy Waters, 30
Mulloy Brothers, 142, 143
Mulloy, Elizabeth, 143
Mulloy, Enda, 144
Mulloy, Pat, 143, 145
Mumford and Sons, 130–132
Mumford, Marcus, 130–132
Mundy (Eamon Enright), 146
Murphys, Dropkick, 161
Murray, Larry, 16
Murry, John, 32–33, 139, 149–150, 178–179
Music Managers Forum, 37
My Aim is True, 156, 157

N

NAMM tradeshow, 102
Nashville
  Grand Ole Opry, 48
Nashville Skyline, 50
Nashville Songwriters Association, 39
The Nashville Sound, 13, 81
National Academy of Recording Arts and Sciences, 14
National Public Radio (NPR), 75
National Recordings Registry, 54
Nature, 113
Nelson, Willie, 43, 51, 55, 153, 176
Netherlands
  Americana music, 181
Newman, Paul, 178
New Rose, 100
Newton, Dobe, 98, 99–100
Nicholls, Danni, 87, 126, 127, 197
Nico, 115
Ninepin, 163
Nitty Gritty Dirt Band (NGDB), 71
Nixon, Richard, 21–22
Noah and the Whale, 130
Noble, Peter, 96
Nolden, John (Cadillac), 64
Not Pretty Enough, 104, 111

O

Oberst, Conor, 201
O Brother Where Art Thou? (movie), 59–60, 62, 136, 203
Odgers, Phil (Swill), 159–161
O'Keeffe, Elly, 147–148, 195
Okie from Muskogee, 19–21
Old Crow Medicine Show, 72
The Oldest Story in the Book, 108
The Old Grey Whistle Test, 121
O'Looney, Maureen, 145–146
On the Road Again, 176
On the Shoulders of Giants (OSOG), 184

Oprys, 48
The Order of Time, 88
O'Riordan, Cait, 150, 159
Örjansson, Johan, 177
Ortega, Lindi, 169–171
"Outlaw Country" movement, 51–56
Out on the Weekend, 96
Outside El Paso, 90
Owens, Buck, 47
Owens, Oscar, 203
Oxford, Keven, 95

P

Page, Jimmy, 30
Pamper Records, 51
Parish, Lincoln, 200
parlour music, 166
Parsons, Gram, 55–56, 68–69, 129, 204
Parton, Dolly, 170, 198
Passionate Kisses, 58
Patterns, 101
Patton, Charley, 64
Paul, Brad, 56
Pay the Devil, 153
Peel, John, 40, 136, 160
Peer, Ralph, 46
Petrusich, Amanda, 28, 59
Petty, Tom, 84, 149–150
The Phantom Empire (movie), 47
Phillips, Leslie Ann (Sam), 129
Phipps, Martin, 137
Pigram, Alan, 104, 200
Pink, 202
Piticco, Paul, 131
Plaine, Belle, 166–168
Plant, Robert, 117, 128–129
Plumb, Jason, 167
The Pogues, 99, 159
Police Dog Hogan, 141
Poole, Tony, 133
Pop music, 18, 65

Presley, Elvis, 120, 150, 155–156, 157, 161
Price, Margo, 138
Pride, Charley, 150
Prine, John, 12, 64, 71–73, 75, 83, 154
Prophet, Chuck, 58
Proud to be a Coal Miner's Daughter, 22
Pub Rock, 109, 113, 156

R

Race records market, 35
racial diversity, 79
Rackhouse, Pilfer, 148
Radcliffe, Mark, 192
radio, 46
Radio Corporation of America (RCA), 48
Radio Geronimo, 40
Rage Against the Machine, 179
Raising Sand, 129
Raitt, Bonnie, 72, 74, 75, 96
Randolph, Marcus, 85
Randolph, Robert, 84–85, 86
Rateliff, Nathaniel, 79
Rawlings, David, 61–63
Razor Wire, 87
Reagan, Ronald, 21, 163
Recording Academy (RA). See National Academy of Recording Arts and Sciences
Red Clay Halo, 136
Red-Headed Stranger album, 54
Reeves, Jim, 49
Rennie-Hynes, Josh, 101
Reshen, Neil, 54
Resilient, 194
Reunions, 81
Revival, 62
Riley, Jim, 148
Rising Appalachia, 193–194
Ritter, Tex, 21, 48

Riviera, Jake, 155, 157
Roach, Archie, 109
Robbins, Marty, 25
Robertson, Robbie, 49
Robinson, Dave, 100, 155–156
Robinson, Tom, 125
Robson, Cheryl, 8
Robson, Steve, 8
Rock & Roll, 65, 112, 120
Rodgers, Jimmie, 46, 47, 199
Rodgers, Nile, 38, 202
Rogers, Kenny, 13
Rogers, Maggie, 72
Rogers, Tammy, 84
Rogue State of Mind, 178
Rolling Stones, 29
Ronstadt, Linda, 71
Roosevelt, Franklin D., 20
roots music, 18
Ross, Ricky, 118
Ross-Spang, Matt, 138
Rubarth, Amber, 137
Rubin, Rick, 82
Ruins, 176
Rum, Sodomy, and the Lash, 159
Ryman Auditorium, 18

S

Sad-Eyed Lady of the Lowlands, 50
A Sailor's Guide to Earth, 66, 67
Sainte-Marie, Buffy, 166–167
The Saints, 100
Santana, Carlos, 86
Saving Country Music blog, 108, 176
Scandinavian Americana, 175–179
Scott, Eric, 94
Scott, Hazel, 48
Scott, Michael, 56
Scruggs, Earl, 71
Seasonal Shift, 90
Secunda, Tony, 40
Seeger, Peggy, 121
Seeger, Pete, 145

Sexton, Paul, 38, 141, 191
Shadow Box, 138
Shake your Hips, 59
Shannon, Sharon, 146
Sheeran, Ed, 38, 115, 197
Shepherd, Catherine, 83
Shires, Amanda, 79, 80, 190, 191
Sholes, Steve, 13
A Short History of Decay, 150
Shtibelman, Yoav, 184
Sigh No More, 131
Silver, Sara, 191–193
Simmonds, Paul, 159
Simon and Garfunkel, 80
Simpson, Sturgill, 65–67, 84
Sister Rosetta Goes Before Us, 129
Skaggs, Ricky, 203
Smith, Caitlyn, 123
Smith, Chloe, 193–194
Smith, Harry, 18
Smith, Leah, 193–194
Smith, Patti, 135
Smith, Slim, 22
Smith, Stevie, 124–125, 127
Smucker, Dylan, 101
Smulian, Mark, 51–54, 182–183
Snider, Todd, 74
Solitude, 104
Songbird, 153
Song of the Old Rake, 112
Son House, 135
Son Little, 134
Son Volt, 57
Soul Journey, 62
Sound and Fury, 67
South by Southwest (SXSW) festival, 28, 76, 195
Southeastern, 80–81
Southern Music/American Music, 23
Speace, Amy, 137
The Speed of Now Part 1, 202
Spencer, Paul, 125

Spice Girls, 190
The Spinning Jennies, 177
Spotify, 37–38, 79
Spottswood, Richard, 18
Spragg, Rob, 203
Springsteen, Bruce, 177
Stanley Brothers, 18
Stanley, Ralph, 60, 203
Staples, Mavis, 27, 29
Stapleton, Chris, 12, 83
Stapleton, Morgane, 84
Staton, Candi, 15
The Steeldrivers, 83
Steenburgen, Mary, 123
Stick in the Wheel, 41
Stiff, Denise, 61
Stiff Records, 100
The Story, 82
Strange Prison, 171
streaming services, 36
Streets of Laredo, 25–27
Strings, Billy, 90–91
Studholme, James 141
Stuff of Dreams, 178
SubmitHub, 41
subscription services, 36
Summertime, 101
Sundberg, Ellen, 177
Sure Got Me, 110
Sur un Volcan, 179
Swann, Matthew, 170
Sweeney, Joel Walker, 145
Sweetheart of the Rodeo album, 56
Sweet Kind of Blue, 138

T
Tabatznik, Risa, 197
Tamworth, Australia, 95–96
Tandy, Larissa, 101
Taranto, Brian, 96, 99
Taylor, Mark, 36–37
Telecommunications Act of 1996, 16

Tench, Benmont, 84
Thank You Mr President, 21
Tharpe, Rosetta, 120
theatrical cinema, 60
They Don't Know, 123
Thirty Tigers, 191
Thomas, Benjamin Folke, 178, 179
Thomas, Helen, 191
Thomas, Kamara, 88
Thomas, Mick, 113–114
Thomson, Graeme, 155
Thompson, Graham, 98
Thompson, Hunter S., 138–139
Thompson, Richard, 121
Thompson, Sara, 154
Thompson, Stephen, 76
Thriving Roots 2020, 172
Til the Goin' Gets Gone, 170
Timberlake, Justin, 84
Timmins, Michael, 150
Tiny Desk concerts, 75–79, 195
To Be Good Takes a Long Time, 110
Tooke, Jay, 171
Took the Children Away, 108
Toussaint, Allen, 129
Townshend, Pete, 30
The Tragically Hip, 161
Traveller, 84
Tribal Voice, 100
Triffids, 113
Trigger instrument, 55
Tritt, Travis, 83
Trudell, John, 33
Trump, Donald, 58
Trust, Gary, 16
Tucker, Shonna, 80
Tudhope, Adam, 130
Turk, Nathan, 48
Turner, Othar, 33
TV entertainment, 48
Twain, Shania, 17, 149
21 (Adele), 83

2TM radio station, 94–95
Tyminski, Dan, 59

U
Uh Huh, 134
Ullman, Tracey, 123
Umphrey's McGee, 90
Uncle Tupelo, 57
The Unfortunate Rake, 25–26
United Kingdom (UK)
    Irish artists in, 151–162
Up Where We Belong, 166
Urban, Keith, 84, 97, 100, 107–109, 111, 153, 201–203
Urquhart, Felicity, 98
US Americana
    alt-country, 57–63
    Country Music industry, 43–50
    different strands in, 43–74
    family, 64–68
    Grievous Angel, 68–73
    modern, 75–92
    "Outlaw Country" movement, 51–56
user-centric algorithm, 37
user-centric payment system (UCPS), 37

V
Valenzuela, Jacob, 89–90
Vallely (family), 148
Vance, Aaron, 77–79
Van Halen, 13
Van Hoek, Maurice, 181
VanWyck, 180
Van Zandt, Townes, 129
Victor Talking Machine Company, 46, 48
Vincent, Gene, 30
The Voice (BBC reality show), 148

W

Wainwright, Loudon III, 165
Wainwright, Martha, 165
Wainwright, Rufus, 140, 165–166
Walker, Tim, 129
Walker, Wily Bo, 41
Walking Proof, 200
Walk Through Fire, 119–120
Wallace, George, 22
Wallace, Mark (Squeeze-box Wally), 114
Wallander (BBC drama), 137
Wall, Colter, 166
The Waltons, 168
Wanted! The Outlaws, 54–55
Waterson, Mary, 138
Waters, Roger, 74
Watson, Doc, 71, 90, 129
Watson, Rosa Lee, 129
The Waves, The Wake, 172
Ways and Means, 108, 109
Weddings, Parties Anything (Wed-dos), 113–114
We Banjo 3, 146
The Weekend, 79
Weir, Bob, 63
Welch, Gillian, 57, 60–63
Wenk, Martin, 90
West, Kanye, 98
We Walk This Road, 85
Wexler, Jerry, 71
WhiteFlag project, 184
White, Jack, 135
Whitley, Keith, 203
Wilco, 29
Wilco and Nick Lowe, 29
Wilco (band), 29, 58
Wild Rose, 122
Wildwood Kin, 192–194
Wilkes, JD, 59
Williams, Andy, 49
Williams, Hank, 155
Williams, Hank, Jr., 49

Williams, Jade, 123
Williams, Kathryn, 179
Williams, Lee, 39
Williams, Lucinda, 57–58, 67, 191, 198
Williamson, John, 97, 98
Williams, Stanley Miller, 57
Wills, Bob, 32, 47
Will the Circle be Unbroken, 71
Willy Clay Band, 177
Wilson, Danny George, 133
Wilson, Julian, 133
A Window to Other Ways, 138
Winehouse, Amy, 197
Winnipeg Folk Festivals, 171
Woke Up This Morning, 203
women, in Americana music, 34, 187–198
The Wood Brothers, 79
Workingman's Dead, 63
Workman, Hawksley, 38, 172
Wray, Doug, 29–30
Wray, Link, 29–32, 109
Wrecking Ball, 62
Wright, Jon, 196
Wright Smith, Ben, 101

X

XERA, 44

Y

Y'alternative, 59
Years to Burn, 90
Yoakam, Dwight, 17, 65
yodelling, 47, 80
Yola, 75, 117–120, 190–191
York, Kate, 123
Yothu Yindi, 100
Young, Neil, 7, 96, 115, 164
YouTube, 41

Z

Zeppelin, Led, 128

Other books on Music
www.supernovabooks.co.uk

50 Women in the Blues
Jennifer Noble
Zoë Howe

9781913641191
£19.99

The British Beat Explosion:
Rock 'n' Roll Island
Ed. JC Wheatley

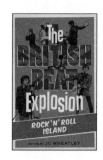

9781906582470
£9.99

Women Make Noise: Girl Bands
from Motown to the Modern
Ed. Julia Downes

9780956632913
£15.99